W9-AZH-054

Temples of Knowledge

Andrew Carnegie's Gift to Indiana

B35

"Fowler Public Library"

Drawing by Brett Volpp

Alan McPherson

"Shelbyville-Shelby County Public Library"

Temples of Knowledge: Andrew Carnegie's Gift to Indiana

COPYRIGHT 2003 BY ALAN MCPHERSON, AUTHOR, COMPILER, PHOTOGRAPHER

ISBN # 0-9636978-4-6

PUBLIC LIBRARY BUILDINGS-INDIANA-HISTORY

FOR ADDITIONAL COPIES, WRITE HOOSIER'S NEST PRESS, POB 38, KEWANNA, IN 46939

FRONT COVER PHOTO: MORGAN COUNTY PUBLIC LIBRARY, MARTINSVILLE

BACK COVER PHOTO: MUNCIE-CENTER TOWNSHIP PUBLIC LIBRARY

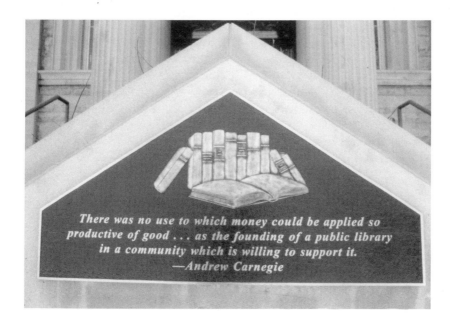

"Shelbyville-Shelby County Library"

"There was no use to which money could be applied so productive of good, as the founding of a public library in a community which is willing to support it."

ANDREW CARNEGIE (1835-1919)

CONTENTS

"Andrew Carnegie (1835-1919)"

"Just Show Me Indiana, Where To Set It Down."

DRAWING BY BRETT VOLPP, ADAPTED FROM 1908 ORIGINAL

CARNEGIE LIBRARIES IN INDIANA: A LISTING

Carnegie Blessed: A Century of Service

CARNEGIE ALTERED: SERVICE IN ANOTHER CAPACITY

CARNEGIE ALTERED: FORMER ACADEMIC LIBRARIES

CARNEGIE RAZED: GONE WITH THE WIND, FIRE & BULLDOZER

APPENDIX: A-G

" Washington Carnegie Public Library"

FOREWORD

"A Public Library is the never-failing spring in the desert."

ANDREW CARNEGIE

IT WAS RECOGNIZED A LONG TIME AGO THAT ANDREW CARNEGIE HAD FUNDED THE CON-
STRUCTION OF MORE LIBRARY BUILDINGS IN INDIANA THAN IN ANY OTHER STATE. ALTHOUGH HE
NEVER SPOKE OR WROTE OF IT, MANY OTHERS HAVE SPECULATED UPON HIS REASON FOR DOING SO.
DID HE HAVE SOME PARTICULAR LIKING FOR THE HOOSIER STATE, SOME HAVE WONDERED, OR WAS
HE INFLUENCED BY FRIENDS OR ACQUAINTANCES THERE? OTHERS HAVE SOUGHT PSYCHOLOGICAL
AND EVEN PSYCHIC REASONS FOR HIS GENEROSITY TO IT. HAVING SPENT MANY FRUITLESS HOURS
WORKING THROUGH THE CARNEGIE ARCHIVES PRESERVED AT COLUMBIA UNIVERSITY, HOWEVER,
THIS WRITER HAS CONCLUDED, TO HIS OWN SATISFACTION AT LEAST, THAT INDIANA JUST HAP-
PENED TO COME OF AGE BIBLIOTHECALLY AT EXACTLY THE RIGHT TIME TO BENEFIT FROM HIS GEN-
EROSITY MORE THAN OTHER STATES.

BY THE TIME CARNEGIE INITIATED HIS LIBRARY BUILDING CAMPAIGN, THE NATION'S LONGER
ESTABLISHED CITIES EAST OF INDIANA, HAVING ALREADY CONSTRUCTED MANY LIBRARY BUILDINGS
WITH LOCAL RESOURCES, HAD LESS NEED FOR HIS HELP. MEANWHILE THE STATES WEST OF THE
WABASH RIVER HAD NOT YET DEVELOPED ADEQUATELY EDUCATED POPULATIONS OR THE NECES-
SARY INFRASTRUCTURES TO BENEFIT FULLY FROM HIS BENEFACTIONS. FIRST AND FOREMOST, THE
ERSTWHILE BOBBIN BOY FROM DUNFERMLINE WAS A CANNY INVESTOR, AND HE REGARDED HIS
LIBRARY DONATIONS AS JUST THAT... I.E. INVESTMENTS IN THE NATION'S FUTURE. INDIANA AT THE
TURN OF THE CENTURY HAD A FIRMLY ESTABLISHED BOOKISH CULTURE, WIDESPREAD LITERACY, AN
UNDERSTANDING OF THE KINDS OF BENEFITS LIBRARIES COULD GENERATE AMONG ITS POPULACE,
AND SUFFICIENT EXPERIENCE WITH RENTAL AND SOCIAL LIBRARIES TO ASSURE THE EXTENSIVE
FUTURE USE OF FREE PUBLIC LIBRARIES WHEN THEY SHOULD BECOME AVAILABLE. CARNEGIE SIM-
PLY PUT HIS MONEY TO WORK IN INDIANA BECAUSE HE FELT IT WOULD GENERATE A GREATER SOCIAL
PROFIT THERE THAN IT WAS LIKELY TO DO ELSEWHERE AT THAT TIME.

THE 164 LIBRARY BUILDINGS THAT CARNEGIE FUNDED IN INDIANA BETWEEN 1900 AND 1920
CERTAINLY ALTERED PROFOUNDLY AND FOR A LEAST A CENTURY THE READING TOPOGRAPHY OF
HOOSIERDOM. ALTHOUGH HE NEVER WROTE OR SPOKE OF HIS UNUSUAL GENEROSITY OF THE STATE
OF INDIANA, HE DID SPEAK AND WRITE ON A NUMBER OF OCCASIONS OF HIS MOTIVATION FOR CON-
STRUCTING LIBRARY BUILDINGS IN GENERAL. PERHAPS NOWHERE ARE THOSE COMMENTS MORE
REVEALING THAN IN HIS DEDICATORY ADDRESS AT THE HOWARD UNIVERSITY LIBRARY ON APRIL 25,
1910, WHERE HE TOLD THE ASSEMBLED STUDENTS:

"BOOKS ARE MOST PERFECT INSTRUMENTS OF PHILANTHROPY THAT EXISTS. I WILL TELL YOU
WHY. THEY DO NOT DO ANYTHING FOR NOTHING... IF YOU ARE GOING TO GET ANY BENEFIT OUT OF
THESE BOOKS, YOU MUST WORK FOR IT... I WISH TO HELP THOSE WHO HELP THEMSELVES."

THE PEOPLE OF INDIANA, HE RIGHTLY DIVINED WERE PREPARED TO WORK FOR WHAT THEY COULD
OBTAIN FROM LIBRARY BOOKS. AS USUAL, HIS PRESCIENCE IN THIS MATTER WAS ACCURATE. THERE
ARE VERY FEW PERSONS IN INDIANA WHO HAVE NEVER SEEN, OR ADMIRED, OR USED, OR BEEN
AFFECTED BY A CARNEGIE LIBRARY. MOREOVER, ALTHOUGH MANY OF HIS BENEFACTIONS ARE STILL
IN USE AS LIBRARIES, MANY OTHERS NOW GRACE OUR URBAN LANDSCAPES AFTER HAVING BEEN
EFFECTIVELY ALTERED FOR OTHER CIVIC AND CULTURAL USES. FORTUNATELY ONLY A SMALL NUM-
BER HAVE BEEN DEMOLISHED BY MAN AND NATURE. WE OWE ANDREW CARNEGIE A GREAT DEBT OF
GRATITUDE.

WE ALSO OWE OUR GRATITUDE TO THE COMPILERS OF THIS FINE VOLUME, DOCUMENTING, AS IT
DOES IN SO HANDSOME A WAY, THE PRESENCE OF THESE LANDMARK STRUCTURES AMONG US OVER
THE PAST CENTURY.

DAVID KASER, DISTINGUISHED PROFESSOR EMERITUS, INDIANA UNIVERSITY

"Kewanna-Union Township Public Library"

PREFACE

"The taste for reading is one of the most precious possessions of life."

ANDREW CARNEGIE

I WAS RAISED IN A SMALL, NORTH CENTRAL INDIANA TOWN. OUR COMMUNITY CLAIMED A CARNEGIE LIBRARY, LIKE MANY OF THE NEIGHBORING TOWNS. LOOKING BACK, I REALLY DID NOT APPRECIATE THE OLD 1913 CARNEGIE LIBRARY UNTIL ADULTHOOD. DURING THE 1950S, THE LIBRARY WAS IN COMPETITION WITH THE MOVIES, COMIC BOOKS, AND TELEVISION FOR MY INTELLECTUAL ATTENTION. HOWEVER, THE LOCAL PUBLIC SCHOOL TEACHERS MADE SURE THAT STUDENTS WITH RESEARCH PAPERS FOR HOMEWORK BECAME FAMILIAR WITH THE WORLD OF BOOKS AT THE LOCAL CARNEGIE LIBRARY.

ONCE EXPOSED TO THE WORLD OF BOOKS IN THE LOCAL LIBRARY DURING MY SCHOOL BOUND YOUTH, MY LESS-THAN-ENTHUSIASTIC JUVENILE ATTITUDE SAW THE LIBRARY AS NO MORE A PLACE ONE MIGHT VISIT FROM TIME TO TIME. SPORTS, EXPLORING OUTDOORS, AND THOUGHTS OF GIRLS COMPETED FOR MY PRECIOUS MOMENTS, ESPECIALLY DURING MY TEENAGE YEARS AND WARM SUMMER MONTHS. FOR YEARS, I CARRIED THE SAME LIBRARY CARD THAT I HAD WHEN I WAS A KID WAY INTO ADULTHOOD. I DIDN'T WEAR IT OUT FROM OVERUSE.

FAVORABLE LIBRARY MEMORIES OF MY YOUTH CARRIED OVER INTO ADULTHOOD, AND I STILL VISIT THE LOCAL CARNEGIE LIBRARY IN SEARCH OF AN ANSWER TO A REFERENCE QUESTION OF THE MOMENT, OR TO FIND A BOOK THAT CONNECTS TO MY LATEST INTEREST. WHEREVER I DRIVE, I ALWAYS NOTICE THE CARNEGIE LIBRARIES AS I PASS THROUGH UNFAMILIAR TOWNS. I NEVER THOUGHT I WOULD "GROW UP" AND VISIT EVERY EXISTING CARNEGIE LIBRARY IN THE INDIANA OF MY TIME, BUT I HAVE. IT HAS BEEN AN EDUCATIONAL ODYSSEY.

MY JOURNEY TO DOCUMENT INDIANA CARNEGIE LIBRARIES BEGAN IN LIBRARY SCIENCE SCHOOL AT INDIANA UNIVERSITY DURING THE MID 1980S, WHEN A LIBRARIAN FRIEND SUGGESTED THAT, IF I WOULD PHOTOGRAPH INDIANA'S CARNEGIE LIBRARIES IN MY TRAVELS ABOUT THE STATE, SHE WOULD FEATURE THEM IN SLIDE PROGRAMS TO LOCAL COMMUNITY SOCIAL CLUBS. I AGREED. AFTER PHOTOGRAPHING TEN OR SO, I STARTED TO ENVISION A REFERENCE BOOK ON INDIANA CARNEGIE LIBRARIES.

DURING THE WARM MONTHS OF 2001, I MADE AN EFFORT TO VISIT, ON SUNNY DAYS WHENEVER POSSIBLE, EVERY EXISTING CARNEGIE LIBRARY BUILDING IN INDIANA. I WAS SUCCESSFUL IN SHOOTING OVER 1,500 EXTERIOR AND INTERIOR PHOTOGRAPHS. IN SPRING OF THE FOLLOWING YEAR, I RETURNED TO COMPLETE THE PHOTOGRAPHIC TASK. DURING THE WINTER OF 2002-2003, I FINISHED COMPILING AND WRITING THE MANUSCRIPT.

WITH A SINCERE DEBT OF GRATITUDE, I ACKNOWLEDGE ALL THE LIBRARIANS WHO CONTRIBUTED TO THIS BOOK, AND ALLOWED ME TO FREELY PHOTOGRAPH THEIR LIBRARIES AND COMPILE THEIR HISTORIES. I AM ALSO INDEBTED TO NUMEROUS PEOPLE WHO GRANTED ME PERMISSION TO REPRINT THEIR MATERIALS. A DEEP GRATITUDE GOES TO KATHIE SCOTT FOR ALL HER ENTHUSIASM, ORIGINAL RESEARCH, AND WRITING EFFORTS. A SPECIAL THANK YOU GOES TO DR. DAVID KASER, INDIANA UNIVERSITY EMERITUS AND DISTINGUISHED PROFESSOR OF LIBRARY SCIENCE, WHO WROTE THE FOREWORD TO THE BOOK. FINALLY, I WANT TO THANK MY PARENTS AND BROTHERS WHO FIRST READ BOOKS TO ME.

ALAN MCPHERSON

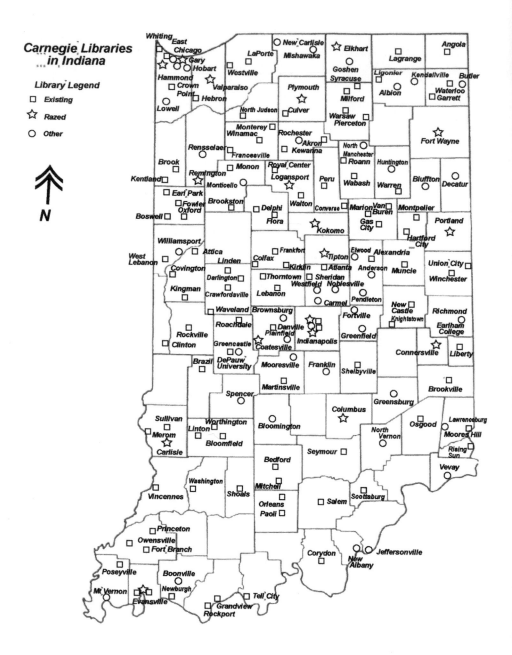

Carnegie Libraries in Indiana

"Muncie-Center Township Public Library"

OVERVIEW

"There is not such a cradle of democracy upon this earth as the Free Public Library."

ANDREW CARNEGIE

INDIANA HAS THE GREATEST NUMBER OF CARNEGIE FUNDED LIBRARY BUILD-INGS OF ANY STATE IN THE UNITED STATES, A FACT THAT HOOSIERS CAN BE PROUD OF. U. S. STEEL MANUFACTURER AND PHILANTHROPIST ANDREW CARNEGIE (1835-1919), THE "PATRON SAINT OF LIBRARIES," LOVED BOOKS IN HIS YOUTH, HAVING HAD ACCESS TO PRIVATE COLLECTIONS TO READ AND ENJOY. HIS LOVE OF BOOKS CARRIED OVER INTO HIS WEALTHY ADULTHOOD, CULMINAT-ING IN HIS WORLDWIDE LIBRARY PHILANTHROPY THAT INDIANIANS SHARED IN DURING THE EARLY 20TH CENTURY, AND ARE CONTINUING TO ENJOY IN THE 21ST CENTURY.

BEFORE CARNEGIE'S PHILANTHROPY, INDIANA'S PUBLICLY FUNDED TOWN-SHIP AND COUNTY LIBRARIES WERE RATHER LIMITED IN LITERARY SELECTION, POORLY HOUSED, AND OFTEN MEAGERLY STAFFED, BUT THEY WERE IN DEMAND BY A LITERATE READING PUBLIC. BEFORE 1880, INDIANA POSSESSED HARDLY ANY MAJOR PUBLIC COLLECTIONS OF BOOKS DESPITE THE GENEROSITY OF PRI-VATE ASSOCIATIONS SUCH AS THE WILLIAM MACLURE-FUNDED MECHANIC AND WORKINGMEN'S LIBRARIES, OF WHICH NEARLY EVERY INDIANA COUNTY HAD ONE. LITERARY AND WOMEN'S CLUBS GAVE THE LIBRARY MOVEMENT OF THE

LATE 19TH CENTURY MOMENTUM AND SUCCESS. STILL, WITHOUT ANDREW CARNEGIE'S FINANCIAL GIFTS, IT IS BELIEVED THAT MANY SMALLER INDIANA COMMUNITIES WOULD HAD TO DELAY ESTABLISHING THEIR LIBRARIES, OR WOULD NEVER HAVE HAD A PUBLIC LIBRARY.

A TOTAL OF 164 CARNEGIE FUNDED LIBRARY BUILDINGS WERE CONSTRUCTED FROM 1901 TO 1922 IN 155 INDIANA COMMUNITIES, RANGING FROM UNDER 1,000 RESIDENTS TO THE LARGEST CITY IN HOOSIERDOM, INDIANAPOLIS. ANOTHER PROUD HOOSIER FACT IS THAT NOT ONE OF THE INDIANA CARNEGIE COMMUNITIES DEFAULTED ON THE PLEDGE OF PROVIDING FOR A BUILDING ONCE IT WAS CONSTRUCTED.

THE "GOLDEN STATE" OF CALIFORNIA (142 LIBRARIES) AND NEIGHBORING ILLINOIS (106 LIBRARIES) RAN A DISTANT SECOND AND THIRD TO INDIANA IN THE NUMBER OF CARNEGIE LIBRARY BUILDINGS. THE "EMPIRE STATE" OF NEW YORK ALSO HAD 106 CARNEGIE LIBRARY BUILDINGS, ADJACENT OHIO HAD 105, AND NEARBY IOWA HAD 101. WHY DID INDIANA HAVE THE MOST CARNEGIE LIBRARIES?

A STRONG PUBLIC LIBRARY FERVOR ROLLED ACROSS INDIANA FROM 1900 TO 1929, THE HEYDAY OF THE "CARNEGIE ERA." A SYMPATHETIC PRESS REPORTED ON IT, AND THE POWER ELITE SUPPORTED IT. INDIANA AND OTHER MIDWEST STATES WERE CULTURALLY READY AND GEOGRAPHICALLY POSITIONED FOR MORE LIBRARIES, NOW THAT THE NORTHEASTERN STATES HAD LIBRARIES ALREADY IN PLACE. PRIOR TO THE CARNEGIE FREE PUBLIC LIBRARY, THE FORMER 19TH CENTURY SUBSCRIPTION, COUNTY, TOWNSHIP, AND SCHOOL LIBRARIES HAD FAILED TO PROVIDE THE FULFILLING COMMUNITY ROLE OF A PUBLIC LIBRARY.

IN 1891, THE INDIANA LIBRARY ASSOCIATION WAS ORGANIZED TO PROMOTE THE ESTABLISHMENT OF LOCAL LIBRARIES AND PRESS FOR MORE LIBERAL LEGISLATION IN THE MATTER OF LIBRARIES. A LEGISLATIVE ACT IN 1899 EXTENDED PERMISSION TO LEVY LOCAL TAXES FOR LIBRARIES AND ESTABLISH THE PUBLIC LIBRARY COMMISSION. THE EXCELLENT LEADERSHIP OF THE PUBLIC LIBRARY COMMISSION ADDED ENORMOUSLY TO THE LIBRARY MOVEMENT IN INDIANA BY WORKING WITH COMMUNITIES THAT SOUGHT CARNEGIE GIFT MONEY TO BUILD LIBRARIES. PROGRESSIVE HOOSIER COMMUNITIES PREFERRED A FREE CARNEGIE FUNDED LIBRARY.

THE CARNEGIE ERA OF LIBRARY BUILDING COINCIDED WITH THE NATIONAL CONSCIOUSNESS OF THE PROGRESSIVE ERA (1900-1920), WHICH HELD THAT MEMBERS OF SOCIETY HAVE A SOCIAL RESPONSIBILITY TO IMPROVE THEIR COMMUNITIES AND HOMES, AND TO RESPECT FAMILIES, NEIGHBORS, AND SHARED INSTITUTIONS. THE LIBRARIES WERE LANDMARKS OF PUBLIC AND PRIVATE ACHIEVEMENT AND PRIDE.

ON THE GRASSROOTS LEVEL, COMMUNITY PRIDE RANKS HIGH IN THE MOTIVATIONS OF LOCAL LIBRARY BOARDS AND THEIR CONSTITUENTS TO PURSUE THE CARNEGIE LIBRARY BUILDING GIFT. LIBRARIES, AFTER ALL, WERE INTELLECTUAL AND DEMOCRATIC INSTITUTIONS THAT WERE "FREE TO ALL," CHERISHED BY FREETHINKING HOOSIERS. RURAL FOLKS GENERALLY HAD LIMITED ACCESS TO BOOKS AND LIMITED MONEY TO BUY THEM. HOWEVER, THE BOOKS AT THE LOCAL PUBLIC LIBRARY PROVIDED TAX SUPPORTED, RECREATIONAL READING AND SOCIALIZING. A SMALL NUMBER OF INDIANA COMMUNITIES THAT DESIRED A CARNEGIE LIBRARY DID NOT SUCCEED IN OBTAINING ONE FOR A VARIETY OF REASONS, PRIMARILY ADMINISTRATIVE. STILL, DESPITE ORGANIZED LABOR 'S OPPOSITION TO CARNEGIE AND HIS "BLOOD MONEY" FOR LIBRARIES AFTER THE HOMESTEAD, PENNSYLVANIA STRIKE OF 1892, UNION ACTIVITY DID NOT DETER THE ESTABLISHMENT OF ANY INDIANA CARNEGIE LIBRARY.

Wm Maclure

"Indiana's First Library Philanthropist"

WILLIAM MACLURE (1763-1840)

WILLIAM MACLURE WAS BORN IN AYR, SCOTLAND AND CAME TO THE UNITED STATES AT AGE 33 IN 1796. SELF-TRAINED IN GEOLOGY, MACLURE WAS A WEALTHY, EMINENT SCIENTIST. HE WAS EMPLOYED BY THE UNITED STATES GOVERNMENT TO MAP A NATIONWIDE GEOLOGICAL SURVEY THAT WAS PUBLISHED IN 1809, EARNING HIM THE TITLE, "FATHER OF AMERICAN GEOLOGY." MACLURE WAS ONE OF THE FOUNDERS AND PRESIDENTS OF THE PHILADELPHIA ACADEMY OF NATURAL SCIENCE.

IN 1827, MACLURE WAS INVITED TO NEW HARMONY BY SOCIAL REFORMER ROBERT OWEN TO BE A PARTNER IN HIS UTOPIAN SOCIALIST VENTURE. IN THE OWEN COMMUNITY, MACLURE BECAME THE HEAD OF EDUCATION, AND THE TOWNSPEOPLE WERE INVITED TO USE HIS PRIVATE LIBRARY. BESIDES GEOLOGY, MACLURE HAD A STRONG INTEREST IN PROGRESSIVE EDUCATION ESPECIALLY, FOR THE WORKING CLASS. HE CREATED THE WORKINGMEN'S INSTITUTE OR PUBLIC LIBRARY THAT STILL EXISTS IN NEW HARMONY TODAY.

AFTER A YEAR, OWEN'S SOCIAL EXPERIMENT AT NEW HARMONY FAILED, AND MACLURE TRAVELED TO MEXICO IN 1828. HE LIVED IN MEXICO FOR TWELVE YEARS AND DIED AT AGE 77 ON MARCH 23, 1840 AT SAN ANGEL, EN ROUTE BACK TO NEW HARMONY, INDIANA. IN HIS CONTROVERSIAL 1839 WILL, MACLURE LEFT $80,000 FOR THE ESTABLISHMENT OF WORKINGMEN'S INSTITUTES OR LIBRARIES IN INDIANA. THE 1838 MISSION STATEMENT OF THE WORKINGMEN'S INSTITUTES CALLED FOR THE "DIFFUSION OF USEFUL KNOWLEDGE, BY MUTUAL INTEREST AMONG THE WORKING CLASSES, THE PRODUCING CLASSES WHO LABORED WITH THEIR HANDS, AND GAIN THEIR BREAD BY THE SWEAT OF THEIR BROW."

BY 1855, 146 LIBRARIES WERE FORMED IN 89 INDIANA COUNTIES, AND $500 PER LIBRARY WAS GRANTED. BOOKS PURCHASED FROM THIS MACLURE FINANCIAL GIFT INCLUDED NOVELS, BIOGRAPHIES, HISTORY, TRAVEL, SCIENCE, AND GOVERNMENT DOCUMENTS. IN TIME, THE MACLURE COLLECTIONS, AT LEAST THE ONES NOT WORN OUT OR SCATTERED, WERE EVENTUALLY ABSORBED, MAINLY BY THE TOWNSHIP LIBRARIES, AND LATER BY THE CARNEGIE LIBRARIES. WILLIAM MACLURE WAS THE FIRST MAJOR PHILANTHROPIST IN INDIANA TO MAKE A SIGNIFICANT CONTRIBUTION TO HOOSIER PUBLIC LIBRARY CULTURE.

INDIANA'S "STRONG" LIBRARY LAW WAS ENACTED THE YEAR IN WHICH MR. CARNEGIE MADE THE FIRST LIBRARY GIFT TO INDIANA AT GOSHEN, JANUARY 15, 1901. THE INDIANA PUBLIC LIBRARY COMMISSION WAS STAFFED BY PROFESSIONALS WHOSE MISSION IT WAS TO BRING LIBRARIES TO THE PEOPLE, AND THEY DID. THE AWARENESS OF CARNEGIE GRANTS AND THE DESIRE OF COMMUNITIES FOR LIBRARIES WAS STRONG; NOT ONLY IN INDIANA, BUT THROUGHOUT THE MIDDLE WEST. THE EASTERN STATES ALREADY HAD LIBRARIES IN PLACE, AND CARNEGIE LIBRARY BUILDINGS WERE NOT AS MUCH IN DEMAND IN THE NEW ENGLAND AND MID ATLANTIC REGION, AND NOR WAS THE REGIONS OF THE SOUTH OR WEST CULTURALLY POISED OR ORGANIZED TO RECEIVE CARNEGIE FUNDED LIBRARIES. AFTER THE CITIZENS OF INDIANA RECEIVED THEIR CARNEGIE LIBRARIES, THEY WERE ADEQUATELY MAINTAINED AND PATRONIZED.

OVER 2.6 MILLION DOLLARS FROM THE CARNEGIE CORPORATION WENT TO BUILD 164 PUBLIC LIBRARIES IN INDIANA. THERE WERE ALSO TWO COLLEGES IN INDIANA THAT CARNEGIE HELPED FUND TO BUILD ACADEMIC LIBRARIES AND A "CARNEGIE HALL" AT MOORES HILL IN DEARBORN COUNTY. ALTHOUGH OFTEN INVITED, MR. CARNEGIE NEVER ATTENDED ONE LIBRARY BUILDING DEDICATION IN INDIANA. LIBRARY GIFTS ENDED ON NOVEMBER 7, 1917, THE DAY WHEN THE UNITED STATES ENTERED WORLD WAR I, BUT MONEY CONTINUED TO BE ALLOCATED DURING THE 1920S FOR PREVIOUS GIFT OFFERS. WHERE GRANTS HAD ALREADY BEEN PROMISED, CONSTRUCTION WAS DELAYED BY THE COUNCIL OF NATIONAL DEFENSE, BUT GRANTS WERE MADE AS LATE AS 1919 FOR HONORED REQUESTS WHICH HAD BEEN MADE BEFORE 1917. THE NORTHWESTERN COMMUNITY OF LOWELL RECEIVED THE LAST INDIANA CARNEGIE GIFT IN MARCH OF 1918. BY 1920, AFTER ANDREW CARNEGIE'S DEATH, THE CARNEGIE CORPORATION DECIDED THE MISSION OF LIBRARY BUILDING THROUGHOUT THE ENGLISH-SPEAKING WORLD HAD BEEN, BY AND LARGE ACCOMPLISHED. IN INDIANA, THE LAST CARNEGIE LIBRARY BUILDING COMPLETED WAS AT NORTH JUDSON IN 1922.

"AN ADVOCATE OF CARNEGIE PUBLIC LIBRARIES"

INDIANA PUBLIC LIBRARY COMMISSION (1899-1925)

THE INDIANA PUBLIC LIBRARY COMMISSION (IPLC) WAS A GUIDING FORCE IN THE GROWING PUBLIC LIBRARY MOVEMENT IN INDIANA FROM THE BEGINNING OF THE 20TH CENTURY TO THE MID 1920S, WHEN THE COMMISSION WAS ABSORBED BY THE INDIANA LIBRARY AND HISTORICAL DEPARTMENT. THE IPLC WAS CREATED BY A TIMELY LEGISLATIVE ACT, WHEREBY THREE COMMISSION MEMBERS, APPOINTED BY THE GOVERNOR, ESTABLISHED AND MAINTAINED A PERMANENT LIBRARY SERVICE FOR INDIANA. THE YEARS DURING WHICH THE IPLC OPERATED CONVENIENTLY COINCIDED WITH THE YEARS THE CARNEGIE GIFTS WERE AVAILABLE. IT WAS THE "GOLDEN AGE" FOR INDIANA'S PUBLIC LIBRARIES.

THE IPLC GOT LIBRARIES STARTED OFF ON THE RIGHT FOOTING. ALTHOUGH THE IPLC PURCHASED BOOKS AND EQUIPMENT, GAVE ADVICE, PREPARED LIBRARIES FOR CIRCULATION, ORGANIZED LIBRARIAN TRAINING SCHOOLS AND INSTITUTES, AND ESTABLISHED TRAVELING LIBRARIES, ITS MOST LASTING ROLE WAS AS A GUIDE TO LOCAL LIBRARY BOARDS BUILDING CARNEGIE LIBRARIES. LIBRARY COMMITTEES WERE ENCOURAGED TO TAKE ADVANTAGE OF THE CARNEGIE FINANCIAL GIFTS BY THE COMMISSION. THE *LIBRARY OCCURRENT*, THE MAGAZINE OF THE IPLC, "NETWORKED" INFORMATION ABOUT INDIANA LIBRARIES AROUND THE STATE, ALLOWING LIBRARIANS TO KEEP ABREAST OF RECENT DEVELOPMENTS SUCH AS GRANTS, DEDICATIONS, AND EACH OTHER.

IN BRIEF, THE MISSION OF THE IPLC WAS THE ESTABLISHMENT AND DEVELOPMENT OF PUBLIC LIBRARIES IN INDIANA DURING THE "CARNEGIE ERA," AND THAT MISSION WAS SUCCESSFUL. TODAY, HOOSIERS ARE STILL RECEIVING THE BENEFITS OF THE EFFORTS OF THE INDIANA PUBLIC LIBRARY COMMISSION.

During the Carnegie building years, from 1901 to 1922, the citizens of Indiana underwent various cultural changes. Indiana produced an astonishing number of writers who earned national literary fame in the "Golden Age of Indiana Literature (1880-1920)." Hoosiers were proud of the Hoosier Writers Group of the late 19th and early 20th century. Such best selling writers as Booth Tarkington, Maurice Thompson, George Ade, Meredith Nicholson, William Vaughn Moody, David Graham Phillips, George Barr McCutcheon, James Whitcomb Riley, Charles Major, Theodore Dreiser, and Gene Stratton Porter were Indianians who were read by a national audience and were rewarded for their literary merit. Partially influenced by Indiana's contribution to the nation's literature by its native sons and daughters, the numerous literary clubs that flourished in Indiana's communities during the "Golden Years" helped to provide an appreciative environment for authors and encourage the growth of public libraries.

Women literary clubs also played an important role in the establishment of Carnegie libraries in Indiana. It was a worthwhile, noble cause they championed. For some women, libraries were a part of the greater women's movement that was taking place in America during the 1890s and early 20th century. Women wanted decent reading material for their families, and with the approval of the men of their communities, organized women clubs were highly successful in their efforts to bring Carnegie public libraries to their communities. The Indiana Union of Literary Clubs was also successful in convincing legislators to establish the Public Library Commission and adopt the 1899 public library law. Over 30 women literary societies founded in 1890 are still in existence and functioning around the state.

From 1900 to 1925, Indiana's library system was changed remarkably and expanded as a result of progressive public policy and bountiful private philanthropy. Once the community met Carnegie's requirements, such as providing a building site and adequate taxation for upkeep, financial gifts were obtained from Andrew Carnegie via his private secretary, James Bertram. Library boards wasted no time in letting contracts for architects and general building contractors. Until 1908, each community built its library as it deemed appropriate, once the site was provided and the annual maintenance pledge was signed. However, in order to prevent costly design errors, the Carnegie Corporation issued a pamphlet entitled, *"Notes on the Erection of Library Buildings"*, which provided certain practical standards for libraries in 1908.

Library architectural design was considered a specialty among architects, and several architects of libraries achieved regional prominence in Indiana. Wilson B. Parker of Indianapolis designed over 20 Carnegie funded libraries, the greatest number of any architect of Carnegie libraries in Indiana. A close second was Clifford Shopbell of Evansville. Additional outstanding architects who designed several Carnegie libraries in Indiana include Patton & Miller of Chicago, True L. Brookie of Indianapolis, Samuel A. Craig of Huntington, and Charles E. Kendrick of Rochester.

The greatest number of Carnegie libraries in Indiana were architecturally designed in the neoclassic Greek and Roman styles or the Craftsman-Prairie Tradition style. These early 20th century architectural styles set the national tone at the 1893 Chicago World's Columbian Exposition, where many of the buildings departed from the 19th century Romanesque movement, thus setting the pattern for

19

THE NEXT THIRTY YEARS OF NEOCLASSICAL REVIVAL OR BEAUX ARTS STYLES. THE RISE OF THE MIDWESTERN PRAIRIE SCHOOL OF DESIGN, OF WHICH FRANK LLOYD WRIGHT WAS THE GREATEST PROPONENT, AND THE ARTS AND CRAFTS MOVEMENT, WERE ALSO REFLECTED IN INDIANA'S CARNEGIE LIBRARY ARCHITECTURE.

CARNEGIE LIBRARY BUILDINGS WERE DISTINCTIVE, AND THE FORMAL EXTERIORS APPEALED TO THE PUBLIC. THEY WERE USUALLY SITUATED ALONG OR NEAR THE MAIN STREETS OF MOST COMMUNITIES, WHERE CITIZENS WOULD CONGREGATE. PATRONS "STEPPED UP" INTELLECTUALLY WHEN THEY WALKED UP THE MAIN ENTRYWAY, ENTERING "HIGHER GROUND" THROUGH THE TEMPLE-LIKE PORTAL INTO THE ROOMS OF KNOWLEDGE. MANY OF THE INTERIORS RETAIN THEIR ORIGINAL FURNISHINGS, SUCH AS STAINED GLASS, BRASS LAMPS, FIREPLACES, CEILING FANS, DARK OAK BOOKSHELVES, MARBLE FLOORS, AND OAK FURNITURE. INDIANA'S NON-CARNEGIE LIBRARIES, SUCH AS THOSE IN AURORA, AUBURN, AND GOODLAND, ALSO BUILT IN EARLY 20TH CENTURY, REFLECT MANY FEATURES OF "CARNEGIE LIBRARY ARCHITECTURE."

AFTER A DESIGN WAS SELECTED, IT WAS UP TO THE GENERAL BUILDING CONTRACTOR TO REALIZE THE ARCHITECT'S PLANS. THE CONTRACTOR USUALLY LIVED AND WORKED LOCALLY IN THE AREA, BUT FREQUENTLY CONTRACTS WERE LET TO CONTRACTORS AND THEIR CONSTRUCTION CREWS WHO CAME FROM A FEW HUNDRED MILES AWAY. CONTRACTORS OFTEN HAD CLOSE WORKING TIES TO THE ARCHITECT. PLUMBING AND ELECTRICITY WERE OFTEN SUBCONTRACTED. SUBJECT TO THE WEATHER AND WORLD WAR I RATIONING, THE CONSTRUCTION OF A LIBRARY USUALLY TOOK A NUMBER OF MONTHS. THE LAYING OF THE CORNERSTONE WAS OFTEN A CELEBRATED MOMENT IN THE CONSTRUCTION PHASE. THE FORMAL SERVICES WERE USUALLY CONDUCTED BY THE LOCAL MASONIC ORDER. UPON COMPLETION, THE LIBRARY WAS NEARLY ALWAYS DEDICATED WITH FANFARE, ESPECIALLY AROUND THE TIME OF A NATIONAL HOLIDAY.

THE BEGINNING OF WORLD WAR I TERMINATED THE CARNEGIE LIBRARY BUILDING PROGRAM FOREVER. SEVERAL LIBRARY PROJECTS THAT HAD MONIES PLEDGED WERE DELAYED BY THE SACRIFICES OF THE GREAT WAR. INFLATION OVER THE YEARS TOOK ITS TOLL, SO THE EARLIER CONSTRUCTED CARNEGIE LIBRARIES ACQUIRED MORE BUILDING FOR EACH DOLLAR INVESTED. THE MORE GRANDIOSE AND ELEGANT BUILDINGS WERE CONSTRUCTED BEFORE 1908 WHEN LOCAL LIBRARY BOARDS HAD GREATER SAY ON HOW THE BUILDING WAS TO BE DESIGNED. TO REDUCE THE WASTEFUL SPENDING OF THE EARLIER YEARS (PRE-1908) OF LIBRARY BUILDING, CARNEGIE PLACED MORE EMPHASIS ON SIMPLE, FUNCTIONAL, OR PRACTICAL BUILDINGS, AND HAD THE FINAL SAY ON AN ARCHITECT'S PLANS.

TODAY, AFTER A CENTURY SINCE THE FIRST CARNEGIE GIFT TO INDIANA, 106 OF THE ORIGINAL 164 LIBRARIES ARE STILL SERVING PATRONS. MANY OF THE ORIGINAL CARNEGIE LIBRARY BUILDINGS HAVE BEEN STRUCTURALLY MODIFIED TO ACCOMMODATE GROWING NUMBERS OF PATRONS, AND THE LATEST TECHNOLOGY, ESPECIALLY IN THE LARGER COMMUNITIES. FORTY OF THE LIBRARY BUILDINGS NO LONGER SERVE AS LIBRARIES PRIMARILY DUE TO A LACK OF SPACE TO ACCOMMODATE NEW MATERIALS. HOWEVER, THE ABANDONED CARNEGIE BUILDINGS NOW SERVE IN OTHER PUBLIC CAPACITIES, SUCH AS GOVERNMENT AND COMMERCIAL OFFICES, RESTAURANTS, YOUTH CENTERS, APARTMENTS, AND HOMES. SOME WERE NOT AS FORTUNATE, FOR EIGHTEEN

CARNEGIE LIBRARY BUILDINGS HAVE BEEN DEMOLISHED BY THE HANDS OF MAN AND THE ELEMENTS OF NATURE.

THE FUTURE OF THE REMAINING CARNEGIE LIBRARIES IN INDIANA IS FAIRLY BRIGHT OVERALL. ALTHOUGH MORE CARNEGIE LIBRARIES WILL BE RETIRED FROM PUBLIC SERVICE AS LIBRARIES, THEY WILL LIKELY BE SPARED THE WRECKING BALL, AND WILL CONTINUE TO SERVE COMMUNITIES IN OTHER BENEFICIAL WAYS. SEVERAL CARNEGIE LIBRARY BUILDINGS HAVE BEEN ADDED TO THE NATIONAL REGISTER OF HISTORIC PLACES.

ANDREW CARNEGIE'S OFFER OF FREE LIBRARIES WENT A LONG WAYS IN INDIANA. THEY WERE HIGHLY APPRECIATED AND HAVE BECOME SIGNIFICANT CULTURAL INSTITUTIONS IN MANY OF INDIANA'S COMMUNITIES. HOOSIERS WILL ALWAYS BE THANKFUL TO ANDREW CARNEGIE FOR HIS GIFTS AND HIS RICH LEGACY TO THEIR HOMETOWNS AND STATE.

"PATRON SAINT OF LIBRARIES"

ANDREW CARNEGIE (1835-1919)

ANDREW CARNEGIE WAS BORN A SON IN DUMFERMLINE, SCOTLAND, OF A WEAVER WHO IMMIGRATED, ALONG WITH HIS FAMILY, TO PITTSBURGH, PENNSYLVANIA AT AGE 12 IN 1848. ANDREW WAS EMPLOYED AS A BOBBIN BOY BUT HE SOON ADVANCED BY SUCCESSIVE PROMOTIONS TO A POSITION OF WEALTH AND POWER. ALTHOUGH HIS FORMAL EDUCATION ENDED WHEN YOUNG ANDREW ARRIVED IN AMERICA, HE CONTINUED HIS LIFELONG LOVE OF EDUCATION BY READING BOOKS. HE ESPECIALLY ENJOYED READING AS A WORKING LAD, AND NEVER FORGOT READING BOOKS FROM THE PRIVATE LIBRARY OF RETIRED MERCHANT COLONEL ANDERSON.

INVESTING WISELY, ANDREW CARNEGIE STROVE FOR SUCCESS AND WENT FROM "RAGS TO RICHES," LIKE THE CHARACTERS IN THE 19TH CENTURY NOVELS BY HORATIO ALGER. HELPING BUILD THE INDUSTRIAL FOUNDATION OF POST CIVIL WAR AMERICA, CARNEGIE BECAME THE "KING OF STEEL" IN 1899, WHEN THE CARNEGIE STEEL CORPORATION CONTROLLED ONE QUARTER OF AMERICAN STEEL PRODUCTION. IN 1901, AT AGE 66, HE SOLD HIS CORPORATION TO U. S. STEEL AND J. P. MORGAN AND RETIRED TO GIVE AWAY HIS AMASSED FORTUNE. IN HIS BOOK *THE GOSPEL OF WEALTH*, HE NOTED THAT "A MAN WHO DIES RICH, DIES DISGRACED." HE SAW IT AS HIS CIVIC DUTY TO INVEST HIS MILLIONS FOR THE GOOD OF HUMANITY.

ONE OF THE GREATEST EXAMPLES OF ANDREW CARNEGIE'S PHILANTHROPY WAS THE $55 MILLION DOLLAR FUNDING OF 2,509 LIBRARIES IN THE LATE 1800s AND EARLY 1900s THROUGHOUT THE ENGLISH-SPEAKING WORLD. OF THIS TOTAL, 1,679 LIBRARIES WERE CONSTRUCTED IN THE UNITED STATES AND INDIANA RECEIVED THE MOST OF ANY STATE: 164 LIBRARIES IN 155 COMMUNITIES AT A COST OF $2,614,000. IN ADDITION, INDIANA HAD TWO CARNEGIE-FUNDED ACADEMIC LIBRARIES AT DEPAUW AND EARLHAM, AND INDIANA HAD ITS OWN "CARNEGIE HALL" AT MOORES HILL COLLEGE.

CARNEGIE BELIEVED THAT THE PUBLIC LIBRARY WAS "THE PEOPLE'S UNIVERSITY," WHICH ALLOWED THOSE WHO WERE ABLE AND WILLING TO EDUCATE THEMSELVES AND BE SUCCESSFUL IN AMERICA, MUCH LIKE HIMSELF. LIBRARIES, HE BELIEVED, ADDED TO THE MERITOCRATIC NATURE OF AMERICA; THEY FAVORED AWARD ON THE BASIS OF ABILITY AND DEMOCRATIC EQUALITY. CARNEGIE ALSO BELIEVED THAT IMMIGRANTS LIKE HIS SELF NEEDED A CULTURAL KNOWLEDGE OF AMERICA THAT PUBLIC LIBRARIES AND THE POWER OF BOOKS OFFERED, IF THEY SO DESIRED.

CARNEGIE'S LEGACY LIVES ON IN THE LIBRARIES HIS WEALTH MADE POSSIBLE. THE MILLIONAIRE BENEFACTOR DISTRIBUTED 90% OF HIS WEALTH FOR THE ELEVATION AND BENEFIT OF THE HUMAN RACE. HE WAS COMMITTED TO WORLD PEACE, EDUCATION, AND FREE ACCESS TO INFORMATION. "THE MAN WHO ENTERS A LIBRARY IS IN THE BEST SOCIETY THE WORLD OFFERS," HE ONCE SAID. ANDREW CARNEGIE DIED AT AGE 83 AND WAS BURIED AT NORTH TARRYTOWN, NEW YORK IN AUGUST, 1919.

"*Andrew Carnegie (1835-1919)*"

Painting by Luis Mora

CARNEGIE BLESSED

A CENTURY OF SERVICE

"Akron Carnegie Public Library, Facade"

AKRON

AKRON CARNEGIE PUBLIC LIBRARY

EXCERPTS FROM THE *"HISTORY OF THE AKRON PUBLIC LIBRARY"* FILE:

"PRIOR TO 1870, AKRON'S SMALL COLLECTION OF BOOKS WAS SHELVED IN MILO BRIGHT'S DRUG STORE. MR. BRIGHT RECEIVED A SMALL SUM FROM THE HENRY TOWNSHIP TRUSTEES TO TAKE CARE OF AND LOAN BOOKS. THE COLLECTION WAS LATER MOVED TO ANOTHER STORE IN NEARBY MILLARK VILLAGE IN SOUTHWEST HENRY TOWNSHIP.

BY 1912, THE REV. M. H. KRAUSE, PASTOR OF THE AKRON METHODIST CHURCH AND A FEW OTHER PUBLIC-SPIRITED CITIZENS OF AKRON BEGAN WORKING TO OBTAIN A PERMANENT LIBRARY BUILDING. PETITIONS WERE CIRCULATED AND THE PROCESS BEGAN. THE AKRON LIBRARY, NOW HOUSED IN ROOMS OVER THE WILHOIT AND HOFFMAN MEAT MARKET IN AKRON, FIRST OPENED ITS DOORS ON AUGUST 19, 1912 WITH 260 BOOKS.

EARLY IN 1913, THE REV. M. H. KRAUSE BEGAN HIS CORRESPONDENCE WITH THE CARNEGIE CORPORATION AND ON MAY 21, 1913, A GRANT OF $12,500 WAS AWARDED TO AKRON FOR ITS NEW LIBRARY BUILDING, PROVIDED THAT THE LOCAL LIBRARY BOARD GUARANTEED A SUFFICIENT AMOUNT EACH YEAR TO SUPPORT THE LIBRARY. A SITE WAS SECURED, ONE SQUARE BLOCK EAST OF THE INTERURBAN LINE ON MAIN STREET FROM MORRETT AND PAXTON, FOR A SUM OF $1,500.

ON OCTOBER 28, 1914, A CROWD OF NEARLY 1,000 RESIDENTS ATTENDED THE LAYING OF THE CORNERSTONE FOR THE NEW CARNEGIE LIBRARY. NEARLY 12 MONTHS AFTER LETTING THE CON-TRACT, THE AKRON LIBRARY MOVED INTO THE BRICK BUILDING THAT WAS FURNISHED WITH LIBRARY BUREAU FURNITURE. THE LIBRARY WAS DEDICATED ON OCTOBER 21, 1915."

TODAY THE AKRON CARNEGIE PUBLIC LIBRARY IS STILL FLOURISHING AND IS CURRENTLY ADDING A SOUTH ADDITION TO THE ORIGINAL BUILDING THAT WILL PROVIDE MORE SPACE IN THE 21ST CEN-TURY.

GIFT: $12,500; MAY 21, 1913
DEDICATION: OCTOBER 21, 1915
ARCHITECT: GRIFFITH & FAIR, FORT WAYNE
CONTRACTOR: MILO CUTSHALL, AKRON
STYLE: NEO CLASSICAL REVIVAL

"Alexandria-Monroe Public Library, Ornate Modillion"

ALEXANDRIA

ALEXANDRIA-MONROE PUBLIC LIBRARY

IN 1901, THE REV. J. CHALLEN SMITH HEADED A COMMITTEE THAT WAS FORMED TO CONTACT THE CARNEGIE LIBRARY FOUNDATION FOR FUNDING FOR A NEW BUILDING. CARNEGIE AGREED TO MAKE A GIFT OF $14,000 TO BUILD THE NEW LIBRARY, INCLUDING SHELVES AND FURNITURE. A SITE WAS PURCHASED FROM ANTHONY E. BENTONE ON EAST CHURCH STREET, AND WORK ON THE NEW BUILDING WAS BEGUN IN 1902.

THE CARNEGIE FUNDED BUILDING WAS OPEN TO THE PUBLIC ON DECEMBER 3, 1903, AND A PUBLIC DEDICATION WAS HELD IN THE METHODIST CHURCH THAT EVENING. THE PRESIDENT OF EARLHAM COLLEGE, ROBERT L. KELLY, DELIVERED THE ADDRESS, *"THE FLOWER OF CIVILIZATION."* AN ACCOUNT OF THE DEDICATION AND THE GRAND OPENING WAS PRINTED IN THE *ALEXANDRIA TIMES* OF DECEMBER 5, 1903. THE FOLLOWING IS AN EXCERPT FROM THAT ACCOUNT:

"ALL FEAR OR LACK OF APPRECIATION FOR THE GOOD WHICH ALEXANDRIA AND MONROE TOWNSHIP HAVE RECEIVED AT THE HANDS OF THE GENEROUS ANDREW CARNEGIE MUST HAVE VANISHED FROM THE MIND OF HIM WHO SAW AND OBSERVED THE GREAT THRONGS ATTENDING THE FORMAL OPENING OF THE NEW CARNEGIE LIBRARY. THE CITY AND THE RURAL DISTRICTS WERE REPRESENTED IN THE HAPPY THRONG, AND FROM EVERY FACE THEY BEAMED THE LIGHT OF COMMON PRIDE IN A PRECIOUS AND PRICELESS POSSESSION."

OVER THE LAST CENTURY, THE ALEXANDRIA-MONROE PUBLIC LIBRARY HAS TRIPLED IN SIZE. A RECENT ADDITION WAS DEDICATED IN 1990. MUCH OF THE ORIGINAL CARNEGIE LIBRARY WAS CONVERTED INTO LIBRARY OFFICE SPACE AND IS OFF LIMITS TO THE GENERAL PUBLIC.

GIFT: $14,000; APRIL 26, 1902
DEDICATION: DECEMBER 3, 1903
ARCHITECT: WING & MAHURIN, FORT WAYNE
CONTRACTOR: JOHN E. BARNES & SON, LOGANSPORT
STYLE: NEO CLASSICAL REVIVAL

"Carnegie Library of Steuben County, Angola, Interior, West Wall"

ANGOLA

CARNEGIE PUBLIC LIBRARY OF STEUBEN COUNTY

DURING THE LATE 1800S, A SMALL CIRCULATING LIBRARY, SUPPORTED BY PRIVATE SUBSCRIPTIONS FROM BOTH TOWN AND TOWNSHIP PATRONS, FORMED THE CORE OF THE FIRST LIBRARY IN ANGOLA. IN THE 1850S, AND 1860S, MACLURE OF NEW HARMONY PROVIDED A COLLECTION OF BOOKS THAT EVENTUALLY BECAME UNACCOUNTED FOR. IN 1895, THE LADIES OF THE VARIOUS CLUBS IN ANGOLA, ESPECIALLY THE SOROSIS CIRCLE, FORMED THE SUPPORT OF A CIRCULATING LIBRARY, WHICH OPENED IN 1898.

IN MARCH OF 1909, ANGOLA WAS AWARDED A $10,000 CARNEGIE GIFT. OVER SIX YEARS LATER, THE CARNEGIE LIBRARY WAS DEDICATED. THE LOCAL NEWSPAPER, THE *ANGOLA REPUBLICAN*, ADVERTISED THE OPENING BY RUNNING A FRONT PAGE ARTICLE WHICH READ AS FOLLOWS:

"THE NEW PUBLIC LIBRARY, IN MCCONNELL PARK ON SOUTH WAYNE STREET, WILL BE OPENED TO THE PUBLIC ON SATURDAY, NOV. 27, 1915. THERE WILL BE NO FORMAL CEREMONIES TO CELEBRATE THE OCCASION, BUT MEMBERS OF THE BOARD WILL BE PRESENT TO WELCOME VISITORS AND SHOW THEM THROUGH THE BUILDING. ALL THE CITIZENS OF THE TOWN AND TOWNSHIP ARE URGED TO CALL ON AND INSPECT THE NEW LIBRARY, AND BEGIN TO USE IT."

NEARLY 73 YEARS LATER, THE DEDICATION OF A BUILDING ADDITION WAS HELD ON DECEMBER 11, 1988. THE DECISION WAS MADE TO PRESERVE THE ORIGINAL BUILDING WHILE NEARLY ENCLOSING THE WEST, EAST, AND SOUTH EXTERIORS, MORE THAN QUADRUPLING THE ORIGINAL CARNEGIE LIBRARY. VISITORS MAY, THUS STILL ENJOY THE ORIGINAL CARNEGIE STRUCTURE THAT HOUSES THE INDIANA AND GENEALOGICAL COLLECTIONS.

GIFT: $10,000; MARCH 27, 1909
DEDICATION: NOVEMBER 27, 1915
ARCHITECT: COSMO C. ELLWOOD, ELKHART
CONTRACTOR: A. H. ELLWOOD & SON, ELKHART
STYLE: CRAFTSMAN-PRAIRIE TRADITION

"Hamilton North Public Library, Library Bureau Furniture"

ATLANTA

HAMILTON NORTH PUBLIC LIBRARY

EXCERPTS FROM THE *"HISTORY OF THE ATLANTA JACKSON TOWNSHIP PUBLIC LIBRARY"* FILE, 1930:

"N. A. RHOADS, A TRAVELING SALESMAN AND CITIZEN OF ATLANTA, SAW THAT PUBLIC LIBRARIES WERE BEING BUILT AROUND THE STATE DURING THE EARLY 1900s AND THOUGHT HIS HOMETOWN WAS ELIGIBLE FOR THE SAME BENEFACTION. ON FEBRUARY 19, 1916, A PETITION WAS CIRCULATED AMONG THE CITIZENS OF JACKSON TOWNSHIP THAT RESULTED IN THE REQUIRED AMOUNT OF SIGNATURES FOR A PUBLIC LIBRARY. A BOARD OF TRUSTEES WERE DULY APPOINTED AND ON MARCH 27, 1916 WERE ORGANIZED.

ON MAY 15, 1916 A GIFT OF $10,000 WAS SECURED FROM THE CARNEGIE CORPORATION. THE PROPERTY FOR THE LIBRARY WAS PURCHASED FROM N. J. GOODYKOONTZ FOR $975, SEPTEMBER 5, 1916. THE CORNERSTONE WAS LAID BY THE ATLANTA LODGE 703 F. & A. M. BY APPROPRIATE CEREMONIES ON NOVEMBER 23, 1916. ON OCTOBER 12, 1917 THE LIBRARY WAS DEDICATED WITH A FITTING CEREMONY. DEMARCHUS BROWN, STATE LIBRARIAN, WAS THE DEDICATION MAIN SPEAKER. THE FIRST ANNUAL REPORT SHOWED 1,560 VOLUMES IN THE LIBRARY WITH A CIRCULATION OF 2,487 BOOKS FOR THE YEAR."

BASICALLY, THE CARNEGIE LIBRARY BUILDING REMAINS PHYSICALLY UNCHANGED FROM ITS ORIGINAL DESIGN. TO EFFICIENTLY SERVE THE DEMANDS OF THE AREA PATRONS, BRANCHES WERE ALSO ESTABLISHED IN NEARBY CICERO AND ARCADIA, AND THE LIBRARY SYSTEM WAS RENAMED THE HAMILTON NORTH PUBLIC LIBRARY.

GIFT: $10,000; MAY 15, 1916
DEDICATION: OCTOBER 12, 1917
ARCHITECT: A. A. HONEYWELL, KOKOMO
CONTRACTOR: UNLOCATED
STYLE: CRAFTSMAN-PRAIRIE TRADITION

"Attica Public Library, Facade"

ATTICA

ATTICA PUBLIC LIBRARY

THE ATTICA PUBLIC LIBRARY HAD ITS EARLIEST BEGINNINGS IN A HISTORY CLASS OF THE SOCIETY TO ENCOURAGE STUDY AT HOME, WHICH WAS FOUNDED IN BOSTON, MASSACHUSETTS. THE LADIES' LIBRARY ASSOCIATION IN ATTICA WAS FORMED AS AN OUTGROWTH OF THIS CLASS. BECAUSE THE MEMBERS HAD TO BORROW THE BOOKS THEY NEEDED, THE LADIES DECIDED TO BEGIN ORGANIZING A LIBRARY OF THEIR OWN.

DUES OF $2.00 ANNUALLY, WHICH WAS LATER REDUCED TO $1.00. ON JULY 9, 1887, THE ATTICA CITY COUNCIL, FOR THE SUM OF $1.00, DEEDED TO THE ASSOCIATION A TRIANGULAR PLOT OF GROUND BOUNDED BY BRADY, MAIN, AND MILL STREETS, UPON WHICH THEY ERECTED A SMALL FRAME LIBRARY BUILDING IN 1889. LATER A CITY LIBRARY WAS MADE POSSIBLE UNDER THE LIBRARY ACT OF 1901, SO THE LADIES DEEDED THEIR LIBRARY BUILDING TO THE CITY OF ATTICA. THE CITY LIBRARY WAS OPENED TO THE PUBLIC IN 1902.

MEANWHILE CONTACT AND NEGOTIATIONS WITH THE CARNEGIE CORPORATION WERE GOING ON FOR A GRANT. IN JANUARY, 1903, ATTICA WAS GIVEN A CARNEGIE GRANT OF $10,000 TO BUILD A NEW BUILDING. THE NEW CARNEGIE LIBRARY WAS ERECTED BETWEEN 1903 AND 1904 ON WHAT HAD PREVIOUSLY BEEN WASHINGTON PARK, AT THE NORTHEAST CORNER OF PERRY AND WASHINGTON STREETS. THE TOLEDO, OHIO FIRM OF L. O. FALLIS DESIGNED THE BUFF BRICK AND CONCRETE BUILDING, WHICH MEASURED 34 X 69 FEET. THE CARNEGIE LIBRARY WAS DEDICATED NOVEMBER 26, 1904.

THE MOST SIGNIFICANT CHANGE MADE TO THE ORIGINAL CARNEGIE BUILDING OCCURRED IN 1994-1995, WHEN A ROOMY, MODERN ADDITION DESIGNED BY ARCHITECT HARRY L. MOHLER WAS CONSTRUCTED OF SIMILAR BUFF BRICK.

GIFT: $10,000; JANUARY 13, 1903
DEDICATION: NOVEMBER 26, 1904
ARCHITECT: L. O. FALLIS, TOLEDO, OHIO
CONTRACTOR: R. N. GROVE & SON, LAFAYETTE
STYLE: RENAISSANCE REVIVAL

"Attica Public Library, Interior, Lobby Area"

"Bedford Public Library, Facade"

BEDFORD

BEDFORD PUBLIC LIBRARY

LIKE SO MANY LIBRARIES IN INDIANA, THE BEDFORD PUBLIC LIBRARY SPENT ITS EARLY YEARS IN VARIOUS TYPES OF BUILDINGS. JUST ONE YEAR AFTER LAWRENCE COUNTY WAS CREATED BY THE STATE LEGISLATURE, A LIBRARY WAS ESTABLISHED. TEN PERCENT OF THE PROFITS FROM THE SALE OF LOTS IN THE THEN COUNTY SEAT OF PALESTINE, WAS SET ASIDE FOR LIBRARY OPERATIONAL COSTS AND TO PURCHASE BOOKS. THE FIRST COLLECTION WAS HOUSED IN THE COURTHOUSE. WHEN THE COUNTY SEAT MOVED TO BEDFORD IN 1825, THE LIBRARY MOVED WITH IT.

IN THE NEW COUNTY SEAT, THE LIBRARY WAS LOCATED IN VARIOUS OFFICES AROUND BEDFORD'S COURTHOUSE SQUARE. IN MARCH, 1898, THE BEDFORD PUBLIC LIBRARY, LOCATED ON THE SECOND FLOOR OF THE A. B. TRESSLAR BUILDING ON THE SOUTH SIDE OF THE COURTHOUSE SQUARE, OPENED ITS DOORS TO THE PUBLIC. THE LIBRARY REMAINED IN THE A. B. TRESSLER BUILDING UNTIL THE CARNEGIE BUILDING WAS COMPLETED IN 1902.

IN THE FALL OF 1897, MRS. A. C. VORIS FORMED A COMMITTEE TO ORGANIZE A PUBLIC LIBRARY. IN 1901, MRS. VORIS WROTE A LETTER TO ANDREW CARNEGIE REQUESTING FUNDS TO BUILD A LIBRARY. SHE RECEIVED A RESPONSE JANUARY OF 1902 STATING THAT HE WOULD PROVIDE BEDFORD WITH A DONATION OF $10,000 FOR THE NEW LIBRARY. CARNEGIE LATER INCREASED THE OFFER TO $20,000 WHEN THE CITY AGREED TO BUY THE LOT AND PROVIDE A $2,000 YEARLY MAINTENANCE FUND. THE LOCATION AT THE NORTHWEST CORNER OF 14TH AND K STREETS WAS PURCHASED FOR $4,000. ON APRIL 6, 1903, THE BUILDING WAS DEDICATED.

A UNIQUE FEATURE OF THE BUILDING'S SECOND LEVEL WAS A DISTINCTIVE, TEXTURED ART GLASS FLOOR, WHICH WAS REMOVED DURING THE 1984 RENOVATION IN ORDER TO DOUBLE THE SIZE OF THE ORIGINAL LIBRARY.

GIFT: $20,000; JANUARY 9, 1902
DEDICATION: APRIL 6, 1903
ARCHITECT: PATTON & MILLER, CHICAGO, ILL.
CONTRACTOR: BAILEY & KOERNER, HENDERSON, KY.
STYLE: NEO CLASSICAL REVIVAL

"Bedford Public Library, Limestone Signage"

"Bedford Public Library, Lincoln Bust"

"Bloomfield-Eastern Greene County Public Library "

BLOOMFIELD

BLOOMFIELD-EASTERN GREENE COUNTY PUBLIC LIBRARY

EXCERPTS FROM *THE BLOOMFIELD NEWS*, DATED JUNE 15, 22 AND 28, 1907:

"A LITTLE MORE THAN TWO YEARS AGO, MISS MERICA HOAGLAND, WHO WAS AT THAT TIME SEC-RETARY OF THE STATE LIBRARY COMMISSION, VISITED BLOOMFIELD, GAVE A PLAIN AND PRACTICAL TALK ABOUT THE VALUE OF THE LIBRARY TO ANY COMMUNITY AND THE STEPS NECESSARY TO THE ORGANIZATION OF A LIBRARY.

AS THE FIRST STEP, A COMMITTEE WAS APPOINTED TO SOLICIT SUBSCRIPTIONS. ONE OF THE FIRST STEPS, TOO, WAS THE APPOINTMENT OF A LIBRARY BOARD, AND, FROM TIME TO TIME, THERE HAS BEEN APPOINTED VARIOUS COMMITTEES TO PUSH THE WORK FORWARD.

IN HONOR OF THE FOURTH ANNIVERSARY OF THE FOUNDING OF THE BLOOMFIELD PUBLIC LIBRARY, THE HANDSOME AND SUBSTANTIAL NEW CARNEGIE BUILDING WAS FORMALLY OPENED TO THE PUBLIC [JUNE 17, 1911]. THE BUILDING IS BEAUTIFULLY DECORATED INSIDE AND APPROPRI-ATELY FURNISHED IN MAHOGANY. THE BUILDING LOT WAS CONTRIBUTED BY DR. H. R. LOWDER AND H. W. LETSINGER. ONE OF THE MOST INTERESTING FEATURES OF THE OPENING WAS A BOOK SHOW-ER GIVEN UNDER THE AUSPICES OF THE ARGONAUT CLUB AND AS A RESULT OF THIS SHOWER ABOUT 250 VOLUMES WERE BROUGHT IN."

ON JUNE 11, 1981, THE BLOOMFIELD CARNEGIE LIBRARY OFFICIALLY BECAME THE BLOOMFIELD-RICHLAND TOWNSHIP PUBLIC LIBRARY. ON OCTOBER 7, 1987, SEVERAL TOWNSHIPS CAME TOGETHER TO FORM THE BLOOMFIELD-EASTERN GREENE COUNTY PUBLIC LIBRARY. A $1.3 MILLION DOLLAR PROJECT COMPLETED IN 1995 TRIPLED THE SIZE OF THE LIBRARY WHILE PRE-SERVING THE INTEGRITY OF THE ORIGINAL CARNEGIE BUILDING.

GIFT: $12,000; JULY 22, 1908
DEDICATION: JUNE 17, 1911
ARCHITECT: HERBERT BASS, INDIANAPOLIS
CONTRACTOR: STEVEN D. MILES, BLOOMFIELD
STYLE: PSEUDO-CRAFTSMAN

"Boswell-Grant Township Public Library, New Addition"

BOSWELL

BOSWELL-GRANT TOWNSHIP PUBLIC LIBRARY

EXCERPTS FROM THE *"HISTORY OF THE BOSWELL-GRANT PUBLIC LIBRARY,"* PAPER BY STELLA LA BOUNTY, FORMER LIBRARIAN:

"IN 1909, A GROUP OF 95 PEOPLE FROM BOSWELL AND THE GRANT TOWNSHIP FORMED AN ORGANIZATION KNOWN AS THE LIBRARY COMMITTEE. TOGETHER THEY PLEDGED $316.48 TO BEGIN PLANS FOR A PUBLIC LIBRARY. CARL H. MILAN, THEN SECRETARY OF STATE AND ORGANIZER OF THE PUBLIC LIBRARY COMMISSION, MET WITH INTERESTED CITIZENS ON NOVEMBER 15, 1909 AT THE COMMERCIAL CLUB.

IN 1910, DR. C. W. ATKINSON WROTE TO THE ANDREW CARNEGIE FOUNDATION ABOUT THE COMMUNITY'S WISH FOR A LIBRARY. IN DECEMBER OF 1910, DR. ATKINSON TOLD THE COMMITTEE THAT MR. CARNEGIE HAD OFFERED TO GIVE $8,000 FOR A LIBRARY BUILDING IN BOSWELL, PROVIDED THE TOWN AND GRANT TOWNSHIP WOULD PLEDGE TO PROVIDE $800 PER YEAR FOR MAINTENANCE AND OPERATION OF THE LIBRARY.

LENORA GILLESPIE APPLIED FOR THE POSITION OF LIBRARIAN AND WAS UNANIMOUSLY ACCEPTED, HER WAGES OF TEN CENTS PER HOUR. UNTIL THE NEW CARNEGIE BUILDING WAS READY, A ROOM ACROSS THE STREET FROM WHERE THE LIBRARY NOW STANDS WAS RENTED FOR $5.00 PER MONTH.

IN APRIL 1911 THE BOSWELL TOWN BOARD PLATTED THE LAND FOR ERECTION OF THE LIBRARY BUILDING. THE CARNEGIE LIBRARY WAS FORMALLY DEDICATED ON AUGUST 13, 1912 WITH A PROGRAM OF TALKS AND MUSIC."

A NEW ADDITION THAT DOUBLED THE SIZE AND A RENOVATION OF THE CARNEGIE LIBRARY BUILDING OCCURRED IN 2002-2003, AN ADDITION BEING DEDICATED APRIL 2003.

GIFT: $8,000; NOVEMBER 30, 1910
DEDICATION: AUGUST 13, 1912
ARCHITECT: ROBERT F. DAGGETT & COMPANY, INDIANAPOLIS
CONTRACTOR: THOMAS HEATON, TIPTON
STYLE: PSEUDO-TUDOR GOTHIC

"Brazil Public Library, Free For The People"

BRAZIL

BRAZIL PUBLIC LIBRARY

THE CITY LIBRARY ASSOCIATION, A COOPERATIVE BOOK SOCIETY, WAS ORGANIZED IN FEBRUARY, 1879. THE ORIGINAL SUM EXPENDED FOR BOOKS WAS $107, WITH WHICH 81 VOLUMES WERE PUR-CHASED. PRIOR TO 1879, A MACLURE LIBRARY AND MECHANICS INSTITUTE EXISTED IN BRAZIL, AND PROVIDED BOOKS TO THE LOCAL SOCIETY MEMBERS. AFTER IT CEASED TO EXIST, THE COL-LECTION WAS EVENTUALLY TURNED OVER TO THE LIBRARY ASSOCIATION. A SMALL ROOM AT THE BACK OF MAYOR COLLINS' OFFICE SERVED AS THE FIRST OF MANY LOCATIONS OF THE LIBRARY.

IN 1901, MRS. CRAWFORD, A LIBRARY BOARD MEMBER, MADE A TRIP TO NEW YORK TO SEEK THE GIFT OF A LIBRARY BUILDING FROM ANDREW CARNEGIE. HOWEVER, HE WAS ABROAD IN EUROPE AND NOTHING COULD BE DONE UNTIL HIS RETURN. IN FEBRUARY OF 1902, A LETTER AND QUES-TIONNAIRE WAS RECEIVED FROM JAMES BERTRAM, MR. CARNEGIE'S PERSONAL SECRETARY. THE INFORMATION WAS RETURNED, AND A GRANT OF $20,000 WAS SOON RECEIVED. THE PRESENT LOCATION WAS PURCHASED FROM MRS. CARTER FOR $2,400.

THE CORNERSTONE WAS LAID BY THE MASONS ON AUGUST 6, 1903. THE INDIANA LIMESTONE BUILDING WAS FORMALLY DEDICATED ON OCTOBER 12, 1904. THE *COUNTY ENTERPRISE* NEWSPA-PER PRINTED THE DEDICATION PROGRAM NOTING THAT "THE PEOPLE OF BRAZIL HAVE A RIGHT TO FEEL PROUD OF THEIR LIBRARY, AND IT IS TO BE HOPED ITS ADVANTAGES WILL BE APPRECIATED AND PARTAKEN OF BY ALL OUR PEOPLE, ESPECIALLY THE YOUNGER GENERATION."

IN 1989, THE LIBRARY ACQUIRED 60% OF THE MAURER WOOD BUILDING ACROSS THE STREET TO OPERATE AS A HANDICAP-ACCESSIBLE ANNEX OF THE MAIN LIBRARY BUILDING. THIS WAS MADE POSSIBLE THROUGH THE GENEROSITY OF DR. ROBERT MAURER AND THE CLAY CIVIC MEMORIAL FOUNDATION.

GIFT: $20,000; MARCH 14, 1902
DEDICATION: OCTOBER 12, 1904
ARCHITECT: H. B. MCMILLAN
CONTRACTOR: BRAZIL STONE COMPANY
STYLE: NEO CLASSICAL REVIVAL

"Brazil Public Library, Tympanum, Ornamental Molding, Arabesque pattern"

"Brazil Public Library, Interior, Heating Radiator"

"Brook-Iroquois Township Public Library, Old & New"

BROOK

BROOK-IROQUOIS TOWNSHIP PUBLIC LIBRARY

THE CARNEGIE LIBRARY IN BROOK WAS BUILT ON HISTORIC GROUND. ON THIS LOCATION, THE FIRST COMPANY OF SOLDIERS THAT WENT TO THE WAR OF THE REBELLION (1861-1865) FROM NEWTON COUNTY WAS ORGANIZED. A BRONZE TABLET IN THE LIBRARY SERVES AS A MEMORIAL TO THEIR CONTRIBUTION.

EARLY IN NEWTON COUNTY'S HISTORY, SMALL LIBRARIES WERE HOUSED IN CHURCHES, SCHOOLS, AND HOMES. BY MARCH OF 1910, PEOPLE OF THE COMMUNITY BEGAN TO RECOGNIZE THE NEED FOR A PUBLIC LIBRARY THAT WOULD BECOME A "UNIFYING AND EDUCATIONAL FACTOR IN THE TOWN." MR. CARL MILAN, A REPRESENTATIVE FROM THE INDIANA STATE LIBRARY COMMISSION SPOKE TO A GROUP OF TOWNSPEOPLE AND THE WHEELS WERE SET IN MOTION FOR A PUBLIC LIBRARY IN BROOK.

IN MAY, 1913, APPLICATION WAS MADE TO THE CARNEGIE FOUNDATION FOR FUNDS TO BUILD A NEW LIBRARY. A GRANT OF $7,000 WAS AWARDED, AND IN AUGUST, 1914, THE BUILDING PROJECT WAS BEGUN ON THE SITE. THE NEW LIBRARY WAS FINANCIALLY SUPPORTED BY THE TOWN AND TOWNSHIP WITH A SPECIAL TAX LEVY. ON FEBRUARY 20, 1915, ON THE LIBRARY'S OPENING DAY, SEVERAL HUNDRED PEOPLE CAME TO ADMIRE THE NEW SHALE BRICK AND SLATE ROOFED BUILDING. A BOOK SHOWER IN MCKINLEY PARK REAPED 300 VOLUMES TO ADD TO THE LIBRARY COLLECTION OF OVER 1,000 VOLUMES. PATRONS CHECKED OUT 962 BOOKS DURING THE FIRST MONTH OF OPERATION. THE LIBRARY HAS A LARGE COLLECTION OF THE BOOKS OF A FORMER BROOK RESIDENT, GEORGE ADE (1866-1944), AUTHOR AND PLAYWRIGHT OF HUMOROUS PROSE.

A 2,000 SQUARE FOOT ADDITION TO THE ORIGINAL STRUCTURE BEGAN IN DECEMBER, 1997 AND WAS COMPLETED A YEAR LATER.

GIFT: $7,000; MAY 21, 1913
DEDICATION: FEBRUARY 20, 1915
ARCHITECT: BROOKIE & MCGINNIS, INDIANAPOLIS
CONTRACTOR: CORY & LATHROP, BROOK
STYLE: ECLECTIC-CRAFTSMAN-NEO CLASSICAL

"Brookston-Prairie Township Public Library, Semi-circular Arch"

BROOKSTON

BROOKSTON-PRAIRIE TOWNSHIP PUBLIC LIBRARY

THE BROOKSTON PRAIRIE TOWNSHIP PUBLIC LIBRARY WAS FOUNDED IN 1915 WHEN THE PROPERTY TAXPAYERS OF THE TOWN OF BROOKSTON AND PRAIRIE TOWNSHIP AGREED TO TAX THEMSELVES TO SUPPORT THE LIBRARY. A LIBRARY BOARD WAS APPOINTED AND DONATIONS OF $1,700 WERE RAISED TO BUY TWO LOTS FROM SARAH AND ZEBRA REDDING IN NOVEMBER, 1915. THE BUILDING WAS CONSTRUCTED IN 1916 THROUGH A $10,000 GRANT FROM THE CARNEGIE CORPORATION.

THE CORNERSTONE OF THE LIBRARY FOUNDATION WAS LAID IN THE FALL OF 1916. THE CARNEGIE BUILDING WAS DESIGNATED A CENTENNIAL BUILDING FOR THE INDIANA STATEHOOD CENTENNIAL. THE LIBRARY WAS DEDICATED ON OCTOBER 6, 1917 WITH 300 BOOKS. THE PRINCIPAL ADDRESS WAS DELIVERED BY HENRY N. SANBORN, SECRETARY OF THE PUBLIC LIBRARY COMMISSION, WHO POINTED OUT THE MANY WAYS THE LIBRARY, IF PROPERLY USED, COULD BENEFIT THE COMMUNITY. THE FIRST LIBRARIAN WAS DOLL HAYES, WHO RECEIVED A SALARY OF $30 A MONTH, RETIRING IN 1946.

OVER TIME, THE LIBRARY OUTGREW THE ORIGINAL CARNEGIE BUILDING. REMODELING, FURNISHINGS AND A NEW ROOF WERE ADDED IN THE 1980S. IN 1992, A SPACIOUS NORTH FACING ADDITION WAS CONSTRUCTED, AND REMODELING OF THE ORIGINAL 1916 STRUCTURE WAS COMPLETED.

GIFT: $10,000; SEPTEMBER 29, 1915
DEDICATION: OCTOBER 6, 1917
ARCHITECT: WILSON B. PARKER, INDIANAPOLIS
CONTRACTOR: JAMES L. BROWN, SHOALS
STYLE: ECLECTIC-CRAFTSMAN-NEO CLASSICAL REVIVAL

37

"Whitewater Valley Community Library District, Brookville, Facade"

BROOKVILLE

WHITEWATER VALLEY COMMUNITY LIBRARY DISTRICT

EXCERPTS FROM THE *"BROOKVILLE LIBRARY GOLDEN 50TH ANNIVERSARY"* LIBRARY BROCHURE, FRANKLIN COUNTY BOOKMOBILE DEDICATION, 1962:

"A BRIGHT DREAM OF A HANDFUL OF BROOKVILLE CITIZENS OVER 50 YEARS AGO AND A $10,000 GRANT FROM ANDREW J. CARNEGIE GAVE THE TOWN ONE OF ITS MOST USEFUL AND ENJOYABLE ASSETS. THE TRIM, BRICK BUILDING AT 929 MAIN STREET IS NOW A VERITABLE 'STOREHOUSE OF KNOWLEDGE' USED EXTENSIVELY BY THE PEOPLE OF THE COMMUNITY——-YOUNG AND OLD ALIKE.

INTEREST IN A PUBLIC LIBRARY IN BROOKVILLE BEGAN AS EARLY AS 1895. IN 1908 A GROUP MET WITH THE AIM OF ESTABLISHING A BROOKVILLE PUBLIC LIBRARY. PLANNING REACHED AN ACTIVE STAGE WHEN MR. SHIRK BEGAN A CORRESPONDENCE WITH THE CARNEGIE FOUNDATION IN 1909. MR. SHIRK AND ANDREW CARNEGIE REACHED AN AGREEMENT WHEREBY CARNEGIE AGREED TO FURNISH $10,000 WITH WHICH TO ERECT AND FURNISH THE PRESENT BUILDING. AT THIS TIME A SUBSCRIPTION FOR FUNDS TO PURCHASE A LOT MET WITH SURPRISINGLY GOOD RESULTS, AND THE MONEY WAS USED TO BUY THE MAIN STREET LOT FOR $15.

SINCE THE ORIGINAL ESTIMATE RAN SLIGHTLY OVER $12,000, IT WAS NECESSARY TO MAKE SOME CHANGES IN PLANS TO KEEP THE COST WITHIN THE $10,000 GRANT. FORMAL DEDICATION OF THE BUILDING ON SEPTEMBER 18, 1912 WAS A WELL-ATTENDED COMMUNITY AFFAIR, WITH DEMARCHUS C. BROWN, STATE LIBRARIAN, SPEAKING."

IN THE 50 YEARS SINCE THE LIBRARY'S FOUNDING, BROOKVILLE HAS DONE MUCH WITH ITS GIFT FROM MR. CARNEGIE. A MODERN, MATCHING ADDITION ON THE EAST WALL OF THE LIBRARY WAS COMPLETED AND DEDICATED 2003.

GIFT: $10,000; NOVEMBER 30, 1910
DEDICATION: SEPTEMBER 18, 1912
ARCHITECT: WILSON B. PARKER, INDIANAPOLIS
CONTRACTOR: ISSAC W. MILLIKAN, INDIANAPOLIS
STYLE: RENAISSANCE REVIVAL

"Whitewater Valley Community Library District, Brookville, Historical Marker"

"Whitewater Valley Community Library District, Brookville, Tablet Flower"

"Clinton Public Library, Former Entry, Balustrade"

CLINTON

CLINTON PUBLIC LIBRARY

EXCERPTS FROM THE *"HISTORY OF THE CLINTON PUBLIC LIBRARY"* FILE:

"IN JANUARY, 1908, THE CLINTON COMMERCIAL CLUB BEGAN AGITATION FOR THE ERECTION OF A FREE PUBLIC LIBRARY AND APPOINTED A COMMITTEE TO WRITE ANDREW CARNEGIE OF NEW YORK CITY, ASKING HIS PARTICIPATION IN THE BUILDING OF A LIBRARY IN CLINTON, INDIANA. AN AGREEMENT WAS REACHED AFTER C. H. LEESON, CHAIRMAN OF THE LIBRARY BUILDING COMMITTEE, NOTIFIED ANDREW CARNEGIE OF PLANS FOR THE ORGANIZATION OF A PUBLIC LIBRARY.

ON APRIL 6, 1909, THE CORNER LOT AT SOUTH FOURTH AND BLACKMAN STREETS WAS PURCHASED FROM BELLE CAMPBELL FOR $1,500 AS A SUITABLE LOT ON WHICH TO ERECT A FREE PUBLIC LIBRARY. IT WAS ALSO AGREED THAT THE CITY OF CLINTON WOULD SUPPORT THE SAME BY A TAX LEVY ON TAXABLE PROPERTY, IF ANDREW CARNEGIE WOULD CONTRIBUTE THE MONIES TO ERECT A FREE PUBLIC LIBRARY BUILDING. BOTH PARTIES AGREED TO THE ARRANGEMENT.

ON NOVEMBER 22, 1911, THE CLINTON PUBLIC LIBRARY OPENED THE DOORS OF ITS NEW CARNEGIE FUNDED BUILDING FOR THE FIRST TIME. MISS AMANDA FAYE TILLOTSON WAS HIRED AS THE FIRST LIBRARIAN AT A SALARY OF $40 PER MONTH."

EXPANSION OF THE CHILDREN'S AREA IN 1947 WAS THE FIRST MAJOR STRUCTURAL CHANGE SINCE ITS INCEPTION. IN 1953, A MEETING ROOM WAS ADDED. IN JUNE, 1993, GROUND WAS BROKEN FOR A NEWLY REMODELED AND EXPANDED 12,000 SQUARE FOOT FACILITY THAT PRESERVED AND EXTENDED THE ORIGINAL CARNEGIE FACADE. THE CONSTRUCTION WAS COMPLETED JULY, 1994 AND A DEDICATION WAS HELD AUGUST 25, 1994.

GIFT: $12,500; FEBRUARY 25, 1908
DEDICATION: NOVEMBER 22, 1911
ARCHITECT: THOMAS DOWDY, CLINTON
CONTRACTOR: THOMAS DOWDY, CLINTON
STYLE: NEO CLASSICAL REVIVAL

Colfax Public Library, Facade"

COLFAX

COLFAX PUBLIC LIBRARY

THE MOVEMENT TO FORM A LIBRARY IN COLFAX BEGUN IN 1913 BY LESLIE BUSENBURG, THE SCHOOL SUPERINTENDENT, AND BY THE P. T. A. A $9,000 CARNEGIE GRANT WAS OBTAINED AND THE CORNERSTONE WAS LAID ON JUNE 15, 1916. THE TOWN BOARD DONATED THE LAND FOR THE LIBRARY, THE LAND BEING THE SITE OF THE FORMER HIGH SCHOOL. THE DOORS OPENED IN LATE APRIL, 1917.

THE FOLLOWING ARTICLE APPEARED IN THE JULY, 1917 ISSUE, PAGE 207, OF THE *LIBRARY OCCURRENT*:

"A NOTABLE FEATURE OF THE OCCASION OF THE LIBRARY DEDICATION AT COLFAX APRIL 20TH, 1917, WAS THE FLAG RAISING AND THE SINGING OF THE STAR SPANGLED BANNER BY THE CHILDREN OF THE PUBLIC SCHOOLS. THIS WAS WITNESSED BY A LARGE GATHERING OF CITIZENS FROM ALL PARTS OF THE TOWNSHIP.

HENRY N. SANBORN, SECRETARY OF THE PUBLIC LIBRARY COMMISSION, DELIVERED THE PRINCIPAL ADDRESS AND MENTIONED AMONG OTHER THINGS THE MANY ADVANTAGES TO THE TOWN THAT POSSESSES AN INSTITUTION THAT STANDS FOR THE ADVANCEMENTS OF ITS COMMUNITY WELFARE. FOLLOWING THE DEDICATION EXERCISES THE BUILDING WAS THROWN OPEN FOR THE INSPECTION OF THE PUBLIC. THE BUILDING COST $9,000, THE GIFT OF THE CARNEGIE CORPORATION. THE ARCHITECTS WERE GRAHAM AND HILL, OF INDIANAPOLIS. THE BUILDING MEASURED 32' X 56', BUILT OF BRICK, TRIMMED WITH STONE."

LITTLE RENOVATION HAS BEEN DONE TO THE ORIGINAL CARNEGIE FUNDED BUILDING. THE COLFAX PUBLIC LIBRARY BUILDING IS LISTED IN THE NATIONAL REGISTER OF HISTORIC PLACES.

GIFT: $9,000; SEPTEMBER 29, 1915
DEDICATION: APRIL 20, 1917
ARCHITECT: GRAHAM & HILL, INDIANAPOLIS
CONTRACTOR: GILL & GILL, INDIANAPOLIS
STYLE: CRAFTSMAN-PRAIRIE TRADITION

"Converse-Jackson Township Public Library, Facade"

CONVERSE

CONVERSE-JACKSON TOWNSHIP PUBLIC LIBRARY

EXCERPTS FROM THE *"HISTORY OF THE CONVERSE JACKSON TOWNSHIP LIBRARY,"* PAPER BY CHARLES NEWBY AND COLEEN J. CARLSON:

"PRIOR TO 1916, ALL ATTEMPTS FOR THE ESTABLISHMENT OF A LIBRARY IN CONVERSE DID NOT BEAR FRUIT. INTEREST IN A LIBRARY BEGAN IN 1916 WHEN A SELF APPOINTED COMMITTEE ACQUIRED THE SIGNATURES OF 50 FREEHOLDERS IN CONVERSE AND JACKSON TOWNSHIP ASKING FOR A LIBRARY TAX. ON DECEMBER 16, 1916 THE FIRST MEETING OF THE LIBRARY BOARD WAS HELD. L. O. ARNOLD AND MRS. MILTON MACY CARRIED THROUGH THE CORRESPONDENCE WITH THE CARNEGIE CORPORATION, SECURING A GIFT OF $9,000 WITH WHICH TO COMPLETE AND FURNISH A LIBRARY BUILDING.

THE $1,150 FOR THE PURCHASE OF THE GROUND WAS OBTAINED FROM PRIVATE SUBSCRIPTIONS. THE BUILDING, INCLUDING HEATING, LIGHTING AND SHELVING, WAS ABOUT $8,000 IN COSTS. THE REMAINING $1,000 COVERED THE ARCHITECT'S FEE OF $350, AND THE COST OF TABLES, CHAIRS, DESKS, ETC. TO EQUIP THE LIBRARY.

THE BUILDING WAS COMPLETED AND EQUIPPED IN NOVEMBER 1918 AND THE FORMAL OPENING OF THE LIBRARY OCCURRED ON DECEMBER 20, 1918. THE CONVERSE SCHOOL'S TURNED OVER TO THE LIBRARY THEIR OWN COLLECTION OF ABOUT 1,200 VOLUMES THAT MADE A CONSIDERABLE NUCLEUS FOR A LIBRARY. THERE WERE ALSO MANY DONATIONS OF BOOKS BROUGHT IN ON THE EVENING OF THE OPENING AND AFTERWARDS, SO THAT THE LIBRARY HAD A VERY GOOD FIRST YEAR. MISS VIVIAN SCHMIDT WAS THE FIRST LIBRARIAN IN THE CARNEGIE BUILDING."

THE CARNEGIE BUILDING HAS REMAINED BASICALLY UNCHANGED OVER THE YEARS AND WAS LISTED ON THE NATIONAL REGISTER OF HISTORIC PLACES MARCH, 1999.

GIFT: $9,000; NOVEMBER 9, 1916
DEDICATION: DECEMBER 20, 1918
ARCHITECT: H. G. BOWSTEAD, MARION
CONTRACTOR: L. E. WICKERSHAM, LOGANSPORT
STYLE: CRAFTSMAN-PRAIRIE TRADITION

"Harrison County Public Library, Interior, Skylight"

CORYDON

HARRISON COUNTY PUBLIC LIBRARY

EXCERPTS FROM THE *"BRIEF HIGHLIGHTS,"* NEWSLETTER OF THE CORYDON-HARRISON COUNTY PUBLIC LIBRARY (1820-1991):

"CORYDON HAS A LONG HISTORY OF LIBRARIES, DATING BACK TO THE TIME OF STATEHOOD AND THE FIRST STATE LIBRARY OF 1820. THE MACLURE'S WORKING MEN'S INSTITUTE OF NEW HARMONY, PROVIDED BOOKS FROM 1855 TO 1858. PROBABLY MORE TYPICAL OF BOOK LENDING OF THIS PERIOD WAS THAT DONE BY MISS OLIVE GRIFFIN BETWEEN 1898 AND 1908 IN A SMALL LENDING LIBRARY IN GRIFFIN'S STORE.

IN 1908 SEVERAL CITIZENS MET TO DISCUSS THE ESTABLISHMENT OF A FREE PUBLIC LIBRARY. A GIFT IN THE AMOUNT OF $7,500 WAS AWARDED BY THE CARNEGIE FOUNDATION ON SEPTEMBER 27, 1912, AN OCCASION, 'HAILED WITH GREAT JOY BY THE CITIZENS' REPORTED THE LIBRARY BOARD. MONEY WAS RAISED BY DONATIONS FOR A NEW BUILDING SITE.

GROUND WAS BROKEN FOR THE NEW CARNEGIE BUILDING ON MAY 4, 1914. ON FRIDAY, JUNE 12, 1914, THE CORNERSTONE WAS LAID WITH CEREMONY. THE LIBRARY WAS DEDICATED ON DECEMBER 22, 1914. IN THE PRAISE-FILLED WORDS OF THE LIBRARY BOARD IN 1915, 'SO LONG AS THIS BUILDING STANDS, THIS WILL REMAIN A MONUMENT OF BENEVOLENCE OF MR. CARNEGIE, AND WE EXTEND OUR GRATITUDE FOR HIS HELP.'

IN 1989, THE CORDYON PUBLIC LIBRARY CARNEGIE BUILDING WAS PLACED ON THE NATIONAL REGISTER OF HISTORIC PLACES. IN SEPTEMBER OF 1998, THE CORYDON PUBLIC LIBRARY MOVED THE ADULT AND CHILDREN'S SERVICES INTO A FORMER BANK, AT THE SOUTHWEST CORNER OF THE COURTHOUSE-SQUARE. THE CARNEGIE BUILDING WAS RETAINED AND RENOVATED AS THE GENEALOGY AND LOCAL HISTORY RESOURCE CENTER."

GIFT: $7,500; SEPTEMBER 27, 1912
DEDICATION: DECEMBER 22, 1914
ARCHITECT: VAL P. COLLINS, LOUISVILLE, KY.
CONTRACTOR: J. FRED BEGGS, SCOTTSBURG
STYLE: NEO CLASSICAL REVIVAL

"Covington-Veedersburg Public Library, Facade"

COVINGTON

COVINGTON-VEEDERSBURG PUBLIC LIBRARY

In 1911, the Public Library Commission contacted the Covington Woman's Club, urging them to organize an effort to form a library in Covington. They accepted the proposal. A library board of directors was formed in 1912 and an appeal was made to the Carnegie Corporation. In July, 1912 a letter of financial appeal to Mr. Carnegie was penned by J. M. Wilkey, secretary of the library board. On March 14, 1913 the Carnegie Corporation pledged a grant of $10,000 with the stipulation that the city agree to maintain the facility with at least $1,000 a year and provide a suitable site.

The first library board was formed May 28, 1912. A tax levy was established February 10, 1913 at ten cents per $100 assessed valuation on city property. The land at Fifth and Crockett streets was purchased from J. B. Martin with $1,250 of raised monies, and construction began July 30, 1913. The library was completed in late fall and opened its doors to the public December 10, 1914. Miss Katie Diffenderfer was the first librarian. Her starting salary was $25 a month. The brick structure cost $10,466 and all but $500 was paid with the Carnegie grant. The library was closed for three months in 1915 because of a smallpox epidemic. The Carnegie building is listed on the National Register of Historic Places.

The Covington Library maintained a branch library in Veedersburg for a number of years. later on the Covington-Veedersburg Public Library became a library that served a number of districts. The district includes the Covington, Veedersburg, Troy Township, and Van Buren Township taxing districts.

Gift: $10,000; March 14, 1913
Dedication: December 9, 1914
Architect: Leese & Ludwig, Danville, Ill.
Contractor: Unlocated
Style: Neo Classical Revival

44

"Crawfordsville District Public Library, Entry lamp"

CRAWFORDSVILLE

CRAWFORDSVILLE DISTRICT PUBLIC LIBRARY

CRAWFORDSVILLE'S LIBRARY HISTORY DATES BACK TO THE 1830S WHEN SUBSCRIPTION LIBRARIES SERVED LOCAL PATRONS. THE LADIES LIBRARY ASSOCIATION WAS FORMED IN THE LATE 19TH CENTURY TO GATHER DONATIONS TO FUND THE CRAWFORDSVILLE PUBLIC LIBRARY THAT IT FOUNDED IN 1898 AT THE CORNER OF MAIN AND WATER STREET. THE COLLECTION TOTALED NEARLY 700 BOOKS AND SEVERAL HUNDRED MAGAZINES. IN OCTOBER 1899, THE COLLECTION WAS TURNED OVER TO THE CITY SCHOOL BOARD, THAT BODY HAVING AGREED TO MAINTAIN THE PUBLIC LIBRARY BY LEVYING A TAX ON THE PROPERTY OF CRAWFORDSVILLE.

ON MARCH 8, 1901, CARNEGIE APPROVED A GIFT OF $25,000 TO CONSTRUCT A FREE PUBLIC LIBRARY PROVIDING THE CITY OF CRAWFORDSVILLE WOULD PROVIDE A SITE AND SUPPORT THE LIBRARY TO THE EXTENT OF $2,500 ANNUALLY. THE HANDSOME ITALIAN RENAISSANCE STYLE BUILDING WAS CONSTRUCTED OF SMOOTH CUT ASHLAR STONE AT THE CORNER OF WASHINGTON STREET AND WABASH AVENUE. THE COST OF THE COMPLETED BUILDING WAS $27,000. CRAWFORDSVILLE WAS THE FIRST CARNEGIE LIBRARY BUILDING COMPLETED IN INDIANA. THE LIBRARY WAS DEDICATED ON JULY 29, 1902 AND THERE WAS MUCH PRAISE OF ANDREW CARNEGIE'S GENEROSITY.

THE LIBRARY HAS BEEN RENOVATED THREE TIMES SINCE IT WAS CONSTRUCTED IN 1902. IN THE MID 1970S, THE AUTOMOBILE DEALERSHIP JUST NORTH OF THE LIBRARY WAS PURCHASED AND A CONNECTING LINK WAS MADE BETWEEN THE TWO TO CREATE MORE SPACE.

GIFT: $25,000; MARCH 8, 1901
DEDICATION: JULY 29, 1902
ARCHITECT: W. F. SHARPE, CRAWFORDSVILLE
CONTRACTOR: W. C. CARR, CRAWFORDSVILLE
STYLE: NEO CLASSICAL REVIVAL-ITALIAN RENAISSANCE

"Crown Point Community Library, East Façade"

CROWN POINT

CROWN POINT COMMUNITY LIBRARY

EXCERPTS FROM *"A LIBRARY HISTORY,"* PAPER WRITTEN BY BARBARA HOUK, SPECIAL SERVICES LIBRARIAN, CROWN POINT COMMUNITY LIBRARY, JULY 18, 2000:

"ON MAY 23, 1906, A NINE MEMBER BOARD WAS FORMED TO ESTABLISH A LIBRARY FOR CROWN POINT. IN DECEMBER, 1906, IT WAS REPORTED AT THE LIBRARY BOARD MEETING THAT 'WORD HAD BEEN RECEIVED FROM MR. CARNEGIE THAT HE WOULD GIVE $12,000 TO THE LIBRARY FUND IF A CORRESPONDING AMOUNT WOULD BE ASSURED BY THE PROPER TAXING BODIES FOR MAINTENANCE.' THE CARNEGIE LIBRARY AT CROWN POINT OPENED ITS DOORS ON THE FORMER O. G. WHEELER PROPERTY AT 223 S. MAIN STREET ON FEBRUARY 12, 1908.

THE REMNANTS OF THE MACLURE LIBRARY ASSOCIATION OF 1857, RESIDENT DONATIONS, AND BOOKS PURCHASED FOR $100 ESTABLISHED THE INITIAL BOOK COLLECTION OF 1,500 VOLUMES OF REFERENCE AND NONFICTION MATERIALS BUT 'VERY FEW WORKS OF THE LIGHTER SORT.' THE FIRST LIBRARIAN, MISS MARIE HANSEN, WAS HIRED AT A SALARY OF $40 PER MONTH.

BY THE 1960S, THE LIBRARY WAS OUTGROWING ITS BUILDING AND A NEW ADDITION TO THE REAR OF THE CARNEGIE BUILDING WAS COMPLETED IN 1972, EXTENDING TO 214 SOUTH COURT STREET. THE OLD CARNEGIE WAS GIVEN A NEW PURPOSE AS A COMMUNITY MEETING CENTER AND AS LIBRARY ADMINISTRATIVE OFFICES. EXTENSIVE IMPROVEMENTS AND DECORATING CREATED ELEGANT AND PRACTICAL MEETING ROOMS, WHICH WERE USED BY THE LIBRARY AND MEMBERS OF THE COMMUNITY. LIBRARY PROGRAMS, MEETINGS, PARTIES, AND EVEN WEDDINGS ARE HELD AT THE CARNEGIE CENTER. A COMPLETE RENOVATION TOOK PLACE IN 1995."

GIFT: $12,000; DECEMBER 28, 1906
DEDICATION: FEBRUARY 19, 1908
ARCHITECT: CHARLES E. KENDRICK, ROCHESTER
CONTRACTOR: WILLIAM PERRY, CROWN POINT
STYLE: NEO CLASSICAL REVIVAL

"Culver-Union Township Public Library, Expansion Project"

CULVER

Culver-Union Township Public Library

In 1914, some civic leaders in Culver decided that the town should have a Carnegie library. The civic leaders were aware that nearby communities of Rochester and Kewanna were building Carnegie libraries, and they wanted their own. The library committee was formed, and it moved quickly to apply for Carnegie funding. In the meantime, the use of three rooms above Dr. Tallman's office were donated rent-free for the library and reading rooms by S. C. Shilling. Later on, the rented Menser rooms over the hardware store were occupied by the library.

On April 2, 1914, an article appeared in the Culver Citizen newspaper announcing that the first steps had been taken to secure a grant from the Carnegie Foundation. A committee of seven was appointed at the Commercial Club meeting that worked closely with the Public Library Commission. By November the library board applied for the Carnegie grant.

On January 6, 1915, a letter from the Carnegie Corporation announced that $10,000 would be given for the new building. The businessmen along Main Street committed themselves to raise the purchase price of $1,450 for the building site.

The building went up swiftly. The library moved from the second floor of the Menser Building across the street to the Carnegie building, and was opened to the public on December 30, 1915 at 2 p.m. without any fanfare. Donated books from the community formed the library collection. Miss Zola Moss earned $25 a month as the first librarian. The money for the furniture came from private donations.

Recently a new addition and renovation to the original building was undertaken and dedicated in 2002.

Gift: $10,000; January 6, 1915
Dedication: December 30, 1915
Architect: True L. Brookie, Indianapolis
Contractor: Milo Cutshall, Akron
Style: Renaissance Revival

"Danville Public Library, Gable End Ventilator"

DANVILLE

DANVILLE-CENTER TOWNSHIP PUBLIC LIBRARY

EXCERPTS FROM THE *"HISTORY OF DANVILLE-CENTER TOWNSHIP LIBRARY,"* ARTICLE WRITTEN BY THE DANVILLE JR. HISTORY CLUB, 2000:

"IN 1902, MORD CARTER WAS PRESIDENT OF THE COMMERCIAL CLUB IN DANVILLE. MR. CARTER WROTE TO MR. ANDREW CARNEGIE ON JANUARY 29, 1902 REQUESTING FUNDS TO BUILD A LIBRARY IN DANVILLE. HE NOTED THAT IN ADDITION TO BEING VALUABLE TO THE DANVILLE CITIZENS, A LIBRARY WOULD ALSO BE A WIDE INFLUENCE ON THE STUDENTS OF CENTRAL NORMAL COLLEGE THAT WAS LOCATED IN DANVILLE. MR. CARNEGIE AGREED TO A GIFT OF $10,000 FOR THE DANVILLE LIBRARY, THE FIRST OF FOUR CARNEGIE LIBRARIES IN HENDRICKS COUNTY.

THE CITIZENS OF DANVILLE, THE COMMERCIAL CLUB, THE LADIES' CLUBS, THE CENTRAL NORMAL COLLEGE FACULTY, THE TOWN TRUSTEES, AND THE SCHOOL BOARD SUPPORTED THE IDEA OF A LIBRARY. A PETITION WAS CIRCULATED AND 38 TOWNSPEOPLE SIGNED AND PLEDGED $465 FOR THE ESTABLISHMENT AND MAINTENANCE OF THE DANVILLE LIBRARY.

THE NEWLY FORMED LIBRARY BOARD ACQUIRED THE PROPERTY AT THE CORNER OF MARION STREET AND INDIANA STREET AS THE BUILDING SITE AT THE PRICE OF $525. THE CORNERSTONE CEREMONY WAS HELD ON OCTOBER 14, 1902 WITH OVER 2,000 PEOPLE ATTENDING. ON DECEMBER 5, 1903, THE LIBRARY WAS FORMALLY DEDICATED."

THE DANVILLE CENTER TOWNSHIP LIBRARY IS STILL HOUSED IN THE CARNEGIE BUILDING. THE LIBRARY BOARD ACQUIRED LAND ADJACENT TO THE LIBRARY IN 1973 AND IN 1979, AN ADDITION WAS STARTED AND THE $350,000 EXPANSION WAS DEDICATED ON OCTOBER 12, 1980. A SECOND ADDITION WAS COMPLETED IN 1999.

GIFT: $10,000; MARCH 14, 1902
DEDICATION: DECEMBER 5, 1903
ARCHITECT: S. C. DARK, INDIANAPOLIS
CONTRACTOR: W. C. HALSTEAD & COMPANY, INDIANAPOLIS
STYLE: NEO CLASSICAL REVIVAL

"Danville Public Library, Historical Marker"

"Danville Public Library, Foyer Floor, Patterned Tile Frets"

"Darlington Public Library, Arching Portal"

DARLINGTON

DARLINGTON PUBLIC LIBRARY

EXCERPTS FROM THE *DARLINGTON JOURNAL* NEWSPAPER, MAY 28, 1915 AND DECEMBER 31, 1915:

"THE MOVEMENT WHICH WILL LATER RESULT IN THE ERECTION OF A NEW LIBRARY HERE WAS ORIGINATED BY A WOMAN'S CLUB IN DARLINGTON ABOUT A YEAR AGO. THE FIRST THING WAS TO GET CARNEGIE'S SECRETARY INTERESTED ENOUGH TO MAKE THE NECESSARY DONATION. THIS WAS ACCOMPLISHED WHEN MR. CARNEGIE OFFERED TO DONATE $10,000 PROVIDED THE TOWN OF DARLINGTON WOULD BUY A TRACT OF GROUND FOR THE BUILDING SITE AND MAINTAIN THE BUILDING AND EMPLOY A LIBRARIAN AFTER THE NEW STRUCTURE WAS ERECTED.

A LOT JUST WEST OF THE RESIDENCE OF ISAAC LARRICK'S HOME WAS PURCHASED. THE PLANS WERE DRAWN BY HUBERT PETERSON OF CHICAGO, FORMERLY OF DARLINGTON. BIDS OF SEVERAL CONTRACTORS WERE OPENED AND THE CONTRACT LET TO LEE. E. WICKERSHAM, LOGANSPORT.

THE NEW LIBRARY BUILDING WAS FORMALLY DEDICATED DECEMBER 31, 1915. THE AFTERNOON SERVICE TOOK ON MORE THE NATURE OF AN OPEN HOUSE AND A BOOK SHOWER. BEST OF ALL, MANY BROUGHT ARMLOADS OF BOOKS FOR THE NEW SHELVES. SEVERAL SELECTIONS OF MUSIC WERE RENDERED DURING THE AFTERNOON BY THE ORCHESTRA. MISS NELLIE SIMMONS IS THE LIBRARIAN. SHE WAS FORMERLY IN THE WORK AT MOORES HILL COLLEGE AND IS IN EVERY WAY QUALIFIED FOR THE WORK. IN THE TWO DAYS THE LIBRARY HAS BEEN OPEN, MORE THAN ONE HUNDRED PERSONS HAVE REGISTERED AS PATRONS AND THE LIST IS STEADILY GROWING."

THE CARNEGIE LIBRARY HAS BEEN THE CENTERPIECE OF MAIN STREET SINCE ITS INCEPTION IN DARLINGTON. THE MOST SIGNIFICANT PHYSICAL CHANGE IN THE BUILDING IS THE CONVERSION OF THE BASEMENT ASSEMBLY MEETING ROOM INTO A LOCAL HISTORY MUSEUM.

GIFT: $10,000; FEBRUARY 6, 1915
DEDICATION: DECEMBER 31, 1915
ARCHITECT: HUBERT W. PETERSON, CHICAGO, ILL.
CONTRACTOR: L. E. WICKERSHAM, LOGANSPORT
STYLE: ECLECTIC-CRAFTSMAN-ITALIANATE

"Delphi Public Library, Palladian Windows"

DELPHI

DELPHI PUBLIC LIBRARY

EXCERPTS FROM THE *"HISTORY OF THE LIBRARY,"* A BROCHURE ON *"DEDICATION DAY FOR THE NEW ADDITION,"* DECEMBER 9, 1990:

"THE DELPHI PUBLIC LIBRARY WAS FIRST ORGANIZED AT THE END OF THE LAST CENTURY, AROUND JUNE 1897, THROUGH THE EFFORTS OF THE ORACLE CLUB, WITH THE SUPPORT OF THE DELPHI CITY COUNCIL AND THE CITIZENS OF DELPHI.

IN 1904, THE LIBRARY WAS REORGANIZED UNDER THE STATE LIBRARY LAW. LATER IN THE SAME YEAR, THE NEWLY FORMED LIBRARY BOARD WROTE TO THE CARNEGIE FOUNDATION REQUESTING FUNDS FOR CONSTRUCTION OF A PUBLIC LIBRARY IN DELPHI. THE CITY COUNCIL APPROPRIATED $2,000 FOR THE PURCHASE OF A LIBRARY SITE. IN 1905, THE LIBRARY BOARD RECEIVED A CARNEGIE GRANT OF $10,000 FOR CONSTRUCTION OF A LIBRARY. THE LIBRARY BOARD ACCEPTED THE OFFER, AND THE CITY PURCHASED THE PRESENT SITE AT MAIN AND INDIANA STREETS. CONSTRUCTION BEGAN IN THE SUMMER OF 1905.

IN 1915, DEER CREEK TOWNSHIP ASKED TO BE SERVED BY THE DELPHI LIBRARY AND LEVIED A TAX TO HELP SUPPORT THE LIBRARY. UP UNTIL 1989, THE DELPHI PUBLIC LIBRARY WAS SUPPORTED BY THE TAXPAYERS OF DELPHI AND DEER CREEK TOWNSHIPS; HOWEVER ADDITIONAL TOWNSHIP MERGERS, JEFFERSON, ADAMS AND ROCK CREEK, RESULTED IN AN EXPANSION OF THE LIBRARY SYSTEM. MRS. MARY C. HOWE PROBABLY GAVE MORE OF HER TIME THAN ANY ONE PERSON TO FURTHER THE ESTABLISHMENT AND GROWTH OF THE LIBRARY."

BADLY OUT OF SPACE IN 1984, A GROUND BREAKING FOR A NEW ADDITION TOOK PLACE IN MARCH, 1990. NOW THE DELPHI PUBLIC LIBRARY IS ABLE TO PLAY AN EVER-GREATER ROLE IN THE EDUCATION, ENTERTAINMENT, AND WELL BEING OF THE PEOPLE OF CARROLL COUNTY.

GIFT: $10,000; DECEMBER 30, 1904
DEDICATION: JUNE 19, 1906
ARCHITECT: CHARLES E. KENDRICK, ROCHESTER
CONTRACTOR: W. C. HALSTEAD & COMPANY, INDIANAPOLIS
STYLE: NEO CLASSICAL REVIVAL

"Earl Park Public Library, Façade"

EARL PARK

EARL PARK PUBLIC LIBRARY

EXCERPTS FROM THE *EARL PARK CENTENNIAL BOOK*, PAGE 29, 1972:

"FEBRUARY 5, 1906 MARKED THE FORMAL OPENING OF THE FIRST LIBRARY IN EARL PARK WHICH WAS FIVE ROOMS ON THE SECOND FLOOR IN THE BRICK BUILDING AT THE CORNER OF OAK AND FIFTH STREETS. WHEN THE LIBRARY OPENED WITH MISS SIMS, FROM DELPHI, AS LIBRARIAN, OVER 400 BOOKS WERE DONATED.

AS EARLY AS 1907, LETTERS WERE BEING WRITTEN TO MR. CARNEGIE CONCERNING A NEW BUILDING. HE AGREED TO CONSIDER THE CLAIM TO A BUILDING DONATION IF THE TOWNSHIP WOULD UNITE WITH THE TOWN IN THE LIBRARY TAX. THE ADVISORY BOARD WAS HOSTILE TO LEVYING THIS LIBRARY TAX AND THE LIBRARY BOARD HAD TO SHOW THAT ONE TENTH OF THE FAMILIES LIVING IN THE TOWNSHIP OUTSIDE OF TOWN USED THE LIBRARY IF THE ADVISORY BOARD WOULD BE FORCED TO LEVY THE TAX. IN 1910, THE TOWNSHIP WAS FIRST TAXED.

IN NOVEMBER 1911, A LETTER WAS RECEIVED FROM MR. CARNEGIE STATING HE WOULD GIVE $7,500 FOR A BUILDING. ON MARCH 30, 1912, LOTS 127-8-9 ON THE CORNER OF ELM AND FIFTH STREET IN EARL PARK WERE PURCHASED FROM KATHRYN A. HORNEY FOR $1,500 FOR THE GROUND OF THE LIBRARY.

NO RECORD WAS KEPT AS TO WHEN THEY STARTED WORK ON THE NEW LIBRARY OR WHEN THE CORNERSTONE WAS LAID BUT ACCORDING TO LOCAL NEWS, THE BUILDING WAS COMPLETED IN THE FALL OF 1913. MISS MYRTLE TIMOTHY TOOK A SIX WEEK COURSE IN LIBRARY SCIENCE AT RICHMOND, INDIANA AND BECAME THE FIRST LIBRARIAN IN THE NEW BUILDING."

THE NEW CARNEGIE LIBRARY AT EARL PARK WAS OPENED INFORMALLY MARCH 23, 1914. THE LIBRARY HAS PHYSICALLY REMAINED THE SAME SINCE ITS INCEPTION.

GIFT: $7,500; NOVEMBER 21, 1911
DEDICATION: MARCH 23, 1914
ARCHITECT: GRANT C. MILLER, CHICAGO, ILL.
CONTRACTOR: UNLOCATED
STYLE: PSEUDO-GEORGIAN REVIVAL

"Earl Park Public Library, Wall Shelving"

"Earl Park Public Library, Interior, Hand Railing, Acorn Cap Tip"

"East Chicago Public Library, Pastrick Branch, Original Entry"

EAST CHICAGO

EAST CHICAGO PUBLIC LIBRARY
ROBERT A. PASTRICK BRANCH

EXCERPTS FROM *"THE EAST CHICAGO PUBLIC LIBRARY, ITS HISTORY AND GROWTH,"* ARTICLE BY FRANK H. WHITMORE, MAIN LIBRARIAN, *EAST CHICAGO* MAGAZINE, AUGUST, 1926:

"THE MOVEMENT TO ESTABLISH A LIBRARY STARTED IN 1908. MR. ANDREW CARNEGIE MADE A GENEROUS GIFT OF $40,000 WHICH WAS EXPENDED FOR THE CONSTRUCTION OF TWO LIBRARY BUILDINGS: ONE AT THE JUNCTION OF BARING AND CHICAGO AVENUES, IN THE WESTERN SECTION OF THE CITY, AND THE OTHER AT THE CORNER OF 136TH STREET AND GRAPEVINE, NOW GRAND BOULEVARD, IN THE EASTERN SECTION OF THE CITY.

THE BARING AVENUE BUILDING WAS DEDICATED, WITH EXTENDED CEREMONIES, ON FRIDAY EVENING, MAY 16, 1913, AND THE INDIANA HARBOR BRANCH BUILDING ON THE FOLLOWING EVENING. THE ADDRESS WAS GIVEN BY MARY ELIZABETH DOWNEY ABOUT THE *'EVOLUTION OF LIBRARIES'*."

AN ADDITION PROVIDING A BOOK STACK AND OTHER NEEDED SPACE WAS LATER MADE TO THE BARING AVENUE BUILDING AND COMPLETED IN 1925. IN 1939, ADDITIONAL EXTENSIONS NEARLY DOUBLE THE SIZE OF THE BUILDING. THE MOST RECENT RENOVATION IN 1986, ADDED CONFERENCE AND MEETING SPACE, A KITCHEN, AN ELEVATOR AND EXPANDED CHILDREN'S AREA. THE BARING AVENUE BRANCH LIBRARY WAS RENAMED THE ROBERT A. PASTRICK BRANCH IN HONOR OF THE CITY'S MAYOR FOR THE KEY ROLE FINANCIAL ROLE HE PLAYED.

PERHAPS THE MOST UNIQUE FEATURE OF THE PASTRICK BRANCH LIBRARY IS THE UPPER WALL MURAL ENTITLED, *"GIFT OF THE BOOK TO MANKIND."* THE MURAL WAS PAINTED IN THE 1930S BY ARTIST ERNEST KASAS, WHO WAS FUNDED BY THE WORKS PROJECT ADMINISTRATION (WPA).

GIFT: $20,000; JANUARY 13, 1911
DEDICATION: MAY 16, 1913
ARCHITECT: ARGYLE E. ROBINSON, CHICAGO, ILL.
CONTRACTOR: UNLOCATED
STYLE: CRAFTSMAN-PRAIRIE TRADITION

"East Chicago Public Library, Pastrick Branch, Interior"

"East Chicago Public Library, Pastrick Branch"

MURAL, 'GIFT OF THE BOOK TO MANKIND', PANEL, 'BEAUTY'"

"EVANSVILLE-VANDERBURGH PUBLIC LIBRARY, CHANDLER BRANCH, FACADE"

EVANSVILLE

EVANSVILLE-VANDERBURGH PUBLIC LIBRARY
CHANDLER BRANCH

EXCERPTS FROM THE *"FIRST FIFTY YEARS: THE EVANSVILLE-VANDERBURGH COUNTY PUBLIC LIBRARIES,"* ARTICLE BY HERBERT GOLDHOR, CENTRAL LIBRARY, 1963:

"IN MARCH, 1909, THE WEST SIDE BUSINESS ASSOCIATION WROTE ANDEW CARNEGIE REQUESTING FUNDS TO BUILD FOUR BRANCHES IN EVANSVILLE: WEST, EAST, NORTH AND IN HOWELL. AFTER CONSIDERABLE CORRESPONDENCE, MR. CARNEGIE AGREED TO GIVE $50,000 FOR TWO BRANCH LIBRARIES, ONE ON THE EAST SIDE AND ONE ON THE WEST SIDE, SUBJECT TO THE CITY PROVIDING THE LAND AND GUARANTEEING TO SUPPORT THE LIBRARIES BY AT LEAST $5,000 A YEAR THEREAFTER.

ON FEBRUARY 20, 1911, THE EVANSVILLE CITY COUNCIL FORMALLY ACCEPTED MR. CARNEGIE'S OFFER AND ITS CONDITIONS. THE GROUND FOR THE EAST BRANCH LIBRARY CONSISTED OF TWO LOTS PURCHASED BY THE CITY FROM THE SCHOOL BOARD.

ON OCTOBER 31, 1911, THE NEWLY APPOINTED MEMBERS OF THE PUBLIC LIBRARY BOARD OF TRUSTEES MET FOR THE FIRST TIME. WHEN THE CHIEF LIBRARIAN, MISS ETHEL MCCOLLOUGH WAS APPOINTED ON MAY 31, 1912, THE TWO BRANCH LIBRARY BUILDINGS WERE UNDER CONSTRUCTION. ON JANUARY 1, 1913, THE TWO BRANCH LIBRARY BUILDINGS WERE FORMALLY DEDICATED AND OPEN TO THE PUBLIC. ON NOVEMBER 24, 1914, THE CHERRY BRANCH LIBRARY BUILDING, ALSO A GIFT FROM CARNEGIE, WAS OPENED EXCLUSIVELY FOR NEGROES, THE ONLY BRANCH LIBRARY NORTH OF THE OHIO RIVER TO DO SO.

THE CHANDLER BRANCH OR EAST BRANCH WAS BUILT IN 1912 IN A BEAUTIFUL PARK SETTING. LOCATED IN THE HISTORIC BAYARD PARK NEIGHBORHOOD, THE CARNEGIE BRANCH OCCUPIES A SPACIOUS AND LOVELY SITE SURROUNDED BY SINGLE FAMILY HOMES."

GIFT: $25,000; JANUARY 6, 1911
DEDICATION: JANUARY 1, 1913
ARCHITECT: CLIFFORD SHOPBELL, EVANSVILLE
CONTRACTOR: INTERNATIONAL STEEL & IRON CONSTRUCTION
STYLE: RENAISSANCE REVIVAL

"Evansville-Vanderburgh Public Library, Chandler Branch, Ornate Entablature"

"Evansville-Vanderburgh Public Library, Chandler Branch, Foyer, Radiators"

57

"Evansville-Vanderburgh Public Library, Franklin Park Branch, South Façade"

EVANSVILLE

EVANSVILLE-VANDERBURGH PUBLIC LIBRARY
FRANKLIN PARK BRANCH

THE SISTER LIBRARY TO THE EAST BRANCH IS THE WEST BRANCH AND THE TWO LIBRARIES HAVE SIMILAR HISTORIES. THE FRANKLIN PARK OR WEST BRANCH, A LOOK ALIKE OF ITS STATELY TWIN, THE EAST OR CHANDLER BRANCH, WAS BUILT IN 1913, LIKE THE WEST BRANCH. THE ITALIAN RENAISSANCE STYLE LIBRARY IS LOCATED IN A SMALL URBAN PARK IN ONE OF EVANSVILLE'S OLDEST NEIGHBORHOODS.

LIKE THE EAST BRANCH, THE WEST BRANCH RECEIVED $25,000 FROM THE CARNEGIE FOUNDATION ON FEBRUARY 20, 1911. THE GROUND FOR THE WEST BRANCH LIBRARY WAS GIVEN BY THE CITY FROM ITS WEST SIDE PARK. THE BUILDING PLANS WERE THE SAME FOR BOTH BRANCHES, AND WERE DRAWN BY CLIFFORD SHOPBELL OF EVANSVILLE. BOTH BRANCH BUILDINGS FEATURED A RECTANGULAR RED BRICK STRUCTURE BASED ON A FOUNDATION OF DRESSED BEDFORD LIMESTONE AND LAVISHLY ORNAMENTED WITH CLASSICALLY INSPIRED CREAM COLORED TERRA COTTA IMPORTED FROM CHICAGO.

BOTH LIBRARIES WERE COMPLETED BY THE END OF 1912 AND DEDICATED ON JANUARY 1, 1913 WITH IMPRESSIVE CEREMONIES. THE WEST BRANCH WAS THE ADMINISTRATIVE CENTER BEFORE THE CENTRAL LIBRARY DOWNTOWN WAS FOUNDED.

GIFT: $25,000; JANUARY 6, 1911
DEDICATION: JANUARY 1, 1913
ARCHITECT: CLIFFORD SHOPBELL, EVANSVILLE
CONTRACTOR: INTERNATIONAL STEEL & IRON CONSTRUCTION
STYLE: RENAISSANCE REVIVAL

"Evansville-Vanderburgh Public Library, Franklin Park Branch, Transom"

"Evansville-Vanderburgh Public Library, Franklin Park Br., Foyer, Tile Floor"

"Flora-Monroe Township Public Library, Facade"

FLORA

FLORA-MONROE TOWNSHIP PUBLIC LIBRARY

IN 1914, THE PEOPLE OF FLORA VOTED IN FAVOR OF BUILDING A PUBLIC LIBRARY UNDER THE CARNEGIE PROGRAM. INTERESTED CITIZENS APPLIED FOR AND RECEIVED A GRANT FROM THE CARNEGIE CORPORATION IN 1917, AND FLORA WAS ELIGIBLE TO RECEIVE $10,000 IF IT MET CERTAIN REQUIREMENTS.

THE LIBRARY BOARD WAS ORGANIZED AND FUNCTIONAL. A LOT NEAR DOWNTOWN WAS PURCHASED FOR $1,183.20, AND A CONTRACT WAS SIGNED WITH THE GENERAL CONTRACTOR, W. R. DUNKIN, WHO HAD AGREED TO ERECT THE BUILDING FOR AN ECONOMICAL $10,000. THE ELECTRICITY WAS WIRED BY THE SANDBORN ELECTRIC COMPANY OF INDIANAPOLIS AND THE PLUMBING AND HEATING WAS INSTALLED BY THE WALLACE BROTHERS OF LAFAYETTE. THE TOTAL COST OF THE PROJECT WAS $11,573.30. THE LIBRARY OPENED WITH NO FANFARE ON OCTOBER 17, 1918.

THE FIRST LIBRARIAN, MISS RUTH DAWSON, REQUESTED A PHONE THE NEXT YEAR BUT IT WAS NOT UNTIL 1929 THAT A PHONE WAS INSTALLED. AFTER 22 YEARS WITHOUT A VACATION, THE LIBRARIAN WAS FINALLY GIVEN A WEEK OFF IN 1940.

THE CARNEGIE LIBRARY WAS RENOVATED AND MODERN MATCHING ADDITIONS WERE CONSTRUCTED IN 1978 AND 1996.

GIFT: $10,000; FEBRUARY 3, 1917
DEDICATION: AUGUST 17, 1918
ARCHITECT: WILSON B. PARKER, INDIANAPOLIS
CONTRACTOR: W. R. DUNKIN, FLORA
STYLE: CRAFTSMAN-PRAIRIE TRADITION

"Fort Branch-Johnson Township Public Library, Bracketed Eaves, Wood Cornice"

FORT BRANCH

FORT BRANCH-JOHNSON TOWNSHIP PUBLIC LIBRARY

THE FIRST SUGGESTION FOR A LIBRARY IN FORT BRANCH CAME FROM A LOCAL WOMAN'S CLUB IN TOWN. ON MARCH 15, 1916, THE FIRST MEETING WAS HELD FOR THE PURPOSE OF ORGANIZING A PUBLIC LIBRARY. MR. SANBORN, THE STATE LIBRARIAN, WAS ASKED TO SPEAK AT THE PUBLIC MEETING AND EXPLAIN HOW THE CITY COULD OBTAIN THE DONATION OF A BUILDING FROM THE CARNEGIE FOUNDATION. THE LIBRARY BOARD AGREED TO FURNISH LIBRARY SERVICES AND BOOKS.

THE CONTRACT FOR THE BUILDING WAS AWARDED TO MR. J. A. BEHRICK OF MOUNT VERNON IN THE AMOUNT OF $8,440. THE HEATING CONTRACT WAS AWARDED TO NOBLE HEATING & PLUMBING COMPANY OF PRINCETON, AND THE FURNITURE, LIGHT FIXTURES AND ARCHITECTS' FEE CONSUMED THE REST OF THE $10,000 CARNEGIE GRANT. THE LIBRARY WAS OPENED TO PATRONS IN JUNE, 1917. ARCHITECT CLIFFORD SHOPBELL DESIGNED A SIMILAR STYLED LIBRARY IN NEARBY CARMI, ILLINOIS IN 1914.

IN THE BEGINNING, THE LIBRARY WAS OPEN FOR BORROWING ON WEDNESDAY AND SATURDAY AND FOR READING ON SUNDAY FROM 2:00 P.M. TO 5:00 P.M. THE FIRST LIBRARIAN WAS A RETIRED TEACHER, AND HER SALARY WAS $12.50 A MONTH. THE FIRST JANITOR WAS PAID $5.00 A MONTH.

GIFT: $10,000; MAY 15, 1916
DEDICATION: JUNE 7, 1917
ARCHITECT: CLIFFORD SHOPBELL, EVANSVILLE
CONTRACTOR: J. A. BEHRICK, MOUNT VERNON
STYLE: CRAFTSMAN-PRAIRIE TRADITION

"Benton County Public Library, Fowler, Cornerstone"

FOWLER

BENTON COUNTY PUBLIC LIBRARY

EXCERPTS FROM *THE HISTORY OF BENTON COUNTY AND HISTORIC OXFORD* BY JESSE SETTINGTON BIRCH (1928) LTD. SESQUICENTENNIAL EDITION, CRAW AND CRAW PUBLISHERS, OXFORD, INDIANA, PAGE 78, 1942.

"DURING A MEETING OF THE SEVERAL LADIES CLUBS, THE MATINEE MUSICALE, THE AFTERNOON, THE CHAMINADE, AND THE COTERIE, HELD IN THE PRESBYTERIAN CHURCH IN MAY, 1904, IT WAS DECIDED TO USE THE ANNUAL DUES OF $1.00 PER MEMBER FOR THE ESTABLISHING OF A PUBLIC LIBRARY IN FOWLER. A BOOK SHOWER FOLLOWED WHICH WAS HELD IN THE FOWLER HOTEL. INTERESTED PERSONS DONATED OVER 200 BOOKS, AND THE FOWLER PUBLIC LIBRARY WAS SET UP IN THE FOYER OF THE OPERA HOUSE. THE LIBRARY LATER MOVED INTO WARMER QUARTERS IN THE MAVITY BUILDING.

IN THE MEANTIME A CORRESPONDENCE WAS CARRIED ON WITH THE CARNEGIE LIBRARY ASSOCIATION AND A GIFT OF $7,500 WAS GRANTED APRIL 11, 1906. THE SITE CHOSEN FOR THE LIBRARY WAS THE CORNER OF FIFTH AND VAN BUREN WITH TWO LOTS DONATED BY JAMES M. FOWLER, JR. OF LAFAYETTE, AND A THIRD LOT PURCHASED FOR $800 FROM MRS. CARR. THE CORNERSTONE WAS LAID MAY 17, 1906 BY THE MASONIC ORDER OF FOWLER AND THE STRUCTURE WAS COMPLETED BY NOVEMBER, 1906. THERE WERE 1,000 BOOKS ON THE SHELVES. IN 1917, UNDER THE NEW INDIANA LIBRARY LAW, THE FOWLER PUBLIC LIBRARY BECAME THE FOWLER-BENTON COUNTY PUBLIC LIBRARY."

A NEW ADDITION OPENED, SEPTEMBER, 1965, DOUBLING THE SIZE OF THE ORIGINAL CARNEGIE BUILDING. IN 1967, THE LIBRARY TRUSTEES MERGED THE FOWLER LIBRARY AND THE BENTON COUNTY LIBRARY, RESULTING IN THE BENTON COUNTY PUBLIC LIBRARY OF TODAY.

GIFT: $7,500; APRIL 11, 1906
DEDICATION: NOVEMBER 21, 1906
ARCHITECT: J. ALBERT. BOONSTRA, LAFAYETTE
CONTRACTOR: ALBERT D. FREEMAN, FOWLER
STYLE: NEO CLASSICAL REVIVAL

"Francesville-Salem Township Public Library, Facade"

FRANCESVILLE

FRANCESVILLE-SALEM TOWNSHIP PUBLIC LIBRARY

EXCERPTS FROM THE *"50TH ANNIVERSARY BOOKLET, AN HISTORICAL SKETCH,"* FRANCESVILLE-SALEM TOWNSHIP PUBLIC LIBRARY, 1966:

"EARLY IN THE YEAR OF 1915, THE PEOPLE OF FRANCESVILLE AND SALEM TOWNSHIP BEGAN MAKING ORGANIZED EFFORTS TO MAKE A PUBLIC LIBRARY.

THE CARNEGIE CORPORATION OF NEW YORK HAD AGREED TO FURNISH $9,000 TO THE TOWN OF FRANCESVILLE AND THE TOWNSHIP OF SALEM TO ERECT A FREE PUBLIC LIBRARY PROVIDING THE TOWN AND TOWNSHIP GIVE 10% SUPPORT OF THE DONATED AMOUNT, OR $900 ANNUALLY TO MAINTAIN THE LIBRARY, AND TO PROVIDE A SUITABLE SITE FOR THE LIBRARY. FORMAL ORGANIZATION WAS MADE FOR THE LIBRARY MAY 15, 1915.

THROUGH DONATIONS AND PROMOTIONS BY CITIZEN, FUNDS WITH WHICH TO PURCHASE A BUILDING SITE WERE OBTAINED. THE TOWN AND TOWNSHIP PURCHASED THE LOT FOR THE BUILDING SITE FROM FRED KOPKA ON JUNE 10, 1915 FOR THE SUM OF $600. A SECOND ADJOINING LOT, WAS PURCHASED FROM WALLACE DODGE, FOR THE SUM OF $700, ON JULY 24, 1916.

THE TWO STORY BRICK BUILDING WAS COMPLETED AND DEDICATED ON THURSDAY, NOVEMBER 2, 1916 AND WAS OPENED FOR CIRCULATION ON NOVEMBER 4, 1916 WITH MISS PETRA, AS LIBRARIAN. MRS. ROSELLA HUBBELL WAS THE FIRST BORROWER. ALL THE SCHOOLS IN THE TOWNSHIP WERE DISMISSED FOR THE DAY TO GIVE PUPILS AN OPPORTUNITY TO VISIT THE BUILDING."

A MAJOR RENOVATION AND ADDITION WAS MADE IN 1999-2000.

GIFT: $9,000; APRIL 19, 1915
DEDICATION: NOVEMBER 2, 1916
ARCHITECT: CHARLES W. NICHOLS, LAFAYETTE
CONTRACTOR: L. E. WICKERSHAM, LOGANSPORT
STYLE: CRAFTSMAN-ECLECTIC

"Frankfort-Clinton County Contractual Public Library, Interior, Stairs"

FRANKFORT

FRANKFORT-CLINTON COUNTY CONTRACTUAL LIBRARY

EXCERPTS FROM THE *"HISTORY OF THE FRANKFORT PUBLIC LIBRARY,"* BY EDITH THOMPSON FROM, *A CENTURY OF PROGRESS.* FRANKFORT, INDIANA, 1930:

"ONE OF THE EARLIEST FRANKFORT LIBRARIES BEGAN WITH THE ORGANIZATION OF A STOCK COMPANY ON MAY 19, 1879. IN 1882, THE FRANKFORT PUBLIC LIBRARY WAS IN A BACK ROOM OF A LAW OFFICE. ABOUT 1888, THE FEW HUNDRED BOOKS, WHICH WERE MOSTLY REMNANTS OF THE MACLURE AND TOWNSHIP LIBRARIES, WERE INSTALLED IN A SMALL ROOM OF THE NEW CITY BUILD-ING WITH THE CITY COUNCIL AS THE LIBRARY BOARD. ON FEBRUARY 6, 1903, THE CITY COUNCIL GAVE MANAGEMENT OF THE LIBRARY TO THE SCHOOL TRUSTEES AND THE LIBRARY WAS HOUSED IN THE HIGH SCHOOL BUILDING.

THE LOCAL CLUB WOMEN CHAMPIONED THE CAUSE OF THE PUBLIC LIBRARY. ESTABLISHMENT OF THE PRESENT BUILDING BEGAN NOVEMBER 24, 1905, WHEN ANDREW CARNEGIE THROUGH SUPERINTENDENT EDWIN S. MONROE, OFFERED TO GIVE THE CITY $17,500 FOR THE ERECTION OF THE LIBRARY BUILDING. THE PURCHASE OF THE LAND WAS MADE APRIL 26, 1906. LATER THAT YEAR, CARNEGIE INCREASED THE GIFT TO $22,500.

THE CORNERSTONE FOR THE BUILDING WAS LAID BY THE GRAND LODGE F. & A. MASONS ON NOVEMBER 26, 1906. THE BUILDING WAS CONSTRUCTED OF BEDFORD STONE AND MEASURES 60' X 70'. THE FORMAL OPENING OF THE CARNEGIE LIBRARY WAS HELD ON FEBRUARY 14, 1908."

IN 1965, THE FIRST FLOOR WAS RENOVATED, AS WAS THE UPSTAIR LEVELS OF THE CHILDREN'S AREA IN 1969-1970. A WEST WING WAS ADDED THAT TRIPLED THE SIZE OF THE ORIGINAL FLOOR SPACE IN 1988, AND IN THE 1990S, THE UPPER LEVELS WERE REMODELED.

GIFT: $22,500; NOVEMBER 24, 1905
DEDICATION: FEBRUARY 14, 1908
ARCHITECT: GRINDLE & STILES, MUNCIE
CONTRACTOR: FRANKFORT CONSTRUCTION COMPANY
STYLE: RENAISSANCE REVIVAL

"Garrett Public Library, Interior, Wood Columns, Corbels & Beams"

GARRETT

GARRETT PUBLIC LIBRARY

IN 1910, GARRETT'S FIRST PUBLIC LIBRARY WAS OPENED ON THE SECOND FLOOR OF THE BUILD-ING NOW OCCUPIED BY J. D. BRINKERHOFF JR. ON WEST KING STREET. THE BOOK COLLECTION WAS MOSTLY FICTION AND CONSISTED OF BOOKS CONTRIBUTED BY PERSONS LIVING IN GARRETT AND SURROUNDING AREAS.

THAT SAME YEAR, D. B. VAN FLEIT, OWNER OF THE GARRETT TELEPHONE COMPANY, BEGAN WORKING WITH A CITIZEN COMMITTEE TO RAISE $5,000 TO BUY THE LAND AT THE LIBRARY'S PRES-ENT SITE. INTERESTINGLY, THIS LOCATION WAS THE COMMITTEE'S SECOND CHOICE. A LOT AT THE INTERSECTION OF KEYSER AND LEE STREETS WAS THE FIRST CHOICE, BUT CITIZEN PROTEST RESULTED IN THE SELECTION AND PURCHASE OF THE DOWNTOWN SITE FROM MRS. LOUISE SHANNON AT 107 WEST HOUSTON.

IN 1914, WITH D. B. VAN FLEIT'S LEADERSHIP AND A $10,000 ANDREW CARNEGIE GRANT, A LIBRARY FACILITY WAS CONSTRUCTED AT ITS PRESENT LOCATION AND MADE AVAILABLE TO THE PUBLIC FROM 2:00 TO 9:00 P.M., SIX DAYS A WEEK. THE ORIGINAL BUILDING WAS CONSTRUCTED IN 1914. THE LIBRARY MEASURES 57.5' LONG BY 38' WIDE. THE LIBRARY OPENED TO THE PUBLIC APRIL 24, 1915 WITH ITS COLLECTION OF 2,342 BOOKS AND 1,346 REGISTERED PATRONS.

A MAJOR RENOVATION OCCURRED IN 1996 AND 1997 THAT NEARLY TRIPLED THE SIZE OF THE LIBRARY AT A COST OF $1.24 MILLION.

GIFT: $10,000; MARCH 14, 1913
DEDICATION: APRIL 24, 1915
ARCHITECT: COSMO C. ELLWOOD, ELKHART
CONTRACTOR: WILLIAM NEWELL, COLUMBIA CITY
STYLE: ECLECTIC-CRAFTSMAN-RENAISSANCE REVIVAL

"Gas City-Mill Township Public Library, Office, Dumb Waiter"

GAS CITY

GAS CITY-MILL TOWNSHIP PUBLIC LIBRARY

EXCERPTS FROM *"A BRIEF HISTORY OF THE GAS CITY-MILL TOWNSHIP PUBLIC LIBRARY,"* PAPER BY DELORIS GRIFFITH, MARCH 14, 1994:

"A LETTER DATED APRIL 25, 1911, TO MR. ISSAC CRIPE, SUPERINTENDENT OF GAS CITY SCHOOLS, FROM A LOCAL CITIZEN, WAS THE BEGINNING OF THE CARNEGIE LIBRARY IN GAS CITY. THE LETTER STATED, THAT IN 1911 THERE WERE 125 PUBLIC LIBRARIES, MANY CARNEGIE-FUNDED, IN TOWNS AND CITIES IN INDIANA AND SUGGESTED NOW WAS THE TIME FOR SUCH A POSSIBILITY IN THE COMMUNITY OF GAS CITY. THE PROMINENT PEOPLE OF THE COMMUNITY FAVORED THE ESTABLISHMENT OF A PUBLIC LIBRARY MAINLY DUE TO THE FACT THAT MANY YOUNG PEOPLE OF THE CITY DROP OUT OF SCHOOL AT AN EARLY AGE TO WORK IN THE GLASS FACTORIES.

IN 1912, AN OFFICIAL REQUEST FOR CARNEGIE FUNDS WAS SENT TO NEW YORK TO REQUEST ASSISTANCE FOR BUILDING THE LIBRARY IN GAS CITY. THE LIBRARY BOARD WAS READY TO GO TO WORK ON JANUARY 1, 1913. WITH THE ADDITION OF MILL TOWNSHIP TO ADD TO THE TOTAL EFFORT OF BUILDING AND SUPPORTING THE LIBRARY, THE CARNEGIE CORPORATION AGREED TO ALLOW $12,500 FOR THE BUILDING PROJECT.

IN THE MEANTIME, TEMPORARY QUARTERS FOR THE NEWLY ORGANIZED LIBRARY WERE ARRANGED BY RENTING THE DOWNSTAIRS ROOM OF MRS. JOHN PHILLIPS. THE NEW CARNEGIE BUILDING WAS ERECTED IN THE MIDDLE OF ELEVEN CITY LOTS ON MAIN STREET. THE LIBRARY WAS COMPLETED IN OCTOBER, 1914. THE LIBRARY WAS OPENED IN NOVEMBER, 1914, WITHOUT A FORMAL DEDICATION."

A WEST ADDITION HAS BEEN COMPLETED IN RECENT YEARS, DOUBLING THE FLOOR SPACE, AND THE ORIGINAL CARNEGIE BUILDING WAS RESTORED.

GIFT: $12,500; JANUARY 2, 1913
DEDICATION: NOVEMBER, 1914
ARCHITECT: HIRAM ELDER, MARION
CONTRACTOR: L. L. JOHNSON & SON
STYLE: CRAFTSMAN-NEO CLASSICAL REVIVAL

"Spencer County Public Library, Grandview Branch, West Facade, Gable"

GRANDVIEW

SPENCER COUNTY PUBLIC LIBRARY
GRANDVIEW BRANCH

EXCERPTS FROM *"HISTORY OF THE GRANDVIEW-HAMMOND TOWNSHIP PUBLIC LIBRARY"* FILE:

"IN DECEMBER 1899, MR. E. V. WILBERN OF CINCINNATI, OHIO, THROUGH HIS FRIEND W. E. KNIGHT, OFFERED TO PRESENT TO HIS FORMER HOMETOWN OF GRANDVIEW A LIBRARY, WITH THE CONDITION THE TRUSTEES TAKE OVER ITS CONTROL. THE OFFER WAS ACCEPTED WITH THANKS.

THE WILBERN LIBRARY, NAMED IN HONOR OF ITS DONOR, WAS FORMED IN 1900 BY AN APPOINTED LIBRARY COMMITTEE AND AFTER SEVERAL MOVES, REMAINED AT THE MONITOR NEWSPAPER OFFICE UNTIL THE LIBRARY MOVED INTO THE NEW CARNEGIE BUILDING IN 1919.

STEPS WERE SOON TAKEN TO OBTAIN THE GIFT OF A BUILDING FOR GRANDVIEW AND HAMMOND TOWNSHIP FROM THE CARNEGIE CORPORATION. THE GIFT OF $8,000 WAS MADE IN SEPTEMBER OF 1917. LAND WAS PURCHASED FROM MOSS FISH COMPANY AT A PRICE OF $400.

THE CARNEGIE BUILDING WAS MOVED INTO JANUARY, 1919 WITH MRS. GRACE BARKER SERVING AS THE FIRST LIBRARIAN. THE DARK BRICK BUILDING WAS SITUATED ON THE CORNER OPPOSITE THE INTERURBAN STATION; EASILY ACCESSIBLE TO EVERYONE ENTERING TOWN.

THERE WERE NO MAJOR IMPROVEMENTS OR CHANGES MADE TO THE ORIGINAL BUILDING UNTIL AFTER THE MERGER WITH THE ROCKPORT-OHIO TOWNSHIP PUBLIC LIBRARY. THE RESOLUTION OF MERGER WAS APPROVED AND SIGNED BY THE GRANDVIEW-HAMMOND TOWNSHIP LIBRARY BOARD IN SEPTEMBER OF 1987. THE LIBRARY UNDERWENT A COMPLETE RENOVATION, REPAIR AND ADDITION DURING THE 1990S, DOUBLING THE SIZE OF THE ORIGINAL CARNEGIE BUILDING."

GIFT: $8,000; SEPTEMBER 14, 1917
DEDICATION: MARCH 1, 1919
ARCHITECT: J. W. GADDIS, VINCENNES
CONTRACTOR: JOHN PYLE, ROCKPORT
STYLE: PSEUDO-GEORGIAN REVIVAL

"Putnam County Public Library, Façade"

GREENCASTLE

PUTNAM COUNTY PUBLIC LIBRARY

EXCERPTS FROM THE *MUNICIPAL AND INSTITUTIONAL LIBRARIES OF INDIANA*, COMPILED BY W. E. HENRY, STATE LIBRARIAN, PAGE 52, *"THE GREENCASTLE CARNEGIE LIBRARY,"* BY BELLE HANNA, LIBRARIAN, 1904:

"THE PUBLIC LIBRARY AT GREENCASTLE, IND. BEGAN AS A SCHOOL LIBRARY, WHEN, UNDER THE LAW OF 1881, A TAX WAS LEVIED TO BUY BOOKS FOR THE USE OF THE SCHOOL CHILDREN. IN 1891, THE BOARD OF EDUCATION DECIDED TO THROW IT OPEN TO THE PUBLIC. THE COMMON COUNCIL GAVE AID AND THE PUBLIC LIBRARY WAS OPENED ON THE SECOND FLOOR OF A BUSINESS BLOCK, ON THE EAST SIDE OF THE PUBLIC SQUARE. IT REMAINED THERE, USED CONSTANTLY BY BOTH CHILDREN AND ADULTS, UNTIL ALL THE AVAILABLE SPACE WAS OCCUPIED.

IN 1902, CHIEFLY THROUGH THE EFFORTS OF MR. D. L. ANDERSON, TREASURER OF THE SCHOOL BOARD, THE CARNEGIE GIFT WAS SECURED. MR. CARNEGIE GAVE AT FIRST $10,000, THEN AN ADDITIONAL $10,000 AFTER A PROMISE OF HIGHER TAXES FOR A GRAND TOTAL OF $20,000. THIS WAS PROMPTLY ACCEPTED BY THE COMMON COUNCIL AND THE NAME WAS CHANGED TO THE GREENCASTLE CARNEGIE LIBRARY. A LOT WAS PURCHASED AT VINE AND WALNUT.

THE CORNERSTONE WAS LAID IN SEPTEMBER, 1902. THE BUILDING WAS DEDICATED WITH APPROPRIATE EXERCISES ON JUNE 5, 1903. THE WHOLE BUILDING IS BEAUTIFULLY DECORATED, WELL LIGHTED, ELEGANTLY FURNISHED, AND VERY CONVENIENT."

IN RECENT YEARS, A RENOVATION AND ADDITION WAS MADE THAT QUADRUPLED THE SIZE OF THE ORIGINAL LIBRARY. THE DEDICATION WAS HELD DECEMBER 1, 1996.

GIFT: $20,000, JANUARY 22, 1902
DEDICATION: JUNE 5, 1903
ARCHITECT: PATTON & MILLER, CHICAGO, ILL.
CONTRACTOR: ROBERT S. GRAHAM, GREENCASTLE
STYLE: NEO CLASSICAL REVIVAL

"Putnam County Public Library, Fanlight, Spider Web Pattern"

"Putnam County Public Library, Interior, Indiana & Genealogy Room"

"Hartford City Public Library, Interior, Fireplace"

HARTFORD CITY

HARTFORD CITY PUBLIC LIBRARY

EXCERPTS FROM *A HISTORY OF BLACKFORD, COUNTY, INDIANA*, BLACKFORD COUNTY HISTORICAL SOCIETY, PAGES 50-51, 1986:

"THE HISTORY OF HARTFORD CITY PUBLIC LIBRARY BEGAN AT A REGULAR MEETING OF THE SCHOOL BOARD IN MARCH, 1901, WHEN SUPERINTENDENT C. H. DRYBREAD PROPOSED THE IDEA OF A PUBLIC LIBRARY. THE ONLY LIBRARY IN HARTFORD CITY AT THAT TIME WAS AT THE HIGH SCHOOL AND WAS INADEQUATE FOR STUDENTS, LET ALONE FOR THE REST OF THE COMMUNITY.

BECAUSE OF AN ABUNDANCE OF NATURAL GAS, HARTFORD CITY WAS THRIVING IN 1901. THE TAX DOLLAR HAD BEEN STRETCHED, HOWEVER, FOR THE NEWLY COMPLETED COURTHOUSE, A NEW CITY HALL ABOUT TO BE STARTED, AND STREET IMPROVEMENTS. THE SCHOOL BOARD AND CITY COUNCIL BACKED A DECISION TO APPLY FOR A CARNEGIE ENDOWMENT OF $15,000. ALMOST A YEAR LATER, HARTFORD CITY RECEIVED A PLEDGE OF $15,000 FROM MR. CARNEGIE'S SECRETARY.

ON MARCH 12, 1902, THE CITY ACCEPTED THE PROPOSAL AND APPROPRIATED $700 TOWARD A BUILDING SITE. IN AUGUST, 1902, THE LOT AT 314 NORTH HIGH STREET WAS PURCHASED FROM DELLA AND EZRA STAHL FOR $1,800. HOME TALENT SHOWS SUPPLIED EXTRA FUNDS AS NEEDED.

THE CORNERSTONE BEARING THE LEGEND, 'DEDICATED TO THE MEMORY OF ANDREW CARNEGIE, JULY 30, 1903,' WAS TO BE LAID AT 5 P.M. ON MONDAY, AUGUST 10, 1903 BUT NONE OF THE DIGNITARIES WHO WERE TO PARTICIPATE IN THE CEREMONY SHOWED UP. NO EXPLANATION WAS EVER OFFERED FOR THEIR ABSENCE. THE STONE WAS FITTED IN THE BUILDING THE NEXT DAY BY ONE LONE BOARD MEMBER AND THE WORKMEN WHO SLAPPED IN THE MORTAR. THE CARNEGIE LIBRARY WAS DEDICATED JULY 7, 1904."

GIFT: $16,000; JANUARY 22, 1902
DEDICATION: JULY 7, 1904
ARCHITECT: J. L. BROWN, HARTFORD CITY
CONTRACTOR: THOMPSON & MILLSPAUGH, ANDERSON
STYLE: NEO CLASSICAL REVIVAL

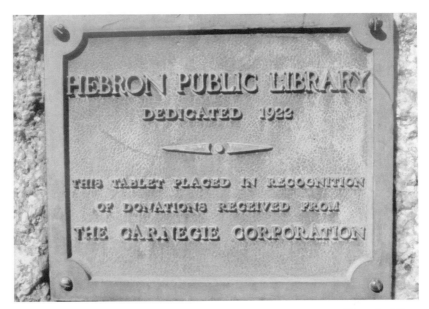

"Porter County Public Library, Hebron Branch, Front Lawn, Historic Plaque"

HEBRON

PORTER COUNTY PUBLIC LIBRARY
HEBRON BRANCH

EXCERPTS FROM THE *LIBRARY OCCURRENT*, *"HEBRON"* BY PHYLLIS J. SAUNDERS, PAGE 326, FEBRUARY 1980:

"THE HEBRON PUBLIC LIBRARY WAS ESTABLISHED IN 1917, ONE OF THE LAST CARNEGIE LIBRARIES TO BUILT IN INDIANA. THE LIBRARY IS A RESULT OF THE EFFORTS OF THE DETERMINED WOMEN OF THE HEBRON FORTNIGHTLY CLUB WHO CANVASSED THE TOWN AND SURROUNDING TOWNSHIPS TO SECURE THE SIGNATURES AND PLEDGES REQUIRED BY LAW. THE PRESIDENT OF THE FIRST BOARD OF TRUSTEES, M. E. DINSMORE, MORTGAGED HIS OWN HOME IN ORDER THAT A PLOT OF GROUND NEAR THE CENTER OF TOWN COULD BE PURCHASED FOR $1,300 FOR A LIBRARY BUILD-ING. BUILDING COSTS WERE VERY HIGH AT THE TIME OF WORLD WAR I, AND AFTER THE GRANT WAS ACCEPTED, THE BUILDING WAS DEFERRED UNTIL 1921.

ON SEPTEMBER 14, 1917, THE CARNEGIE FOUNDATION GRANTED $10,000 BUILDING FUNDS TO THE LIBRARY DISTRICT WHICH INCLUDED THE TOWNSHIPS OF BOONE AND EAGLE CREEK AND THE TOWN OF HEBRON, AND THE BUILDING, STILL IN USE TODAY, WAS DEDICATED APRIL 18, 1922. ARCHITECT WILSON B. PARKER OF INDIANAPOLIS WAS PRESENT FOR THE CELEBRATION. THE ONE-STORY AND BASEMENT-TYPE LIBRARY WAS OF BRICK CONSTRUCTION WITH GLAZED TILE ROOF AND CONTAINED 2,430 SQUARE FEET. THE FIRST LIBRARIAN WAS CARRIE F. NICHOLS, WHO SERVED ON THE FIRST LIBRARY BOARD.

GROUND BREAKING FOR THE 10,370 SQUARE FOOT ADDITION TOOK PLACE ON MAY 21, 1994. THE NEWLY RENOVATED LIBRARY WAS OPENED TO THE PUBLIC ON SEPTEMBER 13, 1995. THE HEBRON PUBLIC LIBRARY IS NOW PART OF THE PORTER COUNTY PUBLIC LIBRARY SYSTEM."

GIFT: $10,000; SEPTEMBER 14, 1917
DEDICATION: APRIL 28, 1922
ARCHITECT: PARKER & HONEYWELL, INDIANAPOLIS
CONTRACTOR: FRED W. MARSDEN, HEBRON
STYLE: CRAFTSMAN TRADITION

"Indianapolis-Marion County Public Library, East Washington Branch, Statue"

INDIANAPOLIS

INDIANAPOLIS-MARION COUNTY PUBLIC LIBRARY
EAST WASHINGTON BRANCH

THE EAST WASHINGTON BRANCH WAS THE FIRST OF FIVE CARNEGIE LIBRARIES THAT WERE BUILT IN INDIANAPOLIS BETWEEN 1911 AND 1914. A CARNEGIE GIFT OF $126,000 WAS DIVIDED AMONG THE FIVE BRANCHES. CONSTRUCTION BEGAN IN 1909 AND THE BUILDING WAS DEDICATED NOVEMBER 14, 1911. THE TUDOR GOTHIC REVIVAL STYLED LIBRARY WAS POSITIONED ALONG THE BUSINESS ROUTE OF U. S. 40, THE OLD NATIONAL ROAD. RESIDENTIAL NEIGHBORHOODS ARE SITUATED TO THE NORTH AND SOUTH OF THE BRANCH AND THE MAJOR THOROUGHFARE.

THE BUILDING IS RICH IN ARTISTIC FLAVOR. A UNIQUE ARCHITECTURAL FEATURE OF THE LIBRARY IS THE TWO HOODED, MONK-LIKE FIGURES OR GROTESQUES THAT HOVER ABOVE THE ENTRANCE ALONG THE PARAPET. THE STOOPED MONK ABOVE THE WEST CORNER OF THE ENTRANCE IS INTENSELY READING A BOOK, WHILE THE MONK ALONG THE EAST CORNER OF THE ENTRANCE HAS JUST FINISHED READING HIS BOOK, AND LOOKS UP, IN ELATED WONDER.

ADDITIONAL CARNEGIE FEATURES INCLUDE THE MATCHING FIREPLACES, THE OAK WOODWORK, AND THE CIRCULATION DESK, AND THE ARCHING PATTERNS OF THE DOORS AND WINDOWS. THE STRUCTURE UNDERWENT RENOVATION IN 1977-1978.

GIFT: $20,000; JANUARY 19, 1909
DEDICATION: NOVEMBER 14, 1911
ARCHITECT: FOLTZ & PARKER, INDIANAPOLIS
CONTRACTOR: UNLOCATED
STYLE: TUDOR GOTHIC REVIVAL

"Indianapolis-Marion County Public Library, Spades Park Branch, Facade"

INDIANAPOLIS

INDIANAPOLIS-MARION COUNTY PUBLIC LIBRARY
SPADES PARK BRANCH

Located at 1801 Nowland Avenue, the Spades Park Branch is the only Carnegie library in Indiana with a unique Italianesque architecture. Dedicated March 22, 1912, the three storied structure sits at a narrow point between Commerce Street and Nowland Avenue, adjacent to the southwest of Brookside Park, west and north about ten blocks from the East Washington Branch library. The property site was a gift from Michael H. Spades.

The Oriental brick walls and terra cotta red tile roof shelter unique Carnegie features such as fireplaces, tin ceilings, and a second floor auditorium. The nearly square building has wide bracketed eaves and an extended or long entryway. The interior underwent a major renovation in 1986-1987. Spades Park Branch Library continues to serve the inner city residential area north of the East Washington Branch library and the historic neighborhood of Woodruff Place.

Gift: $20,000; January 19, 1909
Dedication: March 22, 1912
Architect: Wilson B. Parker, Indianapolis
Contractor: George Weaver, Indianapolis
Style: Italianesque

"Kentland-Jefferson Township Public Library, Director's Office, File Cabinet"

KENTLAND

KENTLAND-JEFFERSON TOWNSHIP PUBLIC LIBRARY

EXCERPTS FROM THE *LIBRARY BOOKMARKER* AND *HISTORY FILE*, KENTLAND PUBLIC LIBRARY:

"THE ESTABLISHMENT OF A PUBLIC LIBRARY IN KENTLAND WAS LONG A DREAM OF MANY OF THE EARLIEST RESIDENTS OF THE COMMUNITY. A SERIOUS EFFORT TO CREATE THE LIBRARY GOT UNDERWAY IN 1909 THANKS TO THE DILIGENT EFFORTS OF THE KENTLAND WOMAN'S CLUB, A DEDICATED BOARD OF TRUSTEES AND MANY OTHERS. IN THAT YEAR, WARREN T. MCCRAY CARRIED OUT CORRESPONDENCE WITH THE ANDREW CARNEGIE FOUNDATION WHICH SUBSEQUENTLY LED TO THE COMMUNITY'S RECEIVING A $10,000 GRANT FROM THE FOUNDATION FOR THE BUILDING'S CONSTRUCTION.

THE KENTLAND WOMEN'S CLUB UNDERTOOK THE COLLECTION OF BOOKS THROUGH DONATIONS, AND A TEMPORARY LIBRARY WAS ESTABLISHED IN THE KNIGHTS OF PYTHIAS LODGE ROOMS. THIS TEMPORARY LIBRARY WAS LATER MOVED TO THE BASEMENT OF THE COURTHOUSE. IN 1910 THE FIRST BOARD OF LIBRARY TRUSTEES WAS APPOINTED.

THE LOTS FOR THE PERMANENT LIBRARY WERE DONATED BY MRS. ELIZA MCCRAY. UPON RECEIPT OF THE CARNEGIE GRANT, LOCAL BUILDER FRED FRIEDLINE RECEIVED THE CONTRACT TO BUILD THE TWO STORY BRICK STRUCTURE. THE KENTLAND PUBLIC LIBRARY WAS INFORMALLY OPENED AT 2:00 P.M., JANUARY 26, 1912 WITH A COLLECTION OF 1,500 BOOKS.

THE OPENING WAS ATTENDED BY HUNDREDS OF CITIZENS OF KENTLAND AND JEFFERSON TOWNSHIP. ALTHOUGH NO CONTRIBUTIONS WERE ASKED FOR, MANY CITIZENS CAME WITH DONATIONS FOR THE NEW LIBRARY."

THE LIBRARY HAS BEEN REMODELED AND RENOVATED SEVERAL TIMES SINCE THE ORIGINAL CARNEGIE STRUCTURE WAS BUILT, BUT THE BUILDING RETAINS ITS FORMER INTEGRITY.

GIFT: $10,000; DECEMBER 2, 1909
DEDICATION: JANUARY 26, 1912
ARCHITECT: PATTON & MILLER, CHICAGO, ILL.
CONTRACTOR: FRED FREIDLINE, KENTLAND
STYLE: CRAFTSMAN-GOTHIC REVIVAL

"Kewanna-Union Township Public Library, Interior"

KEWANNA

KEWANNA-UNION TOWNSHIP PUBLIC LIBRARY

EXCERPTS FROM THE *SESQUICENTENNIAL HISTORY OF KEWANNA*, APRIL, 1967:

"IN MARCH, 1904 THERE WAS TALK OF A PUBLIC LIBRARY FOR KEWANNA, AND IF IT COULD BE SECURED, WOULD PROVE OF MUCH SATISFACTION TO THOSE RESIDING IN THE TOWN AND TOWNSHIP. IN 1905, STEPS WERE TAKEN TOWARD PROVIDING A PUBLIC LIBRARY FOR THE TOWN OF KEWANNA. A TAX LEVY WAS MADE AS PROVIDED BY LAW.

THE BOARD ACCEPTED THE OFFER OF THE SCHOOL BOARD OF A ROOM IN THE SCHOOL BUILDING FOR THE VERY FIRST LIBRARY IN KEWANNA. MRS. JESSIE TONER WAS HIRED AS THE FIRST LIBRARIAN. THE LIBRARY REMAINED AT THE KEWANNA SCHOOL UNTIL SPRING, 1912.

THE LIBRARY BOARD, HEARING THAT ANDREW CARNEGIE THROUGH THE CARNEGIE CORPORATION WAS GIVING MONEY TO BUILD LIBRARIES, CONTACTED THE CORPORATION. A GIFT OF $8,000 WAS GRANTED FOR THE CONSTRUCTION OF THE PRESENT BUILDING. THE KEWANNA PEOPLE WERE JUBILANT OVER THE PROSPECTS OF A NEW CARNEGIE LIBRARY. THE LOT IN THE CENTER OF KEWANNA ON WHICH THE LIBRARY STANDS WAS OWNED BY MRS. JOHN LEITER AND MRS. HENRY HOWELL. THE LOT FRONTAGE MEASURED 71 FEET ON EAST MAIN STREET, OPPOSITE THE EUREKA THEATRE. THE PRICE OF THE LOT WAS $1,000.

THE NEW LIBRARY WAS DEDICATED ON NOVEMBER 24, 1914, WITH DR. STANLEY COULTER OF PURDUE UNIVERSITY GIVING THE ADDRESS ENTITLED, *'THE COMMUNITY VALUE OF THE LIBRARY.'* THE LIBRARY BECAME THE CULTURAL CENTER OF THE COMMUNITY. DURING THE WINTER OF 1914-1915, THERE WAS A SERIES OF FREE LECTURES SPONSORED BY THE STATE LIBRARY COMMISSION, HELD IN THE ASSEMBLY ROOM."

GIFT: $8,000; MAY 21, 1913
DEDICATION: NOVEMBER 24, 1914
ARCHITECT: CHARLES E. KENDRICK, ROCHESTER
CONTRACTOR: J. J. HILL
STYLE: CRAFTSMAN-PRAIRIE TRADITION

"Kingman Public Library, Interior, Original Card Catalog"

KINGMAN

KINGMAN PUBLIC LIBRARY

A GROUP OF CONCERNED CITIZENS BELIEVED THERE WAS A NEED FOR A LIBRARY IN KINGMEN AND MILL CREEK TOWNSHIP. A LIBRARY COMMITTEE WAS FORMED AND HELD A MEETING OCTOBER 4, 1913 TO ELECT THE FIRST OFFICERS OF THE BOARD OF TRUSTEES. THE COMMITTEE HOPED TO SECURE A BUILDING FOR $10,000 FROM MONIES OFFERED BY MR. ANDREW CARNEGIE.

THE BOARD OF TRUSTEES HIRED TRUE L. BROOKIE OF INDIANAPOLIS, AS THE ARCHITECT WHOSE PLANS AND SPECIFICATIONS WERE ACCEPTED. THE BOARD WAS ADVISED THAT THE CARNEGIE CORPORATION WOULD APPROPRIATE NO MORE THAN $8,000. IN FEBRUARY 1914, A LOT OWNED BY ELLISHA PITKOUD, LOCATED AT THE SOUTHWEST CORNER OF STATE AND SECOND STREETS, WAS ACQUIRED FOR $1,000 AS THE BUILDING SITE.

HAVING APPLIED TO THE CARNEGIE FUND FOR $8,000, THE LIBRARY BOARD RECEIVED THE GIFT ON JULY 9, 1913. WORK ON THE NEW BUILDING BEGAN IN APRIL OF 1914. THE BUILDING WAS DEDICATED ON APRIL 24, 1915. THE BOARD APPOINTED MISS JEAN BOONE AS THE FIRST LIBRARIAN. MR. JAMES BERTRAM, CARNEGIE'S PERSONAL SECRETARY, NOTED IN HIS REPLY TO THE LIBRARY BOARD'S REQUEST FOR MORE MONIES FOR BOOKS THAT, "IT WAS THE RESPONSIBILITY OF THE CITIZENS OF KINGMAN TO MAKE THE SACRIFICE TO FILL ITS SHELVES WITH BOOKS."

GIFT: $8,000; JULY 9, 1913
DEDICATION: APRIL 24, 1915
ARCHITECT: TRUE L. BROOKIE, INDIANAPOLIS
CONTRACTOR: UNLOCATED
STYLE: CRAFTSMAN-PRAIRIE TRADITION

"Kirklin Public Library, Rear Exterior, Adding On"

KIRKLIN

KIRKLIN PUBLIC LIBRARY

EXCERPTS FROM THE *"HISTORY OF THE KIRKLIN PUBLIC LIBRARY"* FILE:

"THE KIRKLIN PUBLIC LIBRARY WAS FIRST ORGANIZED IN 1913, SPONSORED BY THE DOUBLE SIX CLUB, WHO FOUND IT FINANCIALLY DIFFICULT TO MAINTAIN A LIBRARY AFTER THEY ORGANIZED IT. THE LIBRARY'S FIRST HOME WAS ABOVE A GENERAL STORE, IN A SPACE PROVIDED BY A CLUB MEMBER. MEMBERS OF THE CLUB TOOK TURNS SERVING AS LIBRARIANS FOR THE DONATED 300 VOLUME COLLECTION, TWO AFTERNOONS A WEEK. MONEY FOR THE BUILDING COULD BE SECURED THROUGH THE CARNEGIE FOUNDATION IF A SITE COULD BE LOCATED. IN 1914, MRS. MCKINNEY AND THE THOMPSON FAMILY GENEROUSLY DONATED THE LOT.

A LIBRARY BOARD WAS QUICKLY ORGANIZED AND A TAX LEVY WAS PUT INTO PLACE. THE SITE FOR THE LIBRARY AND THE TAX LEVY FOR LIBRARY SUPPORT HAVING BEEN SECURED ON APRIL 1, 1914, THE PRESIDENT OF THE LIBRARY BOARD INSTRUCTED THE SECRETARY TO WRITE THE CARNEGIE CORPORATION FOR FUNDS FOR THE BUILDING. NEGOTIATIONS WITH MR. CARNEGIE'S REPRESENTATIVES RESULTED IN A GIFT OF $7,500.

DURING THE TIME THE PLANS WERE BEING MADE FOR THE LIBRARY BUILDING, THE LIBRARY WAS HOUSED IN A RENT-FREE, VACANT ROOM OVER THE BERT MCKINNEY STORE. A BOOK SHOWER PRO-VIDED MORE THAN 300 VOLUMES. THE NEW LIBRARY BUILDING WAS DEDICATED WITH APPROPRIATE CEREMONIES ON DECEMBER 4, 1915. MR. HENRY F. SANBORN, SECRETARY OF THE INDIANA LIBRARY COMMISSION, GAVE THE PRINCIPAL ADDRESS. THE HISTORY OF THE INCEPTION AND DEVEL-OPMENT OF THE LIBRARY IDEA WAS READ BY MRS. H. CAST."

A NEW EAST ADDITION WAS ADDED DURING 2001-2002 THAT DOUBLED THE SIZE OF THE ORIG-INAL LIBRARY.

GIFT: $7,500; MAY 8, 1914
DEDICATION: DECEMBER 4, 1915
ARCHITECT: BROOKIE & MCGINNIS, INDIANAPOLIS
CONTRACTOR: MASTEN LUMBER COMPANY, COATESVILLE
STYLE: CRAFTSMAN-PRAIRIE TRADITION

"Knightstown Public Library, Façade"

KNIGHTSTOWN

KNIGHTSTOWN PUBLIC LIBRARY

EXCERPTS FROM THE *"HISTORY OF THE KNIGHTSTOWN PUBLIC LIBRARY"* FILE:

"BEGINNING AS EARLY AS 1902, THE KNIGHTSTOWN PUBLIC LIBRARY WAS DEVELOPED THROUGH THE EFFORTS OF INTERESTED CLUB WOMEN AND OTHER DEDICATED CITIZENS. A SMALL-POX EPIDEMIC HALTED EFFORTS UNTIL 1904. A TAX LEVY ALLOWED FOR ROOMS TO BE RENTED, A LIBRARY BOARD APPOINTED AND DONATED BOOKS TO BE COLLECTED FOR THE FIRST PUBLIC LIBRARY IN 1906. INTEREST IN A CARNEGIE FUNDED PUBLIC LIBRARY AROSE OVER THE YEARS AND A GIFT OF $10,000 WAS GRANTED APRIL 25, 1911.

THE LAYING OF THE CORNERSTONE FOR THE NEW CARNEGIE LIBRARY WAS CONDUCTED ON JULY 4, 1912, BY THE FREE AND ACCEPTED MASONS OF KNIGHTSTOWN. WITHIN THE CORNER-STONE IN A COPPER RECEPTACLE WERE DEPOSITED THE FOLLOWING ARTICLES: HISTORY OF THE KNIGHTSTOWN LIBRARY; LIST OF DONORS FOR PURCHASE OF THE LIBRARY SITE; DEPOSIT BY EACH OF THE WOMEN'S LITERACY CLUBS; DEPOSIT OF KNIGHTSTOWN FEDERATION OF CLUBS; DEPOSITS BY DIFFERENT LODGES; DEPOSIT OF A ROSTER OF THE TOWN OFFICIALS OF KNIGHTSTOWN; DEPOSIT OF THE KNIGHTSTOWN BANNER.

THE PEOPLE OF KNIGHTSTOWN HAD CAUSE TO BE THANKFUL ON THANKSGIVING DAY, NOVEMBER, 1912, FOR THE NEW CARNEGIE LIBRARY WAS COMPLETED AND DEDICATED ON THAT DAY. THE ATTENDANCE AT THE DEDICATION PROVED THAT PEOPLE WERE TRULY APPRECIATIVE OF THEIR NEW LIBRARY. THE LIBRARY WAS OPENED WITH A RECEPTION AND THOSE WHO REGISTERED THE FIRST DAY WERE GIVEN SOUVENIRS OF MINIATURE FLAGS. AT THE TIME OF THE OPENING, THE ONLY THING THAT WAS LACKING TO BEAUTIFY THE INTERIOR WAS THE FRESCOING OF THE WALLS. AN ADDITIONAL SUM WAS RAISED BY THE CLUBS FOR THIS PURPOSE."

GIFT: $10,000; APRIL 25, 1911
DEDICATION: THANKSGIVING DAY, NOVEMBER, 1912
ARCHITECT: C. H. BYFIELD, INDIANAPOLIS
CONTRACTOR: MARK FESLER, KNIGHTSTOWN
STYLE: RENAISSANCE REVIVAL

"Knightstown Public Library, Interior, Vestibule"

"Knightstown Public Library, Circulation Desk, Lamps"

"LaGrange County Public Library, Cornerstone"

LAGRANGE

LAGRANGE COUNTY PUBLIC LIBRARY

EXCERPTS FROM THE *"HISTORY OF THE LAGRANGE COUNTY LIBRARY"* FILE:

"EARLY SETTLERS IN LAGRANGE COUNTY HAVE MENTIONED THAT THE FIRST LIBRARIAN WAS A WOMAN WHO BROUGHT EIGHT BOOKS IN HER SADDLEBAGS TO LOAN HER NEIGHBORS. BY 1878, CHARLES G. CORNELL, THE DEPUTY POSTMASTER, HAD A BOOKSTORE CONNECTED WITH THE POST OFFICE. PATRONS COULD RENT BOOKS FOR A FEW PENNIES WEEKLY. IN OCTOBER OF 1893, MISS ALICE ELLISON DONATED A BUILDING ON SOUTH DETROIT STREET, WHERE TWO SMALL ROOMS, WERE TO BECOME THE LAGRANGE FREE READING ROOM. IN JANUARY OF 1910, THE WOMAN'S LEAGUE OF LAGRANGE, A UNION OF LITERARY CLUBS, ORGANIZED FOR THE PURPOSE OF ESTABLISHING A LIBRARY. A ROOM IN THE CITY BUILDING SERVED AS LIBRARY OF 400 VOLUMES.

THE CHILDREN OF THE LATE SOLOMON AND CAROLINE ROSE OFFERED TO DONATE A SITE FOR THE LIBRARY ON THE CORNER OF SPRING AND HIGH STREETS IF THE CARNEGIE FOUNDATION WOULD DONATE A STATED SUM FOR THE BUILDING. IN 1917, A GIFT OF $12,500 WAS SECURED FROM THE CARNEGIE FOUNDATION TO FINANCE THE CONSTRUCTION OF THE BUILDING. THE LAYING OF THE CORNERSTONE TOOK PLACE FRIDAY, NOVEMBER 30, 1917. THE LIBRARY WAS COMPLETED IN 1919. THE CONSTRUCTION WAS HINDERED BY THE WAR CONDITIONS. IN 1939, THE LIBRARY WAS BECAME A COUNTY FACILITY, GIVING FREE ACCESS TO ALL CITIZENS OF THE COUNTY."

ADJACENT TO THE CARNEGIE LIBRARY, A FEW YARDS SOUTH WAS THE TOWN HALL, WHICH WAS ABANDONED AND PURCHASED BY THE LIBRARY IN 1965. IN 1976, A NEW TWO-STORY ADDITION CONNECTED THE TWO BUILDINGS. IN 1994, THE SECOND STORY WAS RENOVATED. TODAY, THE LANDLOCKED LIBRARY IS FORCED TO ABANDON THE CARNEGIE BUILDING, AS PLANS ARE BEING MADE FOR A NEW FUTURE LIBRARY BUILDING PROJECT.

GIFT: $12,500; NOVEMBER 9, 1916
DEDICATION: FEBRUARY 9, 1919
ARCHITECT: A. M. STRAUS, FORT WAYNE
CONTRACTOR: ISSAC MILLER, GOSHEN
STYLE: CRAFTSMAN-PRAIRIE TRADITION

"LaGrange County Public Library, Foyer, Hanging Ceiling Lamp"

"LaPorte County Public Library, Façade"

LAPORTE

LaPorte County Public Library

Excerpts from the current library brochure, "LaPorte County Public Library":

"The city's first lending library was formed in 1834-1835 with 300 volumes housed in a corner of the office of John B. Niles, LaPorte's only attorney. The Working Men's Institute was created in 1856 with $500 left by William Maclure for the formation of a library that was found to be especially appealing to railroad workers.

Due to the removal of the railroad shops from LaPorte to Elkhart, the Maclure collection soon merged with the LaPorte Reading Room and Library Association. The Association purchased a lot on Maple Avenue in 1876 for $1,200. In 1876, the first library building was located at 805 Maple Avenue. It was purchase by the LaPorte Library and Natural History Association. In 1896, the building was remodeled and enlarged. In February 1897, the Association turned its property and 7,000 volumes over to the city school board to be operated as a public library.

By 1915, circulation had jumped to almost 52,000 volumes per year and more space was a necessity. Successful application was made to the Carnegie Foundation for funds to erect a new library building, and on November 2, 1920, the new library opened its doors at the corner of Indiana and Maple Avenues. Work on the library building had been delayed by a material shortage and coal strike.

In 1982, the LaPorte County Public Library system was formed. The 1920 Carnegie building has been remodeled and expanded several times."

Gift: $27,500; March 31, 1916
Dedication: November 2, 1920
Architect: Wilson B. Parker, Indianapolis
Contractor: Griewank Brothers, LaPorte
Style: Neo Classical Revival

"LaPorte County Public Library, Front Entrance, Marble Steps"

LA PORTE'S
CARNEGIE LIBRARY
(Continued from other side)
Renovation and expansion designed
by architect William Koster;
building dedicated 1991. Original
1920 section retained. Library
has played a major role in
community's development. One of
1,679 libraries built in U.S. with
funds from philanthropist
Andrew Carnegie. Indiana built
more Carnegie libraries than
any other state.

"LaPorte County Public Library, Historical Marker"

"Lawrenceburg Public Library District, Historic Photo, Circa. 1950"
PHOTO CREDIT LAWRENCEBURG PUBLIC LIBRARY DISTRICT

LAWRENCEBURG

Lawrenceburg Public Library District

EXCERPTS FROM THE LIBRARY BROCHURE, *"HISTORY OF THE LAWRENCEBURG PUBLIC LIBRARY"*:

"THE LAWRENCEBURG PUBLIC LIBRARY WAS ORGANIZED IN 1910 AFTER LOCAL CITIZENS HAD PETITIONED FOR THE ESTABLISHMENT OF A PUBLIC LIBRARY. DUE TO THE UNTIRING EFFORTS OF MISS ADA FITCH AND THE ASSISTANCE OF THE REVIEW CLUB, A LIBRARY WAS FOUNDED. OPENED ON MAY 18, 1910, THE FIRST LIBRARY COLLECTION OF 2,000 BOOKS WAS HOUSED IN A SMALL STORE ON SHORT STREET. IN 1914, A CARNEGIE FOUNDATION GRANT WAS AWARDED AND A LOT ON WEST HIGH STREET NEAR THE COURTHOUSE WAS DONATED FOR THE PURPOSE OF ERECTING A LIBRARY BUILDING. THE CARNEGIE BUILDING WAS DEDICATED OCTOBER 9, 1915, THE SECOND DAY OF THE FARMER'S FAIR.

THE 58' x 36' CARNEGIE BUILDING WAS BUILT OF CHINCHILLA BRICK OF LIGHT SHADE, WITH A ROOF OF RED PANAMA TILE. TWO BEDFORD OOLITIC LIMESTONE PILLARS ADORNED THE ENTRANCE. GOLDEN OAK WAS USED IN ALL THE WOODWORK. CORK LINOLEUM COVERED THE HARD MAPLE FLOORS THAT WERE EIGHTEEN INCHES ABOVE THE 1913 FLOOD LINE; HOWEVER, THE 1937 FLOOD DESTROYED THE ENTIRE COLLECTION."

THE FIRST MAJOR RENOVATION OF THE LIBRARY BUILDING WAS IN 1957-1958. THE SECOND MAJOR RENOVATION AND THE CONSTRUCTION OF A NEW 10,000 FOOT ADDITION WAS DEDICATED MAY 22, 1988. THE NEW ADDITION NEARLY ENCLOSED THE ORIGINAL CARNEGIE STRUCTURE WITH THE EXCEPTION OF THE NORTH WALL THAT FACES THE ALLEY AND PARKING LOT AND A PORTION OF THE WEST WALL THAT IS SURROUNDED BY A WALLED-IN GARDEN.

GIFT: $11,000; APRIL 13, 1914
DEDICATION: OCTOBER 9, 1915
ARCHITECT: TRUE L. BROOKIE, INDIANAPOLIS
CONTRACTOR: MASTEN LUMBER COMPANY, COATESVILLE
STYLE: NEO CLASSICAL REVIVAL

"Lawrenceburg Public Library District, Modern Façade"

"Lawrenceburg Public Library district, Façade, North Side"

Lebanon Public Library, Façade"

LEBANON PUBLIC LIBRARY

EXCERPTS FROM THE *"HISTORY OF THE LEBANON PUBLIC LIBRARY,"* PAPER BY CORA O. BYNUM, LIBRARIAN, 1931:

"THE IDEA OF A LIBRARY IN LEBANON WAS FIRST SUGGESTED BY REV. DEMETRIUS TILLOTSON AT A MEETING OF THE FEDERATED CLUBS IN AUGUST OF 1902. A COMMITTEE WAS APPOINTED TO WRITE MR. CARNEGIE TO ASK FOR LIBRARY BUILDING FUNDS ON OCTOBER 8, 1902. IN JANUARY OF 1903, A REPLY CAME FROM MR. CARNEGIE'S SECRETARY, JAMES BERTRAM, STATING THAT IF CERTAIN CONDITIONS WERE MET, HE WOULD SUPPLY $12,500 FOR THE LIBRARY BUILDING. ON APRIL 22, 1903, MR. CARNEGIE INCREASED HIS DONATION TO $15,000.

THE CORNER HARRISON LOT WAS PURCHASED FOR $4,000, AND THE HOUSE ON THE LOT WAS SOLD TO H. A. MEYER. CONSTRUCTION WAS TO BEGIN IN NOVEMBER, BUT WAS DELAYED; FINALLY THE CORNERSTONE WAS LAID ON APRIL 9, 1904. THE LIBRARY FINALLY OPENED ITS DOORS ON THURSDAY, JUNE 8, 1905, WITH A SMALL COLLECTION OF BOOKS, NUMBERING 1,353.

THE BUILDING IS A GREEK CLASSICAL STYLED STRUCTURE BUILT OF BEDFORD LIMESTONE. THE ELEVATED MAIN ENTRANCE ON THE SOUTH SIDE HAS FLANKING PAIRS OF IONIC COLUMNS SUPPORTING A FULL PEDIMENT OVER AN ARCHED ENTRY. FOUR PAIRS OF ENGAGED TUSCAN COLUMNS FORM BAYS FOR THE ARCHED WINDOWS ON THE WEST EXTERIOR OF THE BUILDING. FOUR BRICK FIREPLACES ARE SITUATED ON THE MAIN FLOOR."

MAJOR RENOVATION AND ADDITIONS TO THE ORIGINAL STRUCTURE OCCURRED IN THE MID-1960S AND IN THE 1980S. THE LIBRARY IS PREPARING TO ADD AN ANNEX TO THE LIBRARY ON THE EAST SIDE OF THE BUILDING.

GIFT: $15,000; APRIL 22, 1903
DEDICATION: JUNE 8, 1905
ARCHITECT: C. A. KRUTSCH & COMPANY, INDIANAPOLIS
CONTRACTOR: CHARLES J. ANDREWS, SHELBYVILLE
STYLE: NEO CLASSIC REVIVAL

"Lebanon Public Library, Pediment"

"Lebanon Public Library, Interior, Fireplace"

"Union County Public Library, Liberty, Historic Plaque"

LIBERTY

UNION COUNTY PUBLIC LIBRARY

EXCERPTS FROM THE *"UNION COUNTY PUBLIC LIBRARY AT A GLANCE"* FILE:

"IN 1887, JOHN W. SHORT, SUPERINTENDENT OF THE UNION COUNTY SCHOOLS, TRIED AND FAILED TO CREATE A LIBRARY FUND. FIVE YEARS LATER IN 1892, SMALL DONATIONS AND A GIFT OF BOOKS BY MRS. ALBERT DAVIS, CREATED A SCHOOL LIBRARY AT LIBERTY. AFTER THE SCHOOL LIBRARY WAS ESTABLISHED, SUPERINTENDENT SHORT AND THE SCHOOL BOARD SET ASIDE A SMALL ANNUAL APPROPRIATION FOR BOOK PURCHASES. IN 1902, THE SCHOOL BOARD ACCEPTED A CASH DONATION FROM THE SOCIETY OF ALUMNI AND OPENED THE SCHOOL LIBRARY TO SOCIETY MEMBERS. THE BOOK COLLECTION AMOUNTED TO OVER ONE THOUSAND VOLUMES.

IN 1913, THE LIBERTY SCHOOL BOARD TRANSFERRED THE LIBRARY TO THE STANLEY MEMORIAL BUILDING IN LIBERTY. THE TRANSFER ALSO INCLUDED A CHANGE IN POLITICAL RESPONSIBILITY FOR THE NOW 'PUBLIC LIBRARY' THAT HAD ITS OWN BOARD OF TRUSTEES. MANY VOLUMES WERE RECEIVED AS GIFTS, AND THE COLLECTION GREW TO 2,290 VOLUMES.

AFTER SEVERAL FAILED ATTEMPTS, THE LIBRARY OBTAINED A $10,000 GIFT FROM THE CARNEGIE FOUNDATION FOR THE CONSTRUCTION OF A NEW BUILDING. GROUND WAS BROKEN MAY 17, 1915 AND THE NEW CARNEGIE BUILDING WAS DEDICATED OCTOBER 8, 1915. MR. HENRY N. SANBORN, SECRETARY OF THE PUBLIC LIBRARY COMMISSION OF INDIANA, WAS THE PRINCIPAL SPEAKER. THE BUILDING MEASURED 48' X 46' WITH VARIEGATED MAT BRICK, STONE TRIMMINGS AND A TILE ROOF. MRS. ESTHER HAMILTON WAS THE FIRST LIBRARIAN.

IN 1917, THE UNION COUNTY COMMISSIONERS LEVIED A MODEST COUNTY TAX AND OPENED THE LIBRARY TO ALL COUNTY RESIDENTS. THE FIRST MAJOR ADDITION WAS COMPLETED IN 1995."

GIFT: $10,000; JANUARY 6, 1915
DEDICATION: OCTOBER 8, 1915
ARCHITECT: WILSON B. PARKER, INDIANAPOLIS
CONTRACTOR: UNLOCATED
STYLE: CRAFTSMAN-RENAISSANCE REVIVAL

"Ligonier Public Library, Façade"

LIGONIER

LIGONIER PUBLIC LIBRARY

THE ORGANIZATION OF THE LIGONIER PUBLIC LIBRARY IN 1907 WAS THE RESULT OF THE EFFORTS OF MR. W. C. PALMER, MR. WILL DAUM, ABRAHAM GOLDSMITH, AND THE NATHANIEL PRENTISS CHAPTER OF THE DAUGHTERS OF THE AMERICAN REVOLUTION. THE FIRST LIBRARY BOARD WAS SELECTED AND A READING ROOM WAS RENTED IN 1907.

MORE ROOM WAS NEEDED IN SHORT TIME AND THE LIBRARY BOARD SOUGHT THE AID OF ANDREW CARNEGIE. THE COMMUNITY MATCHED THE CARNEGIE GRANT OF $10,000, DOLLAR PER DOLLAR. IN 1908, THE CORNERSTONE OF THE BUILDING WAS LAID, WITH IMPRESSIVE CEREMONIES. THE FOLLOWING YEAR THE LIBRARY WAS DEDICATED.

EXPANDED DETAIL OF THE BUILDING IS DESCRIBED BY CLEO HOLLOWAY WOOD IN HER PAPER *"A HISTORICAL SKETCH OF THE LIGONIER LIBRARY"*:

"THE BUILDING IS SUGGESTIVE OF THE RENAISSANCE PERIOD, CONSTRUCTED FROM PRESSED BRICK, WITH DISTINGUISHED LINES OF SIMPLE DIGNITY. IT SETS AMID THE LOVELY SURROUNDINGS OF FINE OLD TREES, SHRUBBERY, WINDING WALKS, A FOUNTAIN, AND FLOWERS. THE APPROACH IS THROUGH TWO LIGHT STANDARDS, BUILT OF ORNAMENTAL BRICK. ALTOGETHER, IT FULFILLS TO THE UTMOST WITHIN, THE TRANQUILITY AND ENJOYMENT THAT IT PROMISES WITHOUT."

IN 1975, A MAJOR ADDITION TO THE LIBRARY WAS BUILT, AND IN 1996 AN ADA RENOVATION WAS COMPLETED.

GIFT: $10,000; APRIL 8, 1907
DEDICATION: SEPTEMBER, 1909
ARCHITECT: CHARLES E. KENDRICK, ROCHESTER
CONTRACTOR: E. F. WAUGH
STYLE: NEO CLASSICAL REVIVAL

"Linden Public Library, North Façade"

LINDEN

LINDEN PUBLIC LIBRARY

EXCERPTS FROM THE *"HISTORY OF THE LINDEN CARNEGIE PUBLIC LIBRARY,"* PAPER BY CHARLOTTE LUCAS, LIBRARIAN, JUNE 1932:

"IN AUGUST OF 1915, THE LINDEN WOMAN'S CLUB, AFTER DISCUSSING THE DESIRABILITY OF A PUBLIC LIBRARY IN LINDEN, APPOINTED A COMMITTEE TO INVESTIGATE THE REQUIREMENTS FOR A LIBRARY, AND TO CALL A MEETING OF THE MEN TAXPAYERS OF THE COMMUNITY. THE QUESTION WAS PUT BEFORE THE MEN TO APPROVE OR DISAPPROVE OF A PUBLIC LIBRARY. THERE WAS A UNANIMOUS INTEREST IN THE PROPOSAL.

WITHIN A SHORT TIME THE FIRST LIBRARY BOARD WAS APPOINTED AND CORRESPONDENCE WITH THE CARNEGIE FOUNDATION WAS BEGUN TO SOLICIT A GIFT. THE GIFT OF $7,500 WAS RECEIVED FROM THE CARNEGIE FUND FOR THE CONSTRUCTION OF THE BUILDING.

THE INTERVENTION OF WORLD WAR I PROVED A MISFORTUNE FOR THE UNDERTAKING. WORK HAD BEEN PREVENTED BY THE ACTION OF THE STATE COUNCIL OF DEFENSE. WHEN THE FIRST PLANS FOR THE BUILDING HAD BEEN APPROVED BY THE CARNEGIE FOUNDATION, PRICES ON BUILDING MATERIAL INCREASED SO RAPIDLY THAT IT WAS IMPOSSIBLE WITH THE $7,500 TO CONSTRUCT THE BUILDING AS PLANNED. THE TAX LEVY HAD BEEN ACCUMULATING, AND WAS USED IN ORDER TO MEET THE COST OF $9,995 FOR THE CARNEGIE BUILDING.

AND SO AFTER LONG EXTENDED EFFORTS FROM 1915 TO 1922, THE LINDEN CARNEGIE PUBLIC LIBRARY WAS READY FOR USE. LINDEN WAS VERY FORTUNATE IN HAVING RECEIVED THE GIFT FROM THE CARNEGIE FUND FOR IT WAS AMONG THE LAST OF SMALL TOWNS TO RECEIVE SUCH A DONATION."

THERE HAS BEEN NO ADDITION OR RENOVATION TO THE LIBRARY.

GIFT: $7,500; JANUARY 28, 1916
DEDICATION: MAY 4, 1922
ARCHITECT: WILSON B. PARKER, INDIANAPOLIS
CONTRACTOR: UNLOCATED
STYLE: CRAFTSMAN-PRAIRIE TRADITION

"Margaret Cooper Public Library, Linton, Leaded Paned Glass Window, Site of Home of Andrew Humphreys, Gift of Mr. and Mrs. Jos. Moss"

LINTON

MARGARET COOPER PUBLIC LIBRARY

EXCERPTS FROM THE *"HISTORY OF THE LINTON CARNEGIE LIBRARY,"* PAPER BY EMILY C. BUNYAN, LIBRARIAN, 1985:

"THE ORIGINS OF THE LIBRARY CAME FROM THE LOCAL BAY VIEW LIBRARY CLUB. THE CLUB STARTED A LIBRARY WITH 75 DONATED BOOKS IN A DEPARTMENT STORE, LOCATED ON THE SECOND FLOOR. CORRESPONDENCE WITH CARNEGIE BEGAN IN JANUARY, 1902. THE LIBRARY WAS PROMISED FUNDING DECEMBER 24, 1907. ANDREW CARNEGIE AGREED TO DONATE $15,000 FOR CONSTRUCTION OF THE LIBRARY.

JOSEPH MOSS DONATED THE LOT UPON WHICH THE LIBRARY BUILDING WAS ERECTED. PATTON AND MILLER OF CHICAGO WERE THE ARCHITECTS. THE CORNERSTONE WAS LAID JUNE, 1908. THE TWO STORY BUILDING WAS COMPLETED MARCH, 1909. THE FIRST FLOOR WAS CONSTRUCTED OF PRESSED BROWN BRICK WITH LIMESTONE TRIMMINGS, WHILE THE SECOND STORY HAS A TIMBERED EXTERIOR. THE LINTON PUBLIC LIBRARY WAS RENAMED THE MARGARET COOPER PUBLIC LIBRARY IN HONOR OF THE FIFTH LIBRARIAN (1925-1983)."

THE LIBRARY IS CURRENTLY UNDERGOING A FEASIBILITY STUDY FOR A NEW 21ST CENTURY LIBRARY BUILDING.

GIFT: $15,000; DECEMBER 24, 1907
DEDICATION: MARCH 10, 1909
ARCHITECT: PATTON & MILLER, CHICAGO, ILL.
CONTRACTOR: HUGH SCHLOAT
STYLE: TUDOR GOTHIC REVIVAL

"Marion Public Library, Pediment"

MARION

MARION PUBLIC LIBRARY

IN 1880, A PRIVATE SUBSCRIPTION LIBRARY OPENED IN THE COUNTY'S OLD BRICK COURTHOUSE. IT WAS OPEN TO SUBSCRIBERS ONLY ON SATURDAY AFTERNOON. THE FIRST TAX LEVY WAS GRANTED IN 1884, BUT THE MARION PUBLIC LIBRARY WAS NOT OPENED UNTIL JULY 1888, WITH 1,500 BOOKS. THE LIBRARY WAS IN SEVEN DIFFERENT LOCATIONS BEFORE MOVING INTO THE BUILDING MADE POSSIBLE BY A GIFT OF $50,000 FROM ANDREW CARNEGIE.

THE CITY COUNCIL AT ONCE PASSED THE NECESSARY RESOLUTION AND THE LIBRARY BOARD'S ACCEPTANCE WAS PROMPTLY FORWARDED TO MR. CARNEGIE. A BUILDING LOT AT THE SOUTHWEST CORNER OF WASHINGTON AND SIXTH STREETS WAS PURCHASED FOR $6,000 FROM OWNER PETER G. FINN. THE CONTRACT FOR THE ERECTION OF THE BUILDING WAS LET MAY 8, 1901. THE LIBRARY WAS DEDICATED DECEMBER 5, 1902, AND THE TOTAL COST OF THE PROJECT WAS $62,445.48.

SINCE THAT TIME, THE CARNEGIE BUILDING HAS PERIODICALLY BEEN REMODELED. IN 1989, WORK BEGAN ON A NEW BUILDING THAT WOULD BE CONNECTED TO THE ORIGINAL CARNEGIE BUILDING. LIBRARY SERVICE MOVED TO THE NEW BUILDING IN MARCH, 1991 AND DEDICATION EXERCISES TOOK PLACE APRIL 5, 1992. THE CARNEGIE STRUCTURE WAS RENOVATED AND NOW HOUSES THE LOCAL HISTORY AND GENEALOGY COLLECTIONS, AND PROVIDES SPACE FOR THE LIBRARY'S MUSEUM SERVICES.

GIFT: $50,000; FEBRUARY 18, 1901
DEDICATION: DECEMBER 5, 1902
ARCHITECT: RICHARDS, MCCARTY & BULFORD, COLUMBUS, OHIO
CONTRACTOR: PHILLIP B. PATTON & JAMES LONG
STYLE: BEAU ARTS CLASSICISM

"Marion Public Library, Museum, Interior"

"Marion Public Library, Foyer, Tile Floor, "Lamp of Knowledge"

"Morgan County Public Library, Martinsville, Stained Glass Dome"

MARTINSVILLE

MORGAN COUNTY PUBLIC LIBRARY

EXCERPTS FROM THE *MARTINSVILLE DAILY REPORTER* NEWSPAPER, JUNE 3, 1931:

"IN 1905, PROFESSOR JEREMIAH E. ROBINSON, SUPERINTENDENT OF THE MARTINSVILLE PUBLIC SCHOOLS HAD A CONVERSATION WITH MR. O. C. TONER, A MEMBER OF THE SCHOOL BOARD, WHO CALLED TO HIS ATTENTION THE FACT THAT ANDREW CARNEGIE WAS GIVING MONIES FOR THE ESTABLISHMENT OF PUBLIC LIBRARIES AROUND THE COUNTRY AND THAT THE CITY OF MARTINSVILLE SHOULD SECURE AS MUCH FINANCIAL ASSISTANCE AS POSSIBLE. IMMEDIATELY AFTER THE CONVERSATION BETWEEN PROF. ROBINSON AND MR. TONER, A LETTER WAS FORWARD-ED TO ANDREW CARNEGIE.

IN DUE TIME, THE CITY OF MARTINSVILLE MET THE REQUIREMENTS OF OBTAINING THE CARNEGIE GRANT. A SUITABLE SITE HAD BEEN FOUND AND PURCHASED FOR THE LIBRARY AND A MAINTE-NANCE TAX LEVY WAS IN PLACE, SUFFICIENT FOR SUCH A LIBRARY. THE GRANT OF $12,500 WAS RECEIVED FEBRUARY 13, 1906, AND ALTHOUGH MORE MONIES WERE REQUESTED, IT WAS DENIED. THE CITY OF MARTINSVILLE ADDED A $2,500 DONATION.

THE BUILDING WAS COMPLETED AT A COST OF $14,900. THE DEDICATION DATE WAS HELD SEPTEMBER 1, 1908. THE ADDRESS, *'RELATION BETWEEN THE LIBRARY AND THE COMMUNITY,'* WAS GIVEN BY CHALMERS HADLEY, SECRETARY OF THE PUBLIC LIBRARY COMMISSION OF INDIANA. THE NEWLY OPENED LIBRARY HAD A COLLECTION OF 1,500 BOOKS."

THE MORGAN COUNTY PUBLIC LIBRARY UNDERWENT EXTENSIVE EXPANSION AND RENOVATION IN 1990, INCREASING THE SIZE OF THE LIBRARY TO MORE THAN FOUR TIMES ITS ORIGINAL SIZE OF 20,000 SQUARE FEET AND RESTORING THE ORIGINAL STRUCTURE.

GIFT: $12,500; FEBRUARY 13, 1906
DEDICATION: SEPTEMBER 1, 1908
ARCHITECT: HARRIS & SHOPBELL, EVANSVILLE
CONTRACTOR: ORA STORM, MARTINSVILLE
STYLE: NEO CLASSICAL REVIVAL

"Morgan County Public Library, Martinsville, Rotunda, Fluted Wood Columns"

"Sullivan County Public Library, Merom Branch, Multi-paned Glass Foyer"

MEROM

SULLIVAN COUNTY PUBLIC LIBRARY, MEROM BRANCH

EXCERPTS FROM THE *"MEROM PUBLIC LIBRARY"* BROCHURE, 2000:

"IN SPITE OF OBSTACLES, DETERMINED CITIZENS OF MEROM ESTABLISHED A LIBRARY. THE FIRST ATTEMPT IN 1905 FAILED WHEN THE PRESIDENT OF UNION CHRISTIAN COLLEGE APPEALED TO ANDREW CARNEGIE FOR $25,000 AND WAS REJECTED. IN SPRING 1916, ANOTHER ATTEMPT BY MEROM RESIDENT, DR. J. J. PARKER MET WITH MORE SUCCESS.

JOHN C. CHANEY, ATTORNEY AND CONGRESSMAN, SUPPORTED THE CAUSE BY WRITING THE CARNEGIE CORPORATION THAT MEROM HAD A RAILROAD TWO MILES TO THE SOUTH, WAS A FAMOUS SUMMER RESORT FOR RECREATION SEEKERS, WAS HOME OF THE MEROM BLUFF CHAUTAUQUA ASSOCIATION, AND A 'FINE PLACE FOR A LIBRARY.'

THE TOWN OF MEROM JOINED WITH GILL TOWNSHIP TO CREATE ADEQUATE FUNDS FROM TAXA-TION. A BUILDING SITE WAS PURCHASED FOR $100. THE BLUEPRINTS WERE FINALLY APPROVED IN APRIL 1917. IT WAS DECIDED BY THE CARNEGIE CORPORATION TO GIVE $10,000 TO THE TOWN OF MEROM AND GILL TOWNSHIP FOR BUILDING, FURNISHING AND ARCHITECTURAL FEES. JOSEPH AND LUTISHE LEE SOLD THE MEROM LIBRARY ASSOCIATION THE EAST HALF OF LOT #164 FOR $100. THE GROUNDBREAKING CEREMONIES WERE HELD MAY 5, 1917.

ON SEPTEMBER 1, 1918 THE LIBRARY OPENED WITH MISS BONNIE MILAM AS LIBRARIAN. THE SHELVES HELD 1,124 BOOKS, 928 OF WHICH WERE GIFTS. CIRCULATION FOR THE FIRST MONTH WAS 725 BOOKS."

THE LAST MEETING OF THE MEROM LIBRARY BOARD WAS HELD ON DECEMBER 28, 1967. THE CARNEGIE BUILDING, CONTENTS, AND PROPERTY WERE TRANSFERRED AS A BRANCH TO THE SULLIVAN COUNTY LIBRARY SYSTEM.

GIFT: $10,000; NOVEMBER 9, 1916
DEDICATION: SEPTEMBER 1, 1918
ARCHITECT: S. LOUIS ALDER & FRED WALLICK, INDIANAPOLIS
CONTRACTOR: W. J. COYNER
STYLE: CRAFTSMAN-PRAIRIE TRADITION

"Milford Public Library, Facade"

MILFORD

MILFORD PUBLIC LIBRARY

EXCERPTS FROM A 1957 LIBRARY PAMPHLET COMMEMORATING THE *"50TH ANNIVERSARY, HISTORY OF THE MILFORD PUBLIC LIBRARY"*:

"IN THE FALL OF 1907, A FEW PUBLIC SPIRITED CITIZENS, AT THE SUGGESTION OF THE COLUMBIAN READING CIRCLE, ORGANIZED WHAT WAS KNOWN AS THE FIRST MILFORD PUBLIC LIBRARY. THE LIBRARY WAS OPENED TO THE PUBLIC ON DECEMBER 5, 1907, IN THE INTERURBAN STATION WAITING ROOM, LOCATED IN THE HOTEL MILFORD. EIGHTY VOLUMES WERE BORROWED FROM THE INDIANA STATE LIBRARY FOR THREE MONTHS, AND CITIZENS SUPPLIED THE SHELVES WITH BOOKS OF ALL DESCRIPTIONS FROM THEIR OWN COLLECTIONS. THE MILFORD PUBLIC LIBRARY MOVED FOUR TIMES BEFORE OCCUPYING THE PRESENT DAY CARNEGIE LIBRARY BUILDING.

GROUND FOR A PERMANENT LOCATION WAS PURCHASED IN 1916 FOR $1,800. THE MEMBERS OF THE LIBRARY BOARD WORKED HARD TO GET THE CARNEGIE GRANT SUFFICIENT TO BUILD THE PRESENT DAY BUILDING. MR. RICHARD VANDERVEER WENT TO NEW YORK AND CONFERRED WITH THE CARNEGIE OFFICIALS AND IN NOVEMBER OF 1916, THE LIBRARY BOARD WAS FINALLY ASSURED OF $10,000 FROM THE ANDREW CARNEGIE FUND.

A CONTRACT WAS DRAWN UP WITH MILFORD, VAN BUREN AND JEFFERSON TOWNSHIPS, WHERE-BY ALL FUTURE MAINTENANCE AND SUPPORT WOULD BE PROVIDED BY THE TAXING GOVERNMENTAL UNITS. THE CORNERSTONE OF THE LIBRARY WAS LAID ON APRIL 12, 1918. THE NEOCOLONIAL BUILDING WAS READY FOR OCCUPANCY JANUARY, 1919. THE LIBRARY FURNITURE WAS DONATED BY THE COLUMBIAN READING CIRCLE AND REDMON FURNITURE COMPANY."

DURING MILFORD'S SEQUICENTENNIAL YEAR, 1986, THE LIBRARY WAS REFURBISHED. A NEW MATCHING ADDITION WAS CONSTRUCTED AND DEDICATED IN 1995.

GIFT: $10,000; DECEMBER 3, 1915
DEDICATION: JANUARY, 1919
ARCHITECT: SAMUEL A. CRAIG, HUNTINGTON
CONTRACTOR: DOTY BROTHERS, MILFORD
STYLE: GEORGIAN REVIVAL-NEO COLONIAL

"Mitchell Community Public Library, Foyer, Iron Balusters"

MITCHELL

MITCHELL COMMUNITY PUBLIC LIBRARY

EXCERPTS FROM THE *"HISTORY OF THE MITCHELL-MARION TOWNSHIP PUBLIC LIBRARY,"* PAPER BY MRS. BEULAH BIGGS-MUNGER, LIBRARY BOARD MEMBER, 1931:

"THE IDEA OF A PUBLIC LIBRARY HAS BEEN FLOATING THROUGH THE MINDS OF MANY FOR SOME YEARS. IN CONVERSATION WITH A MEMBER OF THE BEDFORD LIBRARY BOARD, MR. ISAAC H. CRIM, THE WRITER EXPRESSED A WISH THAT MITCHELL TOO COULD HAVE A PUBLIC LIBRARY. MR. CRIM'S ANSWER WAS SO ENCOURAGING THAT THE WRITER, APPOINTED A COMMITTEE TO INVESTIGATE WAYS AND MEANS OF ESTABLISHING A LIBRARY.

THE FIRST STEPS WERE TAKEN IN NOVEMBER, 1913 WHEN 54 CITIZENS SIGNED A PAPER PLEDGING THEMSELVES TO PAYMENT OF THE SUM OF MONEY REQUIRED BY STATE LAW. THE TOWNSHIP WAS INVITED TO SHARE IN THE SUPPORT AND BENEFITS OF THE LIBRARY. THE LIBRARY BOARD WAS ORGANIZED JANUARY 9, 1914. IT WAS DECIDED TO ASK THE CARNEGIE COMMISSION TO FINANCE THE BUILDING. A FAVORABLE REPORT WAS RECEIVED THAT PROMISED $15,000.

THE FINAL CHOICE FOR THE BUILDING SITE WAS THE BATES CORNER AT THE INTERSECTION OF MAIN AND 8TH STREETS. THE LOT WAS PURCHASED OF DR. J. C. KELLY FOR A SUM OF $2,000.

THE OPENING TO THE ADULT PUBLIC WAS THE MONDAY EVENING OF FEBRUARY 12, 1917. PROFESSOR REYNOLDS OF INDIANA UNIVERSITY GAVE THE ADDRESS. THE BUILDING AND BOOKS WERE INSPECTED AND REFRESHMENTS SERVED. THE ROOMS WERE THRONGED WITH INTERESTED AND HAPPY CITIZENS THROUGHOUT THE EVENING."

IN MAY 1995, AN OPEN HOUSE WAS HELD FOR THE NEWLY REMODELED LIBRARY AND THE EXPANDED THE 8,000 SQUARE FOOT MATCHING BUILDING THAT NEARLY TRIPLED THE SIZE OF THE ORIGINAL CARNEGIE.

GIFT: $15,000; MAY 8, 1914
DEDICATION: FEBRUARY 12, 1917
ARCHITECT: CLIFFORD SHOPBELL, EVANSVILLE
CONTRACTOR: W. H. FIDLER & FRED PEACHER, ORLEANS
STYLE: PSEUDO RENAISSANCE REVIVAL

"Monon Town & Township Public Library, Pediment & Inscribed Freize"

MONON

Monon Town & Township Public Library

Early in 1913, the Monon Current Literature Club began efforts to establish a public library. The Monon Public Library was built with a $10,000 grant from the Carnegie Corporation received December 11, 1914. The completed library was dedicated December 11, 1915.

The following is from the *Library Occurrent*, a magazine publication of the Public Library Commission, page 29, December, 1915:

"The Monon Public Library building was formally opened on Friday, December 11, 1915. Women from the various clubs in town were hostesses at a public reception held at the library from 1:30 to 5:00 p.m. Many visitors inspected the new structure with evident interest and pride. At 8:00 in the evening the dedication exercises were held in the Methodist Church, where the principal address was delivered by Demarchus C. Brown, State Librarian. On Saturday afternoon, December 12th, the school children of the community were invited to the library. Stories were told to the various grades by Carrie E. Scott of the Public Library Commission of Indiana.

The building was designed by T. L. Brookie and Wilson B. Parker of Indianapolis. It measures 32 by 54 feet and was constructed at a cost of $10,000, the gift of the Carnegie Corporation."

On January 3, 1993, ground was broken for an 8,160 square foot addition and renovation. The "new" library was dedicated October 2, 1994.

Gift: $10,000; December 8, 1914
Dedication: December 11, 1915
Architect: Brookie & Parker, Indianapolis
Contractor: Young & Hodshire, Monticello
Style: Craftsman-Renaissance Revival

"Monterey-Tippecanoe Township Public Library, Composite Capital"

MONTEREY

Monterey-Tippecanoe Township Public Library

EXCERPTS FROM THE *"HISTORY OF THE MONTEREY-TIPPECANOE TOWNSHIP PUBLIC LIBRARY"* BY RENITA POTOFF, LIBRARIAN, 2000:

"THE MOVEMENT FOR A LIBRARY AT MONTEREY BEGAN IN LATE 1916, WHEN THE LATE HOMER L. ROGERS, PULASKI COUNTY SUPERINTENDENT OF SCHOOLS, MENTIONED TO ELMER JOHNSON THE IDEA OF REQUESTING CARNEGIE FOUNDATION GRANT MONEY FOR THIS PURPOSE. THE FIRST LIBRARY BOARD MEETING WAS HELD JANUARY 8, 1917.

IN APRIL 1917, THE CARNEGIE CORPORATION OFFERED THE $5,000 DONATION IF A DEED FOR THE GROUND COULD BE PRESENTED AND IF A TAX FOR THE UPKEEP OF THE BUILDING COULD BE ASSURED. LAND FOR THE BUILDING, LOTS SECURED FROM DR. WILLIAM KELSEY, WAS PROBABLY A $250 DONATION. THE MONTEREY CARNEGIE LIBRARY WAS THE SMALLEST UNIT TO HAVE BEEN GRANTED A SUBSIDY FOR A LIBRARY BUILDING BY THE CARNEGIE FOUNDATION.

THE LIBRARY BOARD ACCEPTED THE ARCHITECT'S PLANS AT THE JUNE, 1917 MEETING. SEALED BIDS FOR THE BUILDING WERE RECEIVED AUGUST 17, 1917 AND THE MASTER BROTHERS WERE SELECTED GENERAL CONTRACTOR. THE CARNEGIE GRANT PROVED NOT ENOUGH TO PAY FOR ALL COSTS AND THE COMMUNITY RAISED THE REMAINING SUM BY SUBSCRIPTION. THE LIBRARY OPENED ITS DOORS TO THE PUBLIC ON OCTOBER 16, 1918 WITH NO PLUMBING, ELECTRICITY OR FURNITURE AND ONLY ONE BOOK IN ITS COLLECTION, 'THE ROSE OF ST. LOUIS'."

THE TOWN OF MONTEREY AND TIPPECANOE TOWNSHIP UNITED INTO ONE TAXING UNIT IN SUP-PORT OF THE LIBRARY IN SEPTEMBER 1953. PHYSICAL IMPROVEMENTS TO THE BUILDING WERE MADE IN THE 1970S, 1980S AND 1990S. THE CONSTRUCTION OF A MATCHING 3,280 SQUARE FOOT ADDITION WAS COMPLETED IN 1999, DOUBLING THE FACILITY'S ORIGINAL SIZE.

GIFT: $5,000; APRIL 3, 1917
DEDICATION: OCTOBER 16, 1918
ARCHITECT: SAMUEL A. CRAIG, HUNTINGTON
CONTRACTOR: MASTER BROTHERS, MONTEREY
STYLE: NEO CLASSICAL REVIVAL

"Montpelier-Harrison Township Public Library, Children's Room, Furniture"

MONTPELIER

MONTPELIER-HARRISON TOWNSHIP PUBLIC LIBRARY

MONTPELIER RECEIVED A $10,000 CARNEGIE GIFT ON FEBRUARY 21, 1907. THE LIBRARY OPENED ITS DOORS TO THE COMMUNITY IN SEPTEMBER, 1908. AT THE END OF THE FIRST YEAR, THE LIBRARY HAD 3,611 BOOKS IN ITS COLLECTION.

THE FOLLOWING EXCERPTS ARE FROM THE FRONT PAGE OF THE *EVENING HERALD*, MONTPELIER, INDIANA, SATURDAY, SEPTEMBER 12, 1908, *"LIBRARY OPENING"*:

"PLEASING TO THE EARS OF THE MEMBERS OF THE LIBRARY BOARD WHO ACTED AS A RECEPTION COMMITTEE AT THE FORMAL OPENING OF MONTPELIER'S HANDSOME PUBLIC LIBRARY LAST EVENING, WERE THE MANY EXPRESSIONS OF SURPRISE AND DELIGHT MADE BY THE HUNDREDS OF VISITORS AS THEY FOR THE FIRST TIME, VIEWED THE INTERIOR OF WHAT IS UNDOUBTEDLY ONE OF THE NEATEST AND BEST ARRANGED LITTLE PUBLIC LIBRARIES IN THE STATE.

MR. ANDREW CARNEGIE, THE BUILDER OF PUBLIC LIBRARIES, WHOSE DONATIONS HAVE MADE POSSIBLE THE MANY FINE PUBLIC LIBRARY BUILDINGS THROUGHOUT THE COUNTRY, WAS APPEALED TO AND HE PROMPTLY REPLIED THAT UNDER THE SAME CONDITIONS AS HAD BEEN MET BY OTHER CITIES WHICH HE HAD ASSISTED, HE WOULD PRESENT MONTPELIER WITH A $10,000 LIBRARY BUILDING.

THE LIBRARY IS FOR THE FREE USE OF EVERY CITIZEN OF MONTPELIER AND ALL SHOULD AVAIL THEMSELVES OF THE SPLENDID OPPORTUNITY TO GET THE BEST OF EVERYTHING IN LITERATURE, HISTORY AND SCIENCE, SIMPLY FOR THE ASKING. EVERY CITIZEN IS SURELY AND JUSTLY PROUD OF THE NEW LIBRARY AND THANKFUL TO THE MEMBERS OF THE BOARD WHO HAVE DEVOTED THEIR TIME TO ITS BUILDING."

GIFT: $10,000; FEBRUARY 21, 1907
DEDICATION: SEPTEMBER 11, 1908
ARCHITECT: CUNO KIBELE, MUNCIE
CONTRACTOR: HINES & TOWNSEND, HARTFORD CITY
STYLE: RENAISSANCE REVIVAL

"Muncie-Center Twp. Public Library, Statuary Relief, Law, Science Prose"

MUNCIE

MUNCIE-CENTER TOWNSHIP PUBLIC LIBRARY

EXCERPTS FROM THE *"MUNCIE PUBLIC LIBRARY, 125 YEARS (1875-2000)"* BOOKLET, PAGES 2-12, JANUARY 6, 2000:

"ALTHOUGH MUNCIE PROBABLY HAD SOME SORT OF A LIBRARY AS EARLY AS 1853, IT WAS NOT UNTIL 1875 THAT THE MUNCIE PUBLIC LIBRARY WAS ESTABLISHED. THE FIRST MUNCIE PUBLIC LIBRARY WAS LOCATED IN A ROOM OF THE CITY BUILDING. THE 2,195 BOOKS WERE PURCHASED FROM FORMER COUNTY, TOWNSHIP, PHILALETHIAN AND WORKINGMEN'S LIBRARIES.

THE PLAN TO BUILD THE CARNEGIE LIBRARY BEGAN ON FEBRUARY 21, 1901, WHEN THE LIBRARY BOARD DECIDED TO ASK ANDREW CARNEGIE FOR A GIFT OF $50,000. THE COMMERCIAL CLUB WROTE THE LETTER OF REQUEST AND WITHIN TWO WEEKS A POSITIVE RESPONSE WAS RECEIVED FROM JAMES BERTRAM, THE PRIVATE SECRETARY OF ANDREW CARNEGIE. THE PROPOSITION WAS ACCEPTED BY THE CITY COUNCIL ON MARCH 25, 1901.

THE SEARCH FOR A BUILDING LOT CONCLUDED AT THE PRESENT SITE AT THE CORNER OF JACKSON AND JEFFERSON, WHICH WAS PURCHASED FOR $13,000. ON JUNE 1, 1902, THE FOUNDATION WAS LAID FOR THE NEW BUILDING. THE BUILDING WAS COMPLETED THREE YEARS LATER AT A TOTAL COST OF $55,900.85 AND WAS DEDICATED JANUARY 1, 1904.

A SOUVENIR SPOON WITH THE PICTURE OF THE NEW LIBRARY ENGRAVED IN ITS BOWL WAS PRESENTED TO THE YOUNG DAUGHTER OF ANDREW CARNEGIE. THE GIFT SO PLEASED MR. CARNEGIE THAT IN RETURN HE GAVE AN ADDITIONAL GIFT OF $5,000 THAT WAS USED FOR BUILDING EXPENSES."

GIFT: $55,000; MARCH 8, 1901
DEDICATION: JANUARY 1, 1904
ARCHITECT: WING & MAHURIN, FORT WAYNE
CONTRACTOR: MORROW & MORROW, MUNCIE
STYLE: NEO CLASSICAL REVIVAL

"Muncie-Center Township Public Library, Interior, Greek Ionic Capital"

"Muncie-Center Township Public Library, Interior, Rotunda, Stained Glass Dome"

"Ohio Township Public Library, Newburgh, Fireplace, Capital & Column"

NEWBURGH

OHIO TOWNSHIP PUBLIC LIBRARY

EXCERPTS FROM *A BICENTENNIAL LOOK AT NEWBURGH, INDIANA*, EDITED BY WILLIAM BURLEIGH, PUBLISHED BY NEWBURGH PUBLIC LIBRARY, 1976:

"THE FIRST PUBLIC LIBRARY IN WARRICK COUNTY WAS ESTABLISHED IN 1897 IN NEWBURGH. IT WAS KNOWN AS THE OHIO TOWNSHIP LIBRARY AND WAS HOUSED IN THE TRUSTEE'S OFFICE ON EAST CROSS STREET. THE SMALL GIFT OF 150 BOOKS, FROM THE INDIANA STATE LIBRARY, BECAME THE NUCLEUS OUT OF WHICH EVOLVED THE PRESENT NEWBURGH PUBLIC LIBRARY.

THE TOWNSHIP LIBRARY ALONE SOON PROVED INADEQUATE FOR THE NEEDS OF THE COMMUNITY AND EARLY IN 1908 THE NEWBURGH HISTORY CLUB SET ABOUT TO IMPROVE THE SERVICE. A SUBSCRIPTION LIBRARY WAS ORGANIZED. THE LIBRARY WAS MOVED FROM THE TRUSTEE'S OFFICE TO THE TOWN HALL.

A MAJOR STEP IN THE DEVELOPMENT OF THE LIBRARY CAME IN 1916 WHEN THE TOWN APPLIED FOR AND RECEIVED A GRANT FROM THE CARNEGIE CORPORATION. THE NECESSARY RESOLUTIONS WERE PASSED AND A LOT ON JENNINGS STREET WAS DONATED BY REV. DARBY TO COMPLY WITH THE CONDITIONS OF THE GRANT. THE BUILDING WAS SLOWED TO A STANDSTILL BY THE INTERVENTION OF WORLD WAR I BUT BY NOVEMBER OF 1919, THE BUILDING WAS READY FOR USE. THE FORMAL OPENING OF THE CARNEGIE LIBRARY WAS HELD ON THE EVENING OF NOVEMBER 4, 1919. THE BUILDING HAD BEEN IN PARTIAL USE SINCE AUGUST. THE RED BRICK BUILDING HAS LOW WINDOWS THAT LOOK OUT ON THE OHIO RIVER."

THE LIBRARY HAS MADE ADDITIONS AND RENOVATED SEVERAL TIMES OVER THE COURSE OF ITS NEAR CENTURY HISTORY. A 14,000 FOOT SQUARE ADDITION WAS COMPLETED IN 1984.

GIFT: $10,000; MARCH 15, 1916
DEDICATION: NOVEMBER 4, 1919
ARCHITECT: CLIFFORD SHOPBELL, EVANSVILLE
CONTRACTOR: UNLOCATED
STYLE: CRAFTSMAN-PRAIRIE TRADITION

"New Castle-Henry County Public Library, Foyer, Dedication Plaque"

NEW CASTLE

NEW CASTLE-HENRY COUNTY PUBLIC LIBRARY

EXCERPTS FROM THE *MUNICIPAL AND INSTITUTIONAL LIBRARY OF INDIANA* COMPILED BY W. E. HENRY, STATE LIBRARIAN, PAGES 109-110, *"NEW CASTLE PUBLIC LIBRARY,"* UNDER THE DIRECTION OF THE LOUISIANA PURCHASE EXPOSITION COMMISSION OF INDIANA, 1904:

"RECORDS FAIL TO REVEAL WHEN THE NEW CASTLE PUBLIC LIBRARY WAS FIRST ORGANIZED. NEW CASTLE HAS HAD MANY EXPERIENCES WITH LIBRARIES OF VARIOUS KINDS FROM THE CIRCULATING ONE OF A FEW BOOKS TO THE LARGER COMBINATION OF TOWN AND TOWNSHIP OWNERSHIP, AND WHILE ALL WERE OF VAST BENEFIT IN THEIR SCOPE OF USEFULNESS, THEY WERE ALWAYS LIMITED BY AN INADEQUATE OR UNCERTAIN FINANCIAL SUPPORT AND ONE BY ONE DROPPED OUT OF USE."

IN 1913, A SPIRITED AND SUCCESSFUL CAMPAIGN RESULTED IN THE CITY COUNCIL CREATING A LIBRARY BOARD. A GIFT OF $20,000 WAS RECEIVED FROM THE CARNEGIE FOUNDATION IN JULY FOR THE ERECTION OF A FREE PUBLIC LIBRARY. A BUILDING SITE WAS LOCATED ON SOUTH 15TH STREET AND THE BUILDING WAS CONSTRUCTED BY LOCAL CONTRACTORS, KLUS AND LIMBACH. THE LIBRARY WAS DEDICATED JANUARY 18, 1916, OPENING WITH 4,000 VOLUMES.

THREE ADDITIONS WERE ADDED TO THE REAR OF THE CARNEGIE BUILDING BETWEEN 1938 AND 1968. THROUGH AN ANONYMOUS GIFT TO THE LIBRARY IN 1971, A NEW ADDITION OPENED IN 1976. IN 1980, A LARGE DONATION WAS RECEIVED FROM THE ESTATE OF ALICE RATCLIFFE, A LOCAL HIGH SCHOOL LATIN TEACHER THAT SAVED THE CARNEGIE BUILDING FROM BEING DEMOLISHED. THE DONATION WAS USED TO RENOVATE THE CARNEGIE BUILDING AND A SKYWALK WAS BUILT TO CONNECT THE TWO BUILDINGS IN 1986.

GIFT: $20,000; JULY 9, 1913
DEDICATION: JANUARY 18, 1916
ARCHITECT: TRUE L. BROOKIE, INDIANAPOLIS
CONTRACTOR: KLUS & LIMBACH, NEW CASTLE
STYLE: TUDOR GOTHIC REVIVAL

"North Judson-Wayne Township Public Library, Main Entry, Broken Pediment"

NORTH JUDSON

NORTH JUDSON-WAYNE TOWNSHIP PUBLIC LIBRARY

EXCERPTS FROM *"A GIFT FROM MR. CARNEGIE,"* HISTORY SEMINAR PAPER, SANDRA KUEHL, LIBRARIAN, APRIL 19, 1990:

"THE FIRST OVERTURES CONCERNING A LIBRARY FOR THE TOWN OF NORTH JUDSON CAME FROM THE REVEREND J. J. DAVIS IN JULY OF 1914 WHEN HE WROTE THE CARNEGIE CORPORTION FOR DETAILS ABOUT ACQUIRING FUNDING FOR A LOCAL LIBRARY BUILDING. THERE APPEARS TO BE NO RESPONSE FROM THE CARNEGIE CORPORATION, HOWEVER, ON MARCH 14, 1916 A SECOND LETTER OF REQUEST FOR INFORMATION ON APPLYING FOR A GRANT PROVED FRUITFUL.

AT THE SEPTEMBER 14, 1917 MEETING OF THE CARNEGIE CORPORATION, NORTH JUDSON, AS WELL AS GRANDVIEW, HEBRON AND NEW CARLISLE, INDIANA WERE GRANTED FUNDS FOR THE ERECTION OF FREE PUBLIC LIBRARIES. THE $10,000 GIFT ARRIVED IN NORTH JUDSON FEBRUARY 8, 1918. THE LIBRARY PROJECT WAS SLOWED DOWN DUE TO THE IMPACT OF WORLD WAR I, HELD UP BY THE STATE COUNCIL OF DEFENSE, AND INFLATION TOOK ITS TOLL WHEN CONSTRUCTION BEGAN. BY JUNE OF 1919 THE LIBRARY SITE HAD BEEN PURCHASED.

THE CONTRACTOR, GRIEWANK BROTHERS, FAILED TO INCLUDE ALL COSTS AND THE BID WAS LET TO A LOCAL TOWNSMAN WHO WORKED FOR THE CONTRACTOR AS FOREMAN. AFTER MANY DELAYS, THE EXTERIOR OF THE LIBRARY BUILDING WAS COMPLETED BY JANUARY 21, 1922. BY MAY, 1922, THE LIBRARY WAS READY FOR USE. ALMOST SIX YEARS AFTER SERIOUS NEGOTIATIONS HAD BEGUN ON MARCH 14, 1916, THE NORTH JUDSON-WAYNE TOWNSHIP PUBLIC LIBRARY WAS DEDICATED ON JUNE 8, 1922."

DURING 1995-1996, THE CARNEGIE LIBRARY WAS RENOVATED, AND A 5,500 SQUARE FOOT ADDITION WAS CONSTRUCTED AND DEDICATED.

GIFT: $10,000; SEPTEMBER 14, 1917
DEDICATION: JUNE 8, 1922
ARCHITECT: SAMUEL A. CRAIG, HUNTINGTON
CONTRACTOR: GRIEWANK BROTHERS, LAPORTE
STYLE: GEORGIAN REVIVAL

"Orleans Town & Township Public Library, Façade"

ORLEANS

Orleans Town & Township Public Library

Excerpts from the *Orleans Progress Examiner* newspaper, August, 1965:

"Five years prior to the erection of the present day Carnegie building in 1915, two young ladies of Orleans, Miss Stella Glover and Mrs. Claire Stewart Young, saw the need of making good reading material available to the local citizens. Putting action to their thoughts, the first circulating library was started in the fall of 1910.

The books were place on shelves in the Kress Furniture Store and were circulated by the girls from this point for about three years. Realizing the need for a permanent reading room and more varied library material, a room in the Orleans Grade School was set up as the first permanent library location. A library board was appointed and the first meeting was held June 20, 1913.

As the interest in the library grew, the Library Board realized the need for more space and a permanent building. An application was filed with the Carnegie Library Foundation with favorable results. A $10,000 grant was received and the plot on North Maple Avenue, then known as the Artesian or Sulphur Well Park, was selected, and was to face west.

On October 15, 1915, the library was dedicated. The dedicatory address was delivered by Dr. Will D. Howe of the English Department of Indiana University. One thousand volumes were on the shelves for use when the reading room was opened to the public. A small auditorium with a stage, a lounge room and restrooms were a part of the attractive basement."

Gift: $10,000; January 6, 1915
Dedication: October 15, 1915
Architect: Wilson B. Parker, Indianapolis
Contractor: W. H. Fidler & Fred Peacher, Orleans
Style: Craftsman-Prairie Tradition

"Osgood Public Library, Original Furniture, Original Card Catalog"

OSGOOD

OSGOOD PUBLIC LIBRARY

EXCERPTS FROM *"THE HISTORY OF THE OSGOOD PUBLIC LIBRARY"* FILE:

"IN 1909 THE MEMBERS OF THE ENTRE NOUS CLUB OF OSGOOD FOUND THROUGH CLUB ACTIV-ITIES THAT THERE WAS A NEED FOR FAR MORE READING MATERIAL FOR THEMSELVES AND FOR THE COMMUNITY. THEY AGREED THAT A PUBLIC LIBRARY WAS THE ANSWER. EIGHTY-FIVE SUBSCRIP-TIONS FOR $3.65 EACH WERE SECURED, A TAX LEVY WAS GRANTED, AND THE NECESSARY STEPS WERE MADE TO COMPLETE THE ORGANIZATION. ON JANUARY 21, 1912, THE LIBRARY OPENED IN A ROOM OVER THE OSGOOD BANK. THE ORIGINAL COLLECTION OF THIRTEEN DONATED BOOKS SOON ENLARGED BY NUMEROUS DONATIONS AND 'BOOK SHOWERS.'

DEMAND FOR READING MATERIAL SOON INCREASED AND AT THE SUGGESTION OF MR. R. J. BEER, THE CARNEGIE CORPORATION WAS CONTACTED FOR POSSIBLE FINANCIAL AID IN BUILDING A LIBRARY. THE CARNEGIE CORPORATION AGREED TO GIVE A BUILDING FUND EQUAL TO TEN TIMES THE AMOUNT RAISED BY TAXATION FOR MAINTENANCE. A GIFT OF $9,000 WAS GIVEN TO THE LIBRARY FROM THE CARNEGIE CORPORATION. A LOT WAS SECURED BY PUBLIC SUBSCRIPTION OF $1,500. THE CONTRACT PRICE OF THE NEW BUILDING WAS $8,400. MR. CARNEGIE'S DONATION WAS $9,000, AND THE REMAINING $600 WAS SPENT FOR WINDOWS, SHADES, SCREENS, RUGS, CHAIRS, ELECTRICAL FIXTURES AND MORE. BOOKS WERE MOVED INTO THE NEW BUILDING IN JULY, 1914 AND ON AUGUST 21, 1914, THE BUILDING WAS DEDICATED."

TODAY THE LIBRARY IS WELL INTACT THANKS TO AN AMBITIOUS RENOVATION PROGRAM THAT BEGAN IN 1996. SINCE OCTOBER, 1999, THE DISTRICT HAS EXPANDED FROM ONE TOWNSHIP TO FOUR. A FUTURE RENOVATION AND ADDITIONS ARE PLANNED, BRINGING THE TOTAL AREA OF THE LIBRARY TO NEARLY 14,000 SQUARE FEET.

GIFT: $9,000; JANUARY 9, 1913
DEDICATION: AUGUST 21, 1914
ARCHITECT: GUSTAVE M. DRACH, CINCINNATI, OHIO
CONTRACTOR: CHARLES E. MORRELL, OSGOOD
STYLE: TUDOR GOTHIC MILITARY

"Owensville Carnegie Public Library, Facade"

OWENSVILLE

OWENSVILLE CARNEGIE PUBLIC LIBRARY

EXCERPTS FROM *A HISTORY OF OWENSVILLE, INDIANA*, 1982, CHAPTER VI, *"CULTURE AND BEAUTIFICATION"*:

"BEFORE THE CARNEGIE LIBRARY WAS ESTABLISHED THERE WERE A FEW CIRCULATING LIBRARIES OWNED BY PRIVATE CITIZENS SUCH AS MR. J. P. COX, OR SOCIAL CLUBS, SUCH AS THE FRIDAY CLUB. IN 1916, A FEW OF OWENSVILLE'S CIVIC-MINDED CITIZENS WORKED FOR SEVERAL WEEKS INVESTIGATING HOW THEY COULD SECURE A CARNEGIE LIBRARY FOR OWENSVILLE. A BOARD WAS APPOINTED AND MEETING HELD TO MAKE PLANS FOR THE BUILDING OF THE LIBRARY.

THE BOARD DECIDED THE IDEAL LOCATION FOR THE LIBRARY WOULD BE IN THE CENTER OF THE PARK ON THE TOWN SQUARE. ON JULY 8, 1916, MR. J. L. GOAD WAS GIVEN THE GENERAL CONTRACT FOR BUILDING THE LIBRARY. THE LIBRARY BOARD SUPERVISED THE CONSTRUCTION OF THE BUILDING AND HANDLED ALL THE BUSINESS MATTERS PERTAINING TO THE LIBRARY'S ESTABLISHMENT. NYTOX TAN CHINCHILLA BRICK WITH STONE TRIM AND A RED TILE ROOF WERE SELECTED. THE BUILDING COST $12,500, THE EXACT AMOUNT OF THE CARNEGIE DONATION. MISS ZELLA LOCKHART WAS SELECTED LIBRARIAN AT A SALARY OF $35 A MONTH. THE LIBRARY BUILDING WAS COMPLETED AND DEDICATED ON OCTOBER 1, 1917. THE LIBRARY HAS ADDED TO THE DIGNITY AND BEAUTIFICATION OF THE TOWN."

GIFT: $12,500; DECEMBER 3, 1915
DEDICATION: OCTOBER 1, 1917
ARCHITECT: CLIFFORD SHOPBELL, EVANSVILLE
CONTRACTOR: J. L. GOAD, OWENSVILLE
STYLE: NEO CLASSICAL REVIVAL

"Oxford Public Library, Façade"

OXFORD

OXFORD PUBLIC LIBRARY

EXCERPTS FROM THE *"HISTORY OF THE OXFORD PUBLIC LIBRARY,"* PAPER BY MABLE L. DEEDS, LIBRARIAN, 1931:

"THE FIRST MEETING OF THE MEMBERS ELECT OF THE OXFORD LIBRARY BOARD WAS HELD OCTOBER 21, 1912 AND THE FIRST ITEM OF BUSINESS WAS A TAX LEVY OF FIVE CENTS ON THE ONE HUNDRED DOLLARS ASSESSED VALUATION. AT THE MEETING HELD JANUARY 24, 1914, THE SECRETARY OF THE LIBRARY BOARD REPORTED CORRESPONDENCE WITH THE CARNEGIE CORPORATION, WHICH RESULTED IN A PLEDGE OF $8,000, IF OXFORD WOULD FURNISH THE SITE AND PROMISE TO SUITABLY SUPPORT IT. AFTER THE PURCHASE OF THE LOT ON THE NORTHEAST CORNER OF THE PUBLIC SQUARE, THE GIFT WAS RECEIVED AND THE ARCHITECT SELECTED.

CONSIDERABLE DIFFICULTY WAS ENCOUNTERED IN THE MATTER OF SECURING AN ARCHITECT. TRUE L. BROOKIE, INDIANAPOLIS, WAS THE FIRST ONE EMPLOYED AND THE RECORD STATES THAT HE MET WITH THE BOARD ON JUNE 29, 1914. AFTER THAT MEETING, ALL CORRESPONDENCE WAS BROKEN. J. ALBERT BOONSTRA OF LAFAYETTE WAS THEN EMPLOYED AS ARCHITECT, FEBRUARY 10, 1916. AT THE APRIL 15, 1916 MEETING, T. C. JOHNSON WAS AWARDED THE BUILDING CONTRACT.

IN THE FALL OF 1917, THE NEW BUILDING WAS READY FOR OCCUPANCY AND THE OPENING DAY WAS FIXED FOR OCTOBER 6TH. DR. HENRY N. SANBORN, SECRETARY OF THE PUBLIC LIBRARY COMMISSION, WAS THE MAIN SPEAKER. A FEW VOLUMES OF THE MACLURE LIBRARY, A COLLECTION THAT IN THE EARLY DAYS WAS HOUSED IN THE COURTHOUSE, WERE TURNED OVER TO THE LIBRARY AT THE TIME OF OPENING. THE LIBRARY WAS FURNISHED WITH LIBRARY BUREAU OAK FURNITURE."

GIFT: $8,000; JANUARY 14, 1914
DEDICATION: OCTOBER 6, 1917
ARCHITECT: J. ALBERT BOONSTRA, LAFAYETTE
CONTRACTOR: THOMAS C. JOHNSON, OXFORD
STYLE: NEO CLASSICAL REVIVAL

"Paoli Public Library, Façade, Doric Order"

PAOLI

PAOLI PUBLIC LIBRARY

EXCERPTS FROM *THE REPUBLICAN* NEWSPAPER, PAOLI, INDIANA, APRIL 1, 1958, PAGE FOUR:

"AS EARLY AS 1903, THE LADIES OF THE LOCAL TRI KAPPA SORORITY WORKED TO HAVE A LIBRARY IN THE COMMUNITY OF PAOLI. IN SEPTEMBER OF 1911, THE TRI KAPPAS DECIDED TO OBTAIN A ROOM AND START A LIBRARY. JOHN T. STOUT GAVE TRI KAPPA THE USE FOR ONE YEAR OF THE SOUTH ROOM OVER STOUT'S STORE. A STATE ORGANIZER CAME TO PAOLI TO HELP LAUNCH THE PROJECT AND THE FIRST PAOLI LIBRARY WAS OPENED TO THE PUBLIC NOVEMBER 25, 1911. IN SEPTEMBER 1915, WHEN A TWO MILLS RATE WAS APPROVED, THE SORORITY BEGAN THE MOVE-MENT FOR A CARNEGIE LIBRARY.

THE NEWLY FORMED LIBRARY BOARD MET AT THE ORANGE COUNTY BANK MARCH 10, 1917. SELECTION OF A LIBRARY SITE WAS THE RESULT OF A DEVASTATING HOTEL FIRE ON THE TOWN-SQUARE, DECEMBER 12, 1917. PAOLI BUSINESSMEN SAW THE ADVANTAGES OF REPLACING THE EYESORE RUBBLE WITH A NEW CARNEGIE LIBRARY. IN FEBRUARY 1918 AN OFFER OF $1,000 WAS MADE BY THE PAOLI MERCHANTS TO BUY THE FIRE RAZE SITE AND THE LOCATION WAS RESOLVED.

THE CARNEGIE LIBRARY CONSTRUCTION WAS STARTED SPRING 1918 ON THE NORTHEAST COR-NER OF THE TOWN-SQUARE. THE ARCHITECT WAS NORMAN H. HILL OF INDIANAPOLIS, A FORMER NATIVE OF ORANGE COUNTY. THE CARNEGIE LIBRARY WAS DEDICATED OCTOBER 12, 1918. LIMITED FINANCES FOR THE NEW LIBRARY IN 1918 LIMITED MATERIAL PURCHASES."

TODAY THE ONCE ENVIABLE LOCATION OF THE LIBRARY ON THE TOWN-SQUARE IS LANDLOCKED, AND THUS, HAS NOWHERE TO GO EXCEPT OUTWARD FOR A GROWING COMMUNITY WITH INFORMA-TION-SEEKING PATRONS.

GIFT: $8,000; JANUARY 31, 1913
DEDICATION: OCTOBER 12, 1918
ARCHITECT: NORMAN H. HILL, INDIANAPOLIS
CONTRACTOR: MCVEY & LUTES, PAOLI
STYLE: CRAFTSMAN-PRAIRIE TRADITION

"Peru Public Library, Main Entrance, Elliptical Stained Glass Fanlight"

PERU

PERU PUBLIC LIBRARY

EXCERPTS FROM *THE SEVENTH BIENNIAL REPORT OF THE PUBLIC LIBRARY COMMISSION OF INDIANA, OCTOBER 1, 1910-SEPTEMBER 30, 1912*, PAGE 15, INDIANAPOLIS: WM. BURFORD PRINTING, 1913:

"IN THE YEAR 1897, UNDER THE DIRECTION OF THE SCHOOL BOARD, AND A NUMBER OF OTHER LOVERS OF BOOKS WHOSE NAMES MAY BE FORGOTTEN, BUT WHOSE WORK WILL GO ON FOREVER, A LIBRARY WAS ORGANIZED IN THE CITY OF PERU. AFTER A COMMON STRUGGLE ATTENDANT UPON MOST BEGINNINGS, A FEW BOOKS AND A SMALL ROOM FOR THEIR KEEPING WERE SECURED. TO THE EARNEST, CONTINUED AND UNTIRING ZEAL OF MISS MARTHA G. SHIRK, DOES THE CITY OF PERU OWE THE PRESENT SATISFACTORY CONDITION OF ITS LIBRARY.

THE CARNEGIE GIFT OF $25,000 HAS MADE POSSIBLE A SUBSTANTIAL TWO-STORY BUILDING. ONE SIDE OF THE MAIN ROOM IS GIVEN TO THE CHILDREN. HERE ARE TWO LARGE TABLES; ONE OF LITTLE MORE THAN KINDERGARTEN HEIGHT, THE OTHER HIGHER, EACH EASILY SEATING A DOZEN CHILDREN. AT ONE END OF THIS SPACE ARE NO LESS THAN 1,000 BOOKS ON SHELVES THAT ARE CONVENIENT FOR THE CHILDREN. PICTURES AND STATUETTES ADD TO THE BEAUTY OF THE PLACE AND ON A BEAM THAT CROSSES THE CEILING ARE THESE WORDS: 'THIS ROOM IS UNDER THE PROTECTION OF THE BOYS AND GIRLS OF PERU'."

CONSTRUCTION BEGAN 1902 WITH AN ANDREW CARNEGIE GRANT AND WAS COMPLETED IN 1903. AROUND 1930, THE PUTERBAUGH LIBRARY ROOM WAS ADDED, BUT WAS A MUSEUM UNTIL 1977. THE AUDITORIUM WAS TRANSFORMED INTO A YOUNG PEOPLE'S ROOM IN 1975.

GIFT: $25,000; MARCH 8, 1901
DEDICATION: MAY 21, 1903
ARCHITECT: CRAPSEY & LAMM, CINCINNATI, OHIO
CONTRACTOR: J. B. GOODALL, PERU
STYLE: BEAU ARTS CLASSICISM

"Peru Public Library, Main Entrance, Coupled Columns"

"Pierceton & Washington Township Public Library, Cornerstone"

PIERCETON

PIERCETON & WASHINGTON TOWNSHIP PUBLIC LIBRARY

EXCERPTS FROM THE BOOK, *KOSCIUSKO COUNTY, INDIANA, 1836-1986*, PUBLISHED BY THE KOSCIUSKO COUNTY HISTORICAL SOCIETY:

"THE IDEA OF A PUBLIC LIBRARY FOR THE PIERCETON COMMUNITY WAS BORN IN THE MIND OF MRS. ADDA NICHOLS. AT THAT TIME THE ANDREW CARNEGIE FOUNDATION WAS MAKING GRANTS FOR SUCH FACILITIES ALL OVER THE COUNTRY. IN DECEMBER, 1914, SHE BROUGHT TOGETHER INTERESTED CITIZENS AND INVITED THE SECRETARY OF THE STATE LIBRARY ASSOCIATION TO EXPLAIN THE PROCEDURES TO OBTAIN A CARNEGIE LIBRARY. A CARNEGIE GIFT WAS OBTAINED FOR $10,000 ON DECEMBER 3, 1915.

AN OPTION TO PURCHASE THE CORNER LOT FOR $750 ON WHICH THE LIBRARY NOW STANDS WAS TAKEN, AND A DECISION WAS MADE TO NAME THE NEW LIBRARY THE WASHINGTON TOWNSHIP AND PIERCETON CARNEGIE PUBLIC LIBRARY. TOTAL COST FOR THE LAND AND CONSTRUCTION INCLUDING THE BOOK SHELVING WAS $10,009. ON JULY 22, 1916 BIDS WERE AWARDED TO S. PARCHELL OF ROCHESTER AS GENERAL CONTRACTOR OF THE BUILDING FOR $7,719. THE PLUMBING WAS $1,162 AND THE WIRING WAS $337. FURNITURE WAS PURCHASED LOCALLY THROUGH ASHLEY'S FURNITURE STORE. MARIE SHANTON WAS THE FIRST LIBRARIAN AND HER MONTHLY SALARY WAS $37.00. THE LIBRARY'S MONTHLY ELECTRICAL BILL WAS $5.20 AND THE TELEPHONE WAS $2.50."

TODAY, ALMOST ALL OF THE ORIGINAL STRUCTURE REMAINS. EVEN THE WINDOWS WERE SAVED WHEN REPLACED. THE 1914-BUILT LIBRARY IS ONE OF THREE CARNEGIE LIBRARIES IN KOSCIUSKO COUNTY. IT WAS OFFICIALLY OPENED QUITE INFORMALLY ON APRIL 26, 1918.

GIFT: $10,000; DECEMBER 3, 1915
DEDICATION: APRIL 26, 1918
ARCHITECT: MAHURIN & MAHURIN, FORT WAYNE
CONTRACTOR: S. PARCHELL, ROCHESTER
STYLE: CRAFTSMAN-PRAIRIE TRADITION

"Poseyville Carnegie Public Library, Facade"

POSEYVILLE

POSEYVILLE CARNEGIE PUBLIC LIBRARY

EXCERPTS FROM THE *"HISTORY OF THE POSEYVILLE PUBLIC LIBRARY"* FILE:

"THE FIRST LIBRARY IN POSEYVILLE WAS THE 1855 MACLURE WORKINGMEN'S LIBRARY BUT IT WANED ABOUT THE TIME OF THE CIVIL WAR. THE PUBLIC LIBRARY OF POSEYVILLE WAS ESTAB-LISHED IN 1898, WITH ABOUT 400 VOLUMES. UNTIL APRIL, 1903, IT OCCUPIED TWO ROOMS IN THE OPERA HOUSE BUILDING. THE LIBRARY MOVED TO THE UPPER STORY OF THE NEW TOWN HALL IN LATE 1903.

ACCORDING TO LIBRARY OFFICIALS, BANKER GEORGE WATERS WROTE TO CARNEGIE WITH THE SUGGESTION THAT HE BUILD A LIBRARY IN POSEYVILLE. FINALLY A RESPONSE WAS RECEIVED JANUARY 2, 1904 THAT MR. ANDREW CARNEGIE WOULD PUT UP $5,000 FOR THE LIBRARY. MR. CARNEGIE AGREED TO GIVE AN ADDITIONAL $500 FOR FURNITURE FOR THE LIBRARY FOR A GRAND TOTAL OF $5,500. IN SEPTEMBER OF 1904, A CONTRACT WAS LET TO KOCH & GREISBACHER OF EVANSVILLE, HAVING THE LOWEST BID OF $3,979. MR. LEROY WILLIAMS DONATED A LOT FOR THE BUILDING UPON WHICH STANDS THE PRESENT DAY LIBRARY.

THE BUILDING WAS CONSTRUCTED OF BUFF PRESSED BRICK WITH STONE TRIMMINGS AND A RED TILE ROOF. DEDICATION OF THE COMPLETED LIBRARY TOOK PLACE APRIL 20TH, 1905. THE DEDI-CATION ADDRESS WAS GIVE BY JOHN H. FOSTER, JUDGE OF SUPERIOR COURT, EVANSVILLE. THE HISTORY OF THE LIBRARY WAS READ BY MRS. A. E. JAQUESS."

THE LIBRARY HAS UNDERGONE A MAJOR RENOVATION AND A MATCHING ADDITION IN 2000 AND 2001.

GIFT: $5,500; JANUARY 2, 1904
DEDICATION: APRIL 20, 1905
ARCHITECT: CLIFFORD SHOPBELL, EVANSVILLE
CONTRACTOR: KOCH & GRIESBACHER, EVANSVILLE
STYLE: NEO CLASSICAL REVIVAL

"Princeton Public Library, Façade"

PRINCETON

PRINCETON PUBLIC LIBRARY

EXCERPTS FROM *"THINGS TO KNOW ABOUT THE PRINCETON LIBRARY"* FILE:

"THREE YEARS BEFORE PRINCETON WAS INCORPORATED AS A CITY, THE LIBRARY BEGAN AS A RENTED READING ROOM IN OCTOBER, 1881, LOCATED ON THE TOP FLOOR OF A BUILDING THAT STOOD ON THE SOUTHEAST SIDE OF THE COURTHOUSE SQUARE. THE READING ROOM WAS SUPPORTED BY SUBSCRIPTION FROM 53 STOCKHOLDERS. THE FORMAL TITLE OF THE LIBRARY WAS THE PRINCETON LIBRARY ASSOCIATION. THE ASSOCIATION VOTED IN 1882 TO PERMIT PUBLIC USE OF THE LIBRARY.

IN 1884, A NEW CITY TAX LAW STATED THAT THE LIBRARY HAD TO ALLOW 'FREE ACCESS' TO ALL. THE LIBRARY BURNED IN 1886, AND A NEW LIBRARY WAS EVENTUALLY BUILT ON THE COURTHOUSE-SQUARE. THE PRINCETON LIBRARY ASSOCIATION VOTED UNANIMOUSLY IN MARCH, 1903, TO DISBAND AND RELINQUISH OWNERSHIP OF THE LIBRARY TO THE CITY OF PRINCETON. A NEW LIBRARY BOARD WAS APPOINTED.

ANDREW CARNEGIE WAS WILLING TO GIVE $15,000 TO BUILD A NEW LIBRARY IN PRINCETON, AND DID SO, ON JANUARY 22, 1903. THE JESSUP LOT AT WATER AND HART STREETS WAS THE SELECTED SITE FOR THE NEW CARNEGIE LIBRARY BUILDING. THE CONSTRUCTION FIRM OF BEAN AND DAVIS OF PRINCETON WAS AWARDED THE CONTRACT. THE ARCHITECTURAL FIRM OF HARRIS AND SHOPBELL OF EVANSVILLE WERE THE ARCHITECTS. THE COMPLETED STRUCTURE COST $15,118.65. THE OPENING OF THE PRINCETON PUBLIC LIBRARY TOOK PLACE ON JUNE 8, 1905."

THE ORIGINAL CARNEIGE BUILDING UNDERWENT STRUCTURAL CHANGES FROM JUNE, 1987 TO FEBRUARY, 1988. AN ADDITION WAS BUILT ON THE EAST SIDE OF THE BUILDING, INCREASING THE FLOOR SPACE BY DOUBLE.

GIFT: $15,000; JANUARY 22, 1903
DEDICATION: JUNE 8, 1905
ARCHITECT: HARRIS & SHOPBELL, EVANSVILLE
CONTRACTOR: BEAN & DAVIS, PRINCETON
STYLE: NEO CLASSICAL REVIVAL

"Princeton Public Library, Interior, Ceiling, Stained Glass"

"Princeton Public Library, Circulation Desk Area, Gaslit Chandelier"

"Ohio County Public Library, Rising Sun, Facade"

RISING SUN

OHIO COUNTY PUBLIC LIBRARY

ESTABLISHED BEFORE THE CARNEGIE LIBRARY BUILDING, THE MAHLON BROWN LIBRARY OCCU-PIED A ROOM IN THE PUBLIC SCHOOL BUILDING. THE LIBRARY BOARD WAS ORGANIZED JULY 9, 1915 PRIOR TO RECEIVING A $10,000 GRANT FROM THE CARNEGIE CORPORATION ON DECEMBER 3, 1915. THE LOCAL WOMAN'S CLUB LED THE EFFORT TO ESTABLISH A LOCAL LIBRARY. THE LIBRARY WAS DEDICATED ON APRIL 29, 1918. THE FOLLOWING EXCERPTED SPEECH WAS DELIVERED BY BENJAMIN H. SCRANTON, PRESIDENT OF THE LIBRARY BOARD:

"FRIENDS:

IN THE MIDST OF THE GREAT CONFLICT IN WHICH WE ARE ENGAGED, WITH OUR BOYS TRAIN-ING AND STEADILY MARCHING TO THE FRONT. JUST FOR A SHORT TIME, LET US FORGET THE WORLD'S SORROWS AND MAKE THIS A JOYOUS OCCASION.

FOR MANY YEARS, IT HAS BEEN FELT THAT THIS COMMUNITY SHOULD HAVE A PUBLIC LIBRARY. IT WAS THROUGH THE AMBITION, ENERGY AND PUSH OF A NUMBER OF OUR GOOD WOMEN THAT A MOVEMENT WAS SET ON FOOT BY WHICH WE MIGHT SECURE SUCH A LIBRARY HOME.

AN APPEAL WAS MADE TO THE GREAT AND GENEROUS PHILANTHROPIST, MR. ANDREW CARNEGIE, FOR A DONATION DEEMED NECESSARY FOR THE ERECTION OF A DESIRABLE BUILDING. MR. CARNEGIE IMMEDIATELY ASSURED US WE SHOULD HAVE A DONATION OF $10,000 WITH WHICH TO ERECT AND FURNISH A LIBRARY.

WE, AS A BOARD, HAVE THUS FAR PERFORMED OUR DUTY TO THE BEST OF OUR ABILITY, AND ON BEHALF OF THE BOARD, I WANT TO PRESENT THIS BEAUTIFUL BUILDING WITH ITS VALUABLE COL-LECTION OF BOOKS TO THIS COMMUNITY, THE CITY OF RISING SUN AND RANDOLPH TOWNSHIP."

GIFT: $10,000; DECEMBER 3, 1915
DEDICATION: APRIL 29-30, 1918
ARCHITECT: WILSON B. PARKER, INDIANAPOLIS
CONTRACTOR: TRUIT & PROBST
STYLE: CRAFTSMAN-PRAIRIE TRADITION

"Roachdale-Franklin Township Public Library, Interior"

ROACHDALE

ROACHDALE-FRANKLIN TOWNSHIP PUBLIC LIBRARY

EXCERPTS FROM THE *"HISTORY OF THE ROACHDALE PUBLIC LIBRARY AND THE PHILOMATH CLUB,"* PAPER BY MRS. OSCAR A. SHEPARD, 1954:

"IN THE YEAR 1904, EIGHT WOMEN IN ROACHDALE WHO WERE INTERESTED IN READING AND STUDYING THE CLASSICS, ORGANIZED THE PHILOMATH CLUB ON JULY 29TH. IT WAS IN 1911 AND 1912, WHEN THE PHILOMATH CLUB AND COMMERCIAL CLUB BEGAN THINKING SERIOUSLY OF A PUBLIC LIBRARY. CORRESPONDENCE WITH THE STATE LIBRARY BOARD RESULTED IN ONE OF THE OFFICIALS BEING SENT TO CONFER WITH THE COMMITTEE. FURTHER CORRESPONDENCE AND A VISIT TO THE STATE LIBRARY BOARD BROUGHT ABOUT AN APPOINTMENT OF A LOCAL LIBRARY BOARD THAT SOON SECURED A TAX FROM THE TOWN AND TOWNSHIP. THE FIRST ROACHDALE LIBRARY WAS OPENED TO THE PUBLIC IN A SMALL ROOM OF A HARDWARE STORE AUGUST 13, 1912 ON SOUTH MERIDIAN STREET WITH 140 VOLUMES.

THE ENCOURAGING USE OF THE LIBRARY PROMPTED THE LIBRARY BOARD TO SELECT A SITE FOR PURCHASE. THE CARNEGIE CORPORATION OFFERED $10,000 FOR A BUILDING. THE LOT ON THE NORTHEAST CORNER OF MERIDIAN AND WASHINGTON STREETS WAS PURCHASED AND A TAX LEVIED ON THE REGISTERED BORROWERS IN ROACHDALE AND FRANKLIN TOWNSHIP.

THE SUMMER OF THE FOLLOWING YEAR, THE LAYING OF THE CORNERSTONE OF THE CARNEGIE BUILDING TOOK PLACE ON THE PURCHASED LOT CONDUCTED BY THE ROACHDALE MASONIC LODGE ON WEDNESDAY, JULY 30, 1913. THE DEDICATION AND OPENING OF THE NEW CARNEGIE LIBRARY TOOK PLACE IN THE TOWN HALL, AFTER WHICH A GENERAL RECEPTION WAS HELD IN THE LIBRARY BUILDING, JANUARY 5, 1914, WITH PROFESSOR FRANCIS TILDEN OF DEPAUW DELIVERING THE DEDICATORY ADDRESS."

GIFT: $10,000; JANUARY 31, 1913
DEDICATION: JANUARY 5, 1914
ARCHITECT: J. W. HENNON
CONTRACTOR: C. F. RICE, ROACHDALE
STYLE: CRAFTSMAN-PRAIRIE TRADITION

"Roann-Paw Paw Township Public Library, Façade"

ROANN

ROANN-PAW PAW TOWNSHIP PUBLIC LIBRARY

EXCERPTS FROM THE *1953 ROANN CENTENNIAL BOOK*, ROANN PUBLIC LIBRARY, PAGE 59:

"AN UNSUCCESSFUL ATTEMPT APPEARS TO HAVE BEEN MADE ABOUT 1880 BY GEORGE GUNDER, THEN SUPERINTENDENT OF THE SCHOOL, TO ESTABLISH A CIRCULATING LIBRARY. THEN 32 YEARS LATER, THE NEED FOR A PUBLIC LIBRARY WAS FELT AGAIN. A MRS. DANIEL (MARTHAM.) VAN BUSKIRK MADE INQUIRY AS TO THE PROCEDURE FOR SECURING A GRANT FROM THE CARNEGIE CORPORATION FOR A LIBRARY BUILDING.

SOON AFTER HEARING FROM THE CARNEGIE CORPORATION, THE LIBRARY BOARD PURCHASED THE LOTS FOR THE BUILDING ON JULY 22, 1915, STARTED A PUBLIC LIBRARY IN THE SCHOOL HOUSE IN 1914, AND HAD ASSURANCES FROM THE TOWN AND TOWNSHIP OFFICIALS THAT TAXES WOULD MAINTAIN THE NEW LIBRARY. A GRANT OF $10,000 WAS MADE BY THE CARNEGIE CORPORATION AND THE CORNERSTONE FOR THE NEW BUILDING WAS PLACED IN 1916, WITH COMPLETION OF THE BUILDING THE SAME YEAR.

THE ROANN-PAW PAW TOWNSHIP CARNEGIE LIBRARY BUILDING WAS OPEN TO THE PUBLIC ON SATURDAY, AUGUST 3, 1916. DEDICATORY EXERCISES WERE HELD BOTH IN THE AFTERNOON AND EVENING. THE PRINCIPAL ADDRESS WAS MADE BY MR. HAMILTON, SECRETARY OF THE INDIANA PUBLIC LIBRARY COMMISSION. MISS DAISY SHRADER WAS SELECTED LIBRARIAN."

GIFT: $10,000; JUNE 11, 1914
DEDICATION: AUGUST 3, 1916
ARCHITECT: WILSON B. PARKER, INDIANAPOLIS
CONTRACTOR: MILO CUTSHALL, AKRON
STYLE: CRAFTSMAN-PRAIRIE TRADITION

"Roann-Paw Paw Township Public Library, Original Chair"

"Spencer County Public Library, Rockport, Main Entrance"

ROCKPORT

SPENCER COUNTY PUBLIC LIBRARY

FROM THE *"LIBRARY HISTORY"* FILE & *"TIME LINE"*:

1915 ROCKPORT LEVIED A LIBRARY TAX AND A LIBRARY BOARD WAS APPOINTED.
1916 THE ROCKPORT PUBLIC LIBRARY OPENED A READING ROOM IN THE REAR OF THE FARMER'S
       BANK ON FEBRUARY 16TH WITH 1,000 VOLUMES ON THE SHELVES.
1917 THE OHIO TOWNSHIP ADVISORY BOARD LEVIED A TAX FOR LIBRARY SUPPORT.
1918 THE LIBRARY BOARD ACCEPTED A CARNEGIE GIFT OF $17,000 TO THE TOWN AND OHIO
       TOWNSHIP AND PURCHASED A DESIRABLE LOT.
1919 CLIFFORD SHOPBELL DRAWS PLANS FOR THE NEW ROCKPORT CARNEGIE PUBLIC LIBRARY.
1921 THE LOT NEXT TO THE LIBRARY WAS PURCHASED.
1969 ROCKPORT PUBLIC LIBRARY OFFICIALLY MERGED WITH OHIO TOWNSHIP.
1987 ROCKPORT-OHIO TOWNSHIP PUBLIC LIBRARY MERGED WITH GRANDVIEW-HAMMOND TOWN-
       SHIP FORMING THE SPENCER COUNTY PUBLIC LIBRARY.
1990 GRAND OPENING OF NEWLY REMODELED MAIN BRANCH OF THE SPENCER COUNTY PUBLIC
       LIBRARY WAS HELD OCTOBER 20TH.

GIFT: $17,000; JANUARY 5, 1916
DEDICATION: JUNE 1, 1919
ARCHITECT: CLIFFORD SHOPBELL, EVANSVILLE
CONTRACTOR: JOHN F. PYLE, ROCKPORT
STYLE: RENAISSANCE REVIVAL

"Rockville Public Library, Interior"

ROCKVILLE

ROCKVILLE PUBLIC LIBRARY

EXCERPTS FROM *"A BRIEF HISTORY: 25TH ANNIVERSARY OF THE ROCKVILLE LIBRARY,"* LIBRARY BROCHURE, JANUARY 14-15, 1941:

"AT A MEETING OF THE CURRENT LITERATURE CLUB OF ROCKVILLE, JANUARY 13, 1913, AT THE HOME OF THE PRESIDENT, MRS. FRANK STEVENSON, A MOVEMENT WAS STARTED TO SUPPLY ROCKVILLE WITH A PUBLIC LIBRARY. THE COMMITTEE ADOPTED THE CARNEGIE LIBRARY PLAN AND THE REQUIRED FUNDS WERE RAISED BY POPULAR SUBSCRIPTION. A LIBRARY BOARD WAS APPOINTED, AND ADAMS TOWNSHIP RECEIVED LIBRARY SERVICE.

UNDER THE DIRECTION OF MISS KIRKPATRICK, THE ARDUOUS TASK OF RAISING THE NECESSARY FUNDS FOR PURCHASING A SUITABLE LOT WAS UNDERTAKEN, AND IN MARCH, 1914, THE PROPERTY KNOWN AS THE ANDREW BOARDMAN LIVERY BARN WAS PURCHASED FOR $2,500.

THE CARNEGIE LIBRARY BUILDING SPECIFICATIONS WERE MET BY T. L. BROOKIE, INDIANAPOLIS ARCHITECT, AND JAMES T. BOSWELL, BLOOMINGDALE CONTRACTOR, AND THE BUILDING WAS COMPLETED AT A COST OF $12,500. THE STRUCTURE WAS BUILT OF HYTEX BRICK, LAID WITH DARK MORTAR, TRIMMED IN BEDFORD STONE, WITH A ROOF OF GREEN TILE. MISS CARIE SCOTT, NOW HEAD OF THE CHILDREN'S DEPARTMENT OF THE INDIANAPOLIS PUBLIC LIBRARY, ASSISTED WITH THE BOOK SELECTION. MANY WORTHWHILE BOOKS HAVE BEEN GIVEN TO THE LIBRARY DURING ITS 25 YEARS.

THE LIBRARY WAS DEDICATED WITH PROPER CEREMONIES FRIDAY AND SATURDAY, JANUARY 14 AND 15, 1916."

GIFT: $12,500; APRIL 13, 1914
DEDICATION: JANUARY 14-15, 1916
ARCHITECT: TRUE L. BROOKIE, INDIANAPOLIS
CONTRACTOR: JAMES T. BOSWELL, BLOOMINGDALE
STYLE: PSEUDO-GEORGIAN REVIVAL

"Royal Center-Boone Township Public Library, Stairs, Rail Spindles"

ROYAL CENTER

ROYAL CENTER-BOONE TOWNSHIP PUBLIC LIBRARY

EXCERPTS FROM THE *"HISTORY OF THE LIBRARY"* FILE:

"PRELIMINARY STEPS TO INVESTIGATE THE POSSIBILITIES OF ERECTING A LIBRARY BUILDING FOR ROYAL CENTER AND BOONE TOWNSHIP WERE TAKEN ON JUNE 29, 1914, WHEN THE LIBRARY BOARD WAS FORMED, HEADED BY DR. B. A. CONRAD.

A DONATION OF $10,000 WAS RECEIVED UNDER THE CARNEGIE LIBRARY PLAN AFTER A PROGRAM WAS SET UP TO PROVIDE FOR A TAX LEVY TO MAINTAIN THE LIBRARY. A LOT ON WHICH TO BUILD THE LIBRARY WAS DONATED BY THE ROYAL CENTER SCHOOL BOARD, AND AN $8,195 CONTRACT FOR CONSTRUCTION WAS AWARDED TO A ROYAL CENTER FIRM, WALTERS AND KISTLER.

WITH NEARLY A YEAR'S WORK ON NECESSARY PREPARATIONS AND REQUIREMENTS, THE CORNERSTONE OF THE LIBRARY WAS LAID ON MAY 22, 1915 AND A TIME CAPSULE INSERTED. A SPECIAL CEREMONY WAS ALSO CONDUCTED AND A PARADE HELD WITH SCHOOL CHILDREN OF ROYAL CENTER AND BOONE TOWNSHIP PARTICIPATING.

COMPLETED IN THE LATTER PART OF 1915, THE BUILDING WAS OPENED TO THE PUBLIC ON SATURDAY, NOVEMBER 13 WITH AN INFORMAL RECEPTION ATTENDED BY 200 PEOPLE. THE RECEPTION COMMITTEE INCLUDED THE LIBRARY BOARD AND THE LIBRARIAN, MELLIE MEEKS."

GIFT: $10,000; SEPTEMBER 25, 1914
DEDICATION: NOVEMBER 13, 1915
ARCHITECT: W. S. KAUFMAN & SON, RICHMOND
CONTRACTOR: WALTERS & KISTLER, ROYAL CENTER
STYLE: CRAFTSMAN-PRAIRIE TRADITION

"Salem Public Library, Façade"

SALEM

SALEM-WASHINGTON TOWNSHIP PUBLIC LIBRARY

EXCERPTS FROM THE *"SALEM PUBLIC LIBRARY HISTORY"* FILE:

"DUE TO STRONG RELIGIOUS SENTIMENT AND TO EDUCATIONAL INSTITUTIONS, SALEM, IN PIONEER TIMES, EARNED THE TITLE, 'THE ATHENS OF THE WEST.' ONE OF THE OLDEST LIBRARIES WAS THE JOINT STOCK SALEM LIBRARY COMPANY (1818-1830). THE PEOPLE IN THEIR EFFORTS TO POPULARIZE EDUCATION INDUCED THE TOWNSHIP TRUSTEES TO ESTABLISH A PUBLIC LIBRARY IN 1852. WITH THE DISAPPEARANCE OF THE PRIVATE SCHOOLS, THE TOWNSHIP LIBRARY FELL INTO DISUSE. IN 1855, SALEM RECEIVED $500 FROM THE ESTATE OF WILLIAM MACLURE TO ESTABLISH A WORKINGMEN'S LIBRARY. IN 1903-04, THE FORTNIGHTLY CLUB WORKED TO ESTABLISH A FREE PUBLIC LIBRARY. JUDGE BUSKIRK ORDERED THE SALEM PUBLIC LIBRARY ESTABLISHED ACCORDING TO THE ACTS OF THE LEGISLATURE OF THE YEAR 1901.

THE CARNEGIE BUILDING THAT NOW HOUSED THE SALEM PUBLIC LIBRARY FIRST OPENED ITS DOORS AT 212 NORTH MAIN STREET AFTER A DEDICATION CEREMONY ON JULY 6, 1905. MANY INDIVIDUALS AND ORGANIZATIONS HAD WORKED TOGETHER TO MAKE THIS GRAND OPENING POSSIBLE. THE FORTNIGHTLY CLUB STARTED THE MOVEMENT FOR A PUBLIC LIBRARY IN THE EARLY 1900S; MRS. W. W. STEVENS CHAIRED THE SOLICITING COMMITTEE TO SECURE BUILDING MONEY. JOHN HAY, PRESIDENT LINCOLN'S PERSONAL SECRETARY, CONTRIBUTED THE FIRST $25. ANDREW CARNEGIE DONATED $16,000. THE TOWN OF SALEM BOUGHT THE BUILDING LOT AT THE CORNER OF MAIN AND MULBERRY STREETS FOR $2,400. THE GROUNDBREAKING WAS ON AUGUST 19, 1904 AND THE CORNERSTONE WAS LAID ON OCTOBER 7, 1904."

THE LIBRARY UNDERWENT A MAJOR RENOVATION AND ADDITION PROJECT IN 2001. THE NEWLY REMODELED CARNEGIE AND THE EXPANDED ADDITION WAS DEDICATED FEBRUARY 23, 2002.

GIFT: $16,000; FEBRUARY 20, 1904
DEDICATION: JULY 6, 1905
ARCHITECT: HARRIS & SHOPBELL, EVANSVILLE
CONTRACTOR: AMBROSE SHRUM, SALEM
STYLE: NEO CLASSICAL REVIVAL

"Salem Public Library, Rotunda, Stained Glass Dome"

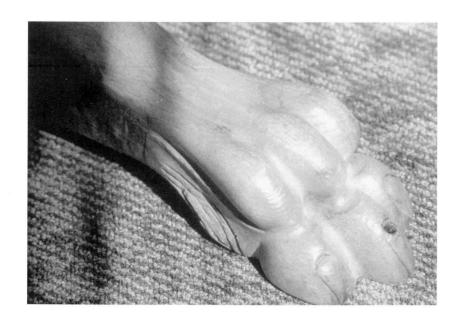

"Salem Public Library, Reading Room, Table, Leg, Animal's Paw"

"Salem Public Library, Looking West, From Foyer to Rotunda"

"Scott County Public Library, Scottsburg, Facade"

SCOTTSBURG

SCOTT COUNTY PUBLIC LIBRARY

EXCERPTS FROM *"A BRIEF HISTORY OF SCOTT COUNTY PUBLIC LIBRARY"* FILE:

"THE PEOPLE IN SCOTT COUNTY BEGAN TO FEEL THAT THERE WAS A NEED FOR A PUBLIC LIBRARY IN THEIR COMMUNITY. THE FIRST RECORDED MENTION OF SUCH A MOVEMENT WAS REPORTED IN THE *SCOTT COUNTY JOURNAL AND DEMOCRAT* NEWSPAPER OF DECEMBER 24, 1913, SAMUEL B. WELLS, EDITOR: 'A PETITION ASKING THE TOWN BOARD TO MAKE A LEVY OF NOT TO EXCEED TWO MILLS ON THE DOLLAR PURCHASE GROUND AND BOOKS FOR A CARNEGIE LIBRARY IS BEING CIRCULATED.' THE CARNEGIE LIBRARY BOARD WAS APPOINTED ON JANUARY 21, 1914. BY 1917, THE LIBRARY FUND HAD GROWN TO $7,500. A .5 MILL LEVY FOR THE MAINTENANCE OF A FREE PUBLIC LIBRARY IN SCOTT COUNTY WAS INSTALLED.

IN JULY OF 1917, THE LIBRARY BOARD SECRETARY WROTE THE CARNEGIE CORPORATION ASKING FOR ASSISTANCE IN THE ERECTION OF A LIBRARY BUILDING. IN NOVEMBER OF 1917 THE CARNEGIE CORPORATION DONATED $12,500 FOR THAT PURPOSE. ON JULY 27,1918, VACANT LOTS 19 AND 20 ON THE SOUTHWEST CORNER OF THE TOWN'S COURTHOUSE SQUARE WERE PURCHASED. BECAUSE OF WORLD WAR I, A BUILDING COULD NOT BE ERECTED, SO ROOM WAS RENTED ON THE EAST SIDE OF THE COURTHOUSE SQUARE. ON AUGUST 25, 1919, A CONTRACT WAS LET TO J. FRED BEGGS TO BUILD THE LIBRARY FOR $20,887. WORK PROGRESSED RAPIDLY AND THE CORNERSTONE WAS LAID ON DECEMBER 14, 1919. BECAUSE OF VARIOUS DELAYS, THE BUILDING WAS NOT READY TO BE OPENED TO THE PUBLIC UNTIL FEBRUARY 5, 1921, WHEN IT WAS DEDICATED WITH APPROPRIATE CEREMONIES."

GIFT: $12,500; NOVEMBER 22, 1917
DEDICATION: FEBRUARY 5, 1921
ARCHITECT: CLIFFORD SHOPBELL, EVANSVILLE
CONTRACTOR: J. FRED BEGGS, SCOTTSBURG
STYLE: RENAISSANCE REVIVAL

"Jackson County Public Library, Seymour, Pediment, H. Vance Swope, East Wing"

SEYMOUR

JACKSON COUNTY PUBLIC LIBRARY

IN 1894, THE FIRST LIBRARY IN SEYMOUR WAS LOCATED AT SHIELDS HIGH SCHOOL. THE SUPER-INTENDENT WAS INSTRUMENTAL IN ITS ORGANIZATION. LATER, IN 1902, THE LIBRARY WAS MOVED TO TWO ROOMS IN THE MASONIC BUILDING. IN 1903, THE ACQUISITION OF A $10,000 CARNEGIE GRANT RESULTED IN THE SEYMOUR PUBLIC LIBRARY BEING ORGANIZED IN 1904. ON JANUARY 5, 1905, THE NEW CARNEGIE LIBRARY BUILDING OPENED. THE FOLLOWING ARTICLE IS FROM THE JANUARY 10, 1905, *SEYMOUR DAILY REPUBLICAN*, ENTITLED *"FORMAL OPENING"*:

"SEYMOUR NOW HAS LIBRARY FACILITIES THAT ARE APPRECIATED BY THE PUBLIC. THE NEW LIBRARY BUILDING WAS FORMALLY OPENED MONDAY EVENING. BETWEEN SEVEN AND TEN O'CLOCK, A GREAT MANY PEOPLE BRAVED THE STORMY WEATHER AND VISITED THE NEW BUILDING. THEY WERE PLEASED WITH THE INTERIOR ARRANGEMENT AND GENERAL CONVENIENCES AND APPEAR-ANCE OF THE LIBRARY. THE BOOK SHOWER RESULTED IN THE ADDITION OF ABOUT 75 BOOKS TO BE PLACED ON THE SHELVES. MISS PEARL CLARK, THE LIBRARIAN WILL BE IN PERSONAL CHARGE.

THE LIBRARY BOARD SHOULD KEEP THE PUBLIC APPRISED OF NEW BOOKS THAT COME TO THE LIBRARY AND OTHER MATTERS OF PUBLIC INTEREST. THE MORE SUCH AN INSTITUTION IS USED THE MORE POPULAR IT BECOMES. ANY COMMUNITY IS BENEFITED BY A GOOD PUBLIC LIBRARY."

THE LIBRARY HAS HAD SEVERAL RENOVATIONS AND ADDITIONS OVER ITS CENTURY-OLD EXIS-TENCE. THE ADDITION OF 14,000 SQUARE FEET AND RENOVATION OF THE ORIGINAL CARNEGIE BUILDING IN SEPTEMBER OF 1992 WAS COMPLETED FOR APPROXIMATELY $2 MILLION DOLLARS. THE SWOPE ART COLLECTION MAY BE VIEWED ON THE LIBRARY'S GROUND FLOOR, EAST WING.

GIFT: $10,000; FEBRUARY 2, 1903
DEDICATION: JANUARY 5, 1905
ARCHITECT: HARRIS & SHOPBELL, EVANSVILLE
CONTRACTOR: TRAVIS CARTER COMPANY
STYLE: NEO CLASSICAL REVIVAL

"Shelbyville-Shelby County Public Library, Interior, Rotunda Area"

SHELBYVILLE

SHELBYVILLE-SHELBY COUNTY PUBLIC LIBRARY

EXCERPTS FROM THE *LIBRARY BROCHURE*, 2000:

"THE CARNEGIE PUBLIC LIBRARY OF SHELBYVILLE WAS ORGANIZED IN NOVEMBER, 1887, UNDER THE NAME OF THE SHELBYVILLE PUBLIC LIBRARY. THE IDEA OF THE PUBLIC LIBRARY ORIGINATED IN THE MINDS OF THE MEMBERS OF THE SCHOOL BOARD WHEN THEY WERE BUILDING THE HIGH SCHOOL BUILDING IN 1895. TWO ROOMS AT THE HIGH SCHOOL WERE SET ASIDE FOR THE SUBSCRIPTION LIBRARY AND WERE OPENED TO THE PUBLIC NOVEMBER 1, 1897. IT BECAME APPARENT IN A FEW YEARS ITS QUARTERS IN THE HIGH SCHOOL BUILDING WERE INADEQUATE.

IN 1901, SCHOOL TRUSTEES APPLIED TO ANDREW CARNEGIE TO FUND A LIBRARY BUILDING. THE DONATION OF $20,000 WAS PROMPTLY ACCEPTED BY THE CITY COUNCIL. A SITE WAS PURCHASED ON THE CORNER OF BROADWAY AND TOMKINS STREETS. ARCHITECTS WERE AT ONCE EMPLOYED TO PREPARE PLANS. EARLY IN 1902 A CONTRACT WAS LET FOR THE CONSTRUCTION OF THE BUILDING. WORK WAS BEGUN ON IN MAY AND IN AUGUST FOLLOWING THE CORNERSTONE WAS LAID WITH APPROPRIATE AND IMPRESSIVE CEREMONIES BY THE MASONIC ORDER OF SHELBYVILLE. LIBRARY SERVICE BEGAN IN THE CITY OF SHELBYVILLE ON JUNE 2, 1903.

THE ORIGINAL BEDFORD STONE CARNEGIE BUILDING SERVED WELL AND IN 1966, A CHILDREN'S ROOM AND ELEVATOR WERE ADDED. COUNTY CONTRACTUAL LIBRARY SERVICE BEGAN IN 1967 USING FEDERAL GRANT MONIES. BOOKMOBILE SERVICE BEGAN SERVING OUTSIDE THE CITY IN 1968. IN 1975, THE LIBRARY DISTRICT EXPANDED TO INCLUDE ALL OF SHELBY COUNTY.

IN 1995, THE LIBRARY DOUBLED IN SIZE WITH AN EXPANSION AND RENOVATION OF THE ORIGINAL CARNEGIE BUILDING. THE GENEALOGY DEPARTMENT HAS MOVED TO THE TOWN HALL, OLD HIGH SCHOOL, ACROSS THE STREET."

GIFT: $20,000; JANUARY 2, 1902
DEDICATION: JUNE 2, 1903
ARCHITECT: HARRIS & SHOPBELL, EVANSVILLE
CONTRACTOR: FEASTER & DAVIS, SHELBYVILLE
STYLE: BEAU ARTS CLASSICISM

"Sheridan Public Library, Original Director's Desk"

SHERIDAN

Sheridan Public Library

Excerpts from the *"History of the Sheridan Library,"* paper by Nellie Pettijohn, Librarian, 1931:

"In June 1910, the ladies of the Tourist Club and Culture Club started a movement for a public library in Sheridan. The movement created much enthusiasm, and soon a board was organized and the first library was established in two small rented rooms on the second floor of the First National Bank Building. Different members acted as librarians. The library started its work with about 300 donated books.

It soon outgrew its quarters, and Mr. Carnegie was appealed to for aid and his gift of $12,500 was accepted. In December of 1911, G. W. Scott was contracted for the purchase of his lot on the corner of Third and Main streets as a site for the Sheridan Public Library. The purchase price was $3,000. The library was completed in November 1913. Over 1,300 books were moved to the Carnegie building. The informal opening was held the afternoon of December 6, 1913."

The dedication was reported in the *Library Occurrent*, page 177, March, 1914:

"The new library building was opened informally at Sheridan on the afternoon of December 6, 1913. This is one of the largest buildings for the money, $12,500, that has been erected in the state. It is located on one of the main streets in town, in the business district, which makes it very accessible to the township borrowers. The building is good in architectural exterior effect and artistic and practicable in its interior arrangement."

Gift: $12,500; December 7, 1911
Dedication: December 6, 1913
Architect: Charles Austin Bond, Carmel
Contractor: O. H. Mann
Style: Craftsman-Prairie Tradition

"Shoals Public Library, Book Press & Glue Pot"

SHOALS

SHOALS PUBLIC LIBRARY

EXCERPTS FROM THE *"SHOALS PUBLIC LIBRARY HISTORY,"* PAPER BY MARIE BROWN, LIBRARIAN, 1930:

"THE IDEA FOR A PUBLIC LIBRARY FOR SHOALS HAD ORIGINATED WITH THE BOOK LOVERS CLUB OF SHOALS AND J. S. JOHNSON, SUPERINTENDENT OF SHOALS PUBLIC SCHOOL. ON MARCH 5, 1912, AN ORGANIZER FROM THE STATE LIBRARY CAME TO SHOALS AND INCORPORATED THE LIBRARY. POPULAR SUBSCRIPTION WAS RAISED AND THE LIBRARY BOARD HAD BEEN APPOINTED.

THE FIRST LIBRARY WAS SHELTERED IN ONE ROOM AT THE SHOALS PUBLIC SCHOOL BUILDING AND J. S. JOHNSON WAS APPOINTED LIBRARIAN. IN APRIL 1913, LIBRARY SERVICE WAS EXTENDED TO HALBERT AND CENTER TOWNSHIPS, CONTRIBUTING TO ITS SUPPORT BY THE LEVY OF A LIBRARY TAX. THE LIBRARY WAS MOVED FROM THE PUBLIC SCHOOL BUILDING TO A ROOM IN THE SECOND STORY OF THE BANK BUILDING IN AUGUST, 1913.

HEARING OF CARNEGIE'S LIBRARY BUILDING PROGRAM, THE LIBRARY BOARD APPLIED FOR A GIFT. ANDREW CARNEGIE MADE POSSIBLE A GIFT OF $10,000 WHEN ALL REQUIREMENTS WERE MET, MARCH 14, 1913. THE SPRING FLOOD OF 1913 DELAYED THE PROGRESS OF THE WORK FOR SOME TIME. THE CORNERSTONE OF THE BUILDING WAS LAID ON FEBRUARY 25, 1915. THE LIBRARY WAS MOVED INTO THE NEW CARNEGIE BUILDING IN JULY 1915 AND THE DEDICATION OF THE BUILDING WAS HELD OCTOBER 1, 1915. THE ADDRESS WAS GIVEN BY EZRA MATTINGLY OF WASHINGTON, AND MUSIC WAS PROVIDED BY THE SHOALS HIGH SCHOOL ORCHESTRA. THE CARNEGIE BUILDING'S DIMENSIONS ARE 46' BY 40', COMPOSED OF CHOCOLATE MATTE BRICK, TRIMMED WITH BEDFORD LIMESTONE, WITH A RED TILE ROOF. MOST OF THE FIRST BOOKS WERE DONATED."

GIFT: $10,000; MARCH 14, 1913
DEDICATION: OCTOBER 1, 1915
ARCHITECT: WILSON B. PARKER, INDIANAPOLIS
CONTRACTOR: UNLOCATED
STYLE: CRAFTSMAN-PRAIRIE TRADITION

"Sullivan County Public Library, Rooftop Ornament, Finial"

SULLLIVAN

SULLIVAN COUNTY PUBLIC LIBRARY

EXCERPTS FROM *A HISTORY OF SULLIVAN COUNTY, INDIANA*, THOMAS J. WOLFE, EDITOR, VOLUME 1, PAGES 310-312, THE LEWIS PUBLISHING COMPANY, 1909:

"THE ESTABLISHMENT OF THE CARNEGIE LIBRARY AT SULLIVAN WAS MAINLY DUE TO THE WOMAN'S CLUB OF THAT TOWN. IN 1899 THE WOMAN'S CLUB APPOINTED A COMMITTEE TO WORK FOR THIS OBJECT. BY ENTERTAINMENTS AND LECTURES A LIBRARY FUND OF ONE HUNDRED DOLLARS WAS ACCUMULATED, BUT THE MOVEMENT PROGRESSED SLOWLY, AND LETTERS TO MR. CARNEGIE MET WITH NO RESPONSE.

IN 1901 THE LEGISLATURE PASSED THE NEW LIBRARY LAW, REQUIRING A TOWN BOARD TO LAY A LIBRARY TAX PROVIDED A FUND EQUAL TO A TAX OF TWO-TENTHS OF A MILLION HAD BEEN RAISED BY POPULAR SUBSCRIPTION. ON NOVEMBER 13, 1902, A READING ROOM OVER MCCLANAHAN'S STORE HAD BEEN OPENED TO THE PUBLIC.

THE CONDITIONS WERE MET IN SULLIVAN, THE FUND RAISED AND A SITE OFFERED FOR THE LIBRARY, AND THE FACTS WERE STATED IN A LETTER TO MR. CARNEGIE. IN ANSWER, CAME A PROMISE POSTDATED JANUARY 13, 1903 OF $10,000 FOR THE LIBRARY BUILDING. ON MARCH 28, 1903, A LOT FOR THE LIBRARY WAS PURCHASED AT THE CORNER OF THOMPSON AND EATON STREETS, WEST END OF JACKSON.

IN MARCH, 1904, THE CONTRACT FOR THE LIBRARY BUILDING WAS LET TO J. F. NICHOLAS FOR $8,276. PAUL MORATZ OF BLOOMINGTON, ILLINOIS WAS SELECTED AS ARCHITECT. ON JUNE 11TH, 1904, THE CORNERSTONE WAS LAID, WITH MASONIC CEREMONIES. THE BUILDING WAS DEDICATED JANUARY 19, 1905 AND ON JANUARY 30, 1905, THE DOORS WERE OPEN."

AN OPEN HOUSE WAS HELD OCTOBER 15, 1995 FOR THE SULLIVAN LIBRARY NEW ADDITION.

GIFT: $11,000; JANUARY 13, 1903
DEDICATION: JANUARY 19, 1905
ARCHITECT: P. O. MORATZ, BLOOMINGTON, IL.
CONTRACTOR: J. F. NICHOLAS
STYLE: PSEUDO MANNERIST

"Syracuse-Turkey Creek Twp. Public Library, Children's Dept., Circulation Desk"

SYRACUSE

SYRACUSE-TURKEY CREEK TOWNSHIP PUBLIC LIBRARY

THE FIRST SYRACUSE LIBRARY WAS STARTED IN A SCHOOL IN 1908, ACROSS FROM TODAY'S LIBRARY. THE FIRST SYRACUSE LIBRARY BOARD MEETING OCCURRED ON OCTOBER 24, 1908 IN THE EAST ROOM OF THE BASEMENT IN THE GRADE SCHOOL BUILDING. IN 1916, C. C. BACHMAN OF THE LIBRARY BOARD ASKED THE CARNEGIE FOUNDATION FOR A $10,000 GRANT THAT WAS GIVEN FEBRUARY 3, 1917. A CARNEGIE GIFT MEANT THE SYRACUSE MUNICIPAL GOVERNMENT HAD TO PROVIDE A SITE AND PASS AN ORDINANCE FOR THE PURCHASE OF BOOKS AND THE MAINTENANCE FOR THE LIBRARY THROUGH TAXATION. THE MAIN STREET BUILDING SITE WAS BOUGHT FROM THE STIFFLER HEIRS FOR $2,000.

DUE TO WORLD WAR I AND A LACK OF FUNDING, THE DELAYED CONSTRUCTION BEGAN IN JULY OF 1920 ON THE BUILDING THAT HAD 4,100 SQUARE FEET. THE CORNERSTONE WAS LAID IN AUGUST OF 1920 ON A WARM SATURDAY AFTERNOON WITH A CEREMONY. THE CARNEGIE LIBRARY BUILDING WAS DEDICATED MARCH 15, 1921 ON A RAINY TUESDAY EVENING. THE TOTAL COST WAS ABOUT $14,000, $4,000 MORE THAN THE CARNEGIE GRANT.

THE MOST RECENT CONSTRUCTION PROJECT WAS THE 1990-1991 REMODELING OF THE ORIGINAL CARNEGIE BUILDING AND A 10,300 SQUARE FEET MATCHING ADDITION.

GIFT: $10,000; FEBRUARY 3, 1917
DEDICATION: MARCH 15, 1921
ARCHITECT: SAMUEL A. CRAIG, HUNTINGTON
CONTRACTOR: J. E. DOTY, MILFORD
STYLE: CRAFTSMAN-PRAIRIE TRADITION

"Tell City-Perry County Public Library, Façade"

TELL CITY

TELL CITY-PERRY COUNTY PUBLIC LIBRARY

EXCERPTS FROM *"A QUICK HISTORY OF THE TELL CITY-PERRY COUNTY PUBLIC LIBRARY"* FILE:

"TELL CITY'S FIRST LIBRARY WAS ORGANIZED IN 1893 BY A GROUP OF 30 RESIDENTS, ORGANIZED UNDER THE NAME OF THE TELL CITY LIBRARY ASSOCIATION. EACH OF THE 30 RESIDENTS DONATED $3.00 FOR THE INITIAL PURCHASE OF LIBRARY BOOKS. THE BOOKS WERE KEPT AT SCHREIBER'S DRUG STORE AND CIRCULATED TO READERS. IN 1905, CHRIS NEWMAN, SUPERINTENDENT OF TELL CITY SCHOOLS, WAS INSTRUMENTAL IN STARTING A CITY LIBRARY SYSTEM. THE PUBLIC LIBRARY WAS ESTABLISHED, OPERATING OUT OF CITY HALL, AND THE LENDING LIBRARY IN SCHREIBER'S DRUG STORE WAS DISCONTINUED.

THE NEED FOR A SEPARATE BUILDING BECAME MORE APPARENT AS THE SCENE CHANGED AT THE BUSY CITY HALL. IN 1916, THE SCHOOL BOARD SECURED A $10,000 GRANT FROM THE CARNEGIE CORPORATION FOR A LIBRARY BUILDING, WITH THE CITY AGREEING TO FURNISH THE SITE NEAR THE PUBLIC SCHOOLS.

THE TELL CITY PUBLIC LIBRARY, AT THE CORNER OF 9TH AND FRANKLIN STREETS, WAS OPENED TO THE PUBLIC IN OCTOBER 1, 1917. THE ARCHITECTURAL STYLE OF THE BUILDING WAS ENGLISH TUDOR GOTHIC REVIVAL WITH RED TAPESTRY BRICK AND RED MORTAR. THE INTERIOR HALLWAYS FEATURED TENNESSEE MARBLE STAIRWAYS AND FUMED OAK WOODWORK. THE OPENING EXERCISES OF THE LIBRARY WERE HELD IN THE BASEMENT LECTURE ROOM."

IN 1968, THE LIBRARY DOUBLED ITS SIZE, OPENING A MAJOR ADDITION FACING FRANKLIN STREET. IN 1982, THE ORIGINAL CARNEGIE BUILDING WAS REMODELED AND A PUBLIC MEETING ROOM WAS ADDED. IN 1996, THE LIBRARY EXPANDED ITS SERVICES AND BECAME KNOWN AS THE TELL CITY-PERRY COUNTY PUBLIC LIBRARY. PLANS FOR A FUTURE FACILITY ARE BEING MADE.

GIFT: $10,000; MARCH 31, 1916
DEDICATION: OCTOBER 1, 1917
ARCHITECT: CLIFFORD SHOPBELL, EVANSVILLE
CONTRACTOR: GEORGE HESS SR.
STYLE: TUDOR GOTHIC REVIVAL

"Thorntown Public Library, Façade"

THORNTOWN

THORNTOWN PUBLIC LIBRARY

THE FIRST LIBRARY TO OPEN IN THORNTOWN IN 1911 WAS OWNED AND OPERATED BY THE PUBLIC SCHOOLS. IN 1912 AND 1913, THE HIGH SCHOOL LIBRARY WAS CONVERTED INTO A PUBLIC LIBRARY, WHICH WAS HOUSED IN THE OFFICE OF SUPERINTENDENT F. B. LONG. TEACHERS ASSISTED BY STUDENTS SERVED AS THE FIRST LIBRARIANS. BY 1914, THE NUMBER OF BOOKS AVAILABLE WAS 2,000.

IN 1912, SUPERINTENDENT LONG, TOGETHER WITH THE SCHOOL BOARD, STARTED PROCEDURES TO OBTAIN ASSISTANCE FROM THE CARNEGIE COMMISSION IN ORDER TO BUILD A LIBRARY IN THORNTOWN. IN MARCH OF 1912, IT WAS ANNOUNCED THAT A CARNEGIE GRANT OF $6,000 WOULD BE RECEIVED. SUGAR CREEK TOWNSHIP JOINED IN THE MOVEMENT TO OBTAIN FUNDS FOR THE LIBRARY AND $10,000 WAS OFFERED AND ACCEPTED. ON DECEMBER 8, 1913, PLANS WERE DRAWN FOR THE LIBRARY BUILDING. THE LOT AT THE CORNER OF MARKET AND BOW STREETS WAS PURCHASED FROM MRS. EMMA NORRIS.

ACCORDING TO THE *LIBRARY OCCURRENT*, A MAGAZINE PUBLISHED BY THE INDIANA PUBLIC LIBRARY COMMISSION, "THE BUILDING IS CONSTRUCTED OF GOLDEN MOTTLED BRICK WITH STONE TRIMMINGS AND TILE WORK AND HAS AN EXCELLENT FLOOR PLAN." DR. STANLEY COULTER OF PURDUE UNIVERSITY GAVE THE ADDRESS ON THE SUBJECT OF THE *"COMMUNITY VALUE OF A LIBRARY."* THE REGISTER OF THE DEDICATION CONTAINED THE SIGNATURES OF 800 VISITORS AND MORE THAN 1,000 PEOPLE VISITED THE BUILDING DURING THE FOUR-DAY OPEN HOUSE. THE NEW LIBRARY OPENED ITS DOORS AT THAT TIME WITH 4,000 BOOKS."

IN 1986 THE BUILDING WAS LISTED IN THE NATIONAL REGISTER OF HISTORIC PLACES. AN ADDITION AND RENOVATION IS PLANNED IN THE FUTURE.

GIFT: $10,000; SEPTEMBER 27, 1912
DEDICATION: JANUARY 10-13, 1915
ARCHITECT: WILSON B. PARKER, INDIANAPOLIS
CONTRACTOR: STATE CONSTRUCTION COMPANY, INDIANAPOLIS
STYLE: CRAFTSMAN-PRAIRIE TRADITION

"Thorntown Public Library, Interior"

"Thorntown Public Library, Interior, Heating Radiator"

"Union City Public Library, Rooftop Elevation, Ornament, Acroteria"

UNION CITY

UNION CITY PUBLIC LIBRARY

EXCERPTS FROM THE *"UNION CITY LIBRARY BUILDING: A LANDMARK FOR 95 YEARS,"* ARTICLE BY VIRGINIA HIATT, LIBRARY DIRECTOR:

"WHAT IS NOW KNOWN AS THE UNION CITY PUBLIC LIBRARY HAD ITS INCEPTION WITH A SOCIETY OF YOUNG, UNMARRIED LADIES KNOWN THE G.G.G. OR THREE G'S SOCIETY, WHO RESOLVED IN APRIL OF 1887, TO ESTABLISH A FOUNDATION FUND FOR A PUBLIC LIBRARY. OTHER LOCAL SOCIAL CLUBS ALSO SECONDED THE MOTION FOR A PUBLIC LIBRARY.

AN EFFICIENT DIRECTOR WAS FOUND IN MR. LINNEAUS N. HINES, SUPERINTENDENT OF SCHOOLS, WHO ORGANIZED AND LOCATED A ROOM IN THE HIGH SCHOOL TO SERVE AS A LIBRARY. A LIBRARY BOARD WAS FORMALLY ORGANIZED APRIL 10, 1902. THE LIBRARY WAS MOVED DOWNTOWN UNION CITY AND LOCATED IN THE WALLACE BUILDING.

PERMANENT QUARTERS FOR THE LIBRARY BECAME APPARENT. THE CITY OWNED FOUR LOTS, CENTRALLY LOCATED, THAT WERE DONATED FOR THE USE OF A PUBLIC PARK OR LIBRARY. AFTER WRITING TO ANDREW CARNEGIE INQUIRING ABOUT POSSIBLE LIBRARY CONSTRUCTION FUNDS EARLY IN 1903, CARNEGIE MADE A PROPOSITION TO THE BOARD TO FURNISH THE CITY OF UNION CITY, $10,000, ON HIS USUAL CONDITIONS, FOR THE PURPOSE OF ERECTING A PUBLIC LIBRARY BUILDING. WITH THE $10,000 GIFT FROM ANDREW CARNEGIE, AND THE PLEDGE OF $1,000 YEARLY APPROPRIATED BY TAXATION FOR THE SUPPORT OF THE LIBRARY BY THE CITY COUNCIL, A BUILDING COMMITTEE WAS APPOINTED. J. M. STEELE WAS THE CONTRACTOR AND WRIGHT AND DUNCAN, THE ARCHITECTS. THE BUILDING WAS COMPLETED IN 1904."

THE MOST IMPORTANT RENOVATION TOOK PLACE IN 1988 WITH THE ADDITION OF AN ELEVATORETTE AND NEW STAIRS IN THE SOUTH ENTRY OF THE BUILDING.

GIFT: $10,000; NOVEMBER 25, 1903
DEDICATION: JUNE 8, 1905
ARCHITECT: WRIGHT & DUNCAN
CONTRACTOR: J. M. STEELE
STYLE: NEO CLASSICAL REVIVAL

"Van Buren Public Library, Façade"

VAN BUREN

VAN BUREN PUBLIC LIBRARY

EXCERPTS FROM THE *"HISTORY OF THE VAN BUREN LIBRARY"* FILE:

"THE VAN BUREN PUBLIC LIBRARY BOARD OF TRUSTEES MET FOR THE FIRST TIME ON FEBRUARY 14, 1917, AND BEGAN DISCUSSION OF ESTABLISHING A LIBRARY FOR THE RESIDENTS OF VAN BUREN TOWNSHIP. THE SEVEN LIBRARY BOARD MEMBERS WERE APPOINTED BY THE GRANT COUNTY CIRCUIT COURT. THE PRESIDENT OF THE LIBRARY BOARD APPOINTED A COMMITTEE TO SEEK THE REQUIRED FIFTY SIGNATURES NEEDED TO ESTABLISH AN ORDINANCE TO CREATE A TAX LEVY FOR A LIBRARY FUND. THE AMOUNT TO BE RAISED BY THE FIFTY PEOPLE WHO SIGNED THE PETITION WAS $160.89 OR $3.21 PER PERSON, DIVIDED INTO EIGHT PAYMENTS OF FORTY CENTS.

A LETTER WAS WRITTEN TO THE CARNEGIE CORPORATION REQUESTING FUNDING TO BUILD THE LOCAL LIBRARY. A REPLY WAS RECEIVED STATING THAT 'IF THE TOWNSHIP WOULD RAISE $1,000 A YEAR IN TAXES FOR THE LIBRARY, MR. CARNEGIE WOULD GRANT AN AMOUNT OF $10,000.' A COMMITTEE WAS SELECTED TO OVERSEE THE LIBRARY BUILDING PROJECT. THE BUILDING SITE WAS SELECTED NEAR THE DOWNTOWN AREA FOR A COST OF $1,500. HIRAM ELDER WAS SELECTED AS THE ARCHITECT AND HIS TOTAL BILL WAS 5% OF THE BUILDING COST OR $428. AUGUST REUDLINGER WAS SELECTED AS THE GENERAL CONTRACTOR. WORLD WAR I SLOWED THE CONSTRUCTION OF THE BUILDING. WILLIAM DOYLE, PRESIDENT OF THE LIBRARY BOARD WAS CHAIRMAN OF THE GENERAL OPENING AND DEDICATION ON SEPTEMBER 3, 1919. LYLA MCMILLIAN WAS APPOINTED AS THE FIRST LIBRARIAN BUT REMAINED IN THE POSITION FOR ONE WEEK BEFORE RESIGNING."

GIFT: $10,000; MAY 3, 1917
DEDICATION: SEPTEMBER 3, 1919
ARCHITECT: HIRAM ELDER, MARION
CONTRACTOR: AUGUST REUDLINGER
STYLE: NEO CLASSICAL REVIVAL

"Knox County Public Library, Vincennes, Façade"

VINCENNES

KNOX COUNTY PUBLIC LIBRARY

EXCERPTS FROM *"LOOKING BACK"* BY BRIAN SPANGLE, HISTORICAL COLLECTION, FRIENDS OF THE LIBRARY NEWSLETTER:

"IN 1901 AND 1902, VINCENNES CITY OFFICIALS WERE BUSY TRYING TO ACQUIRE A CARNEGIE LIBRARY FOR VINCENNES. AT THE FEBRUARY 11, 1901 CITY COUNCIL MEETING, MAYOR GEORGE E. GREENE RECOMMENDED THAT THE COUNCIL PETITION ANDREW CARNEGIE FOR FUNDS TO BUILD A LIBRARY. NO HEADWAY WAS MADE IN GAINING FUNDS FOR THE LIBRARY BUILDING IN 1901, BUT A BOARD HAD BEEN FORMED.

WORD FROM CARNEGIE'S SECRETARY, JAMES BERTRAM WAS RECEIVED IN APRIL, 1902 EXPLAIN-ING THE FUNDING PROCEDURE. AFTER NO WORD IN EIGHT MONTHS, A COMMITTEE FROM VINCENNES WENT TO NEW YORK WHERE THEY MET WITH JAMES BERTRAM, WHO INSTRUCTED THE MEN AS TO WHAT ADDITIONAL MATERIAL THEY NEEDED. THE CARNEGIE CORPORATION OFFERED $30,000 FOR A LIBRARY BUILDING IN MARCH, 1910. DESPITE THESE AMBITIOUS EARLY EFFORTS, THE LACK OF LOCATION FOR A BUILDING SITE MEANT THAT A LIBRARY FOR VINCENNES WAS STILL NEARLY NINE YEARS AWAY.

JAMES BERTRAM RESPONDED TO A 1916 LETTER WITH AN INCREASED OFFER OF $35,000, ACCOUNTING FOR THE POPULATION GROWTH SINCE 1910 AND THE OFFER WAS ACCEPTED. THE LIBRARY LOT AT SEVENTH AND SEMINARY WAS PURCHASED FOR $12,000 AND LET FOR CONTRACT IN OCTOBER, 1917. THE LIBRARY WAS DEDICATED APRIL 15, 1919."

AN ADDITION WAS CONSTRUCTED IN 1976-1977, OPENED ON OCTOBER 17, 1977, AND WAS DEDICATED ON APRIL 16, 1978. A WALL WAS BUILT AROUND THE CARNEGIE BUILDING TO BLEND THE TWO DIVERSE ARCHITECTURAL STYLES.

GIFT: $35,000; MARCH 21, 1910
DEDICATION: APRIL 15, 1919
ARCHITECT: J. B. BAYARD, VINCENNES
CONTRACTOR: T. F. WILLIS, VINCENNES
STYLE: COLLEGIATE GOTHIC REVIVAL

"Knox County Public Library, Vincennes, Grotesque"

"Knox County Public Library, Vincennes, Historical Marker"

"Wabash Carnegie Public Library, Pedimented Gable"

WABASH

WABASH CARNEGIE PUBLIC LIBRARY

In 1890, the Women's Library Association, organized by the Round Table Literary Club, established a library fund. On January 11, 1890, the Women's Library of Wabash was formally opened with 300 volumes on its shelves. The library was first opened in the Probate Courtroom of the Wabash County Courthouse. In 1895, the books were moved to the old Wabash High School building, and in the 1900, the Women's Library Association was dissolved due to a consolidation with the high school library and the new Wabash Public Library. Crowded conditions in the high school forced the library to move again, this time to Memorial Hall where the library remained until the opening of the Carnegie library building.

In 1901, application was made to Andrew Carnegie for funding of a library building. A response from James Bertram, Mr. Carnegie's secretary, stated that the requirements for a free building would be a location and $2,000 a year to maintain a $20,000 building. The Wabash Carnegie Public Library was opened to the public on April 6, 1903, with a collection of 3,000 books.

Designed by the architect J. F. Wing in classic Greek style and constructed of Bedford limestone, the library was built with an $18,000 Carnegie grant. The site was donated by the City of Wabash, which agreed to spend $2,000 a year for its support. The original building was 5,000 square feet but the 1972 addition nearly tripled the size.

Gift: $20,000; March 7, 1901
Dedication: April 6, 1903
Architect: J. F. Wing, Fort Wayne
Contractor: J. H. Hipskind & Son
Style: Neo Classical Revival

"Wabash Carnegie Public Library, Rotunda, stained Glass Dome"

"Wabash Carnegie Public Library, Bust, Andrew Carnegie"

"Walton-Tipton Township Public Library, Stairs, Pierced Wood Balusters"

WALTON

WALTON & TIPTON TOWNSHIP PUBLIC LIBRARY

EXCERPTS FROM THE LIBRARY BROCHURE, *"50TH ANNIVERSARY OF THE DEDICATION OF THE WALTON & TIPTON TOWNSHIP PUBLIC LIBRARY, 1915-1965"*:

"THE LADIES LITERARY CLUB OF 1914 AND 1915 CAN BE GIVEN THE REAL HONOR AND CREDIT FOR OBTAINING FOR WALTON AND TIPTON TOWNSHIP, THE BENEFITS THE LIBRARY HAS AFFORDED THE COMMUNITY OVER THE PAST 50 YEARS. EARLY IN 1914, MRS. G. W. BISHOP OF THE LITERARY CLUB, INITIATED AND CARRIED FORWARD THE MOVEMENT FOR A CARNEGIE LIBRARY.

ON SEPTEMBER 14, 1914, THE FIRST LIBRARY BOARD WAS ORGANIZED. ON OCTOBER 27, 1914 THE LADIES LITERARY CLUB MET AND VOTED TO TURN OVER THE LIBRARY THAT HAD BEEN SUPPORTED AND CARED FOR BY THE CLUB TO THE WALTON-TIPTON TOWNSHIP LIBRARY BOARD. ON NOVEMBER 25, 1914, IT WAS RESOLVED BY THE LOCAL GOVERNMENTAL UNITS THAT A SUITABLE SITE FOR SAID BUILDING WOULD BE FURNISHED, AND AN ANNUAL TAX LEVY WOULD BE MADE ON TAXABLE PROPERTY. THE RESOLUTIONS WERE ACCEPTED BY THE CARNEGIE CORPORATION AND THE CONTRIBUTION OF $10,000 WAS GAINED.

ON JUNE 12, 1915 WITH APPROPRIATE CEREMONIES THE CORNERSTONE WAS LAID AND ON DECEMBER 8, 1915, THE NEW LIBRARY BUILDING WAS DEDICATED. A FEATURE OF THE DEDICATION FOR THE NEW CARNEGIE BUILDING WAS THE PRESENTATION OF A PORTRAIT OF MRS. VORA BISHOP, A LIBRARY BOARD MEMBER, WHO HAS DONE MUCH TO MAKE THE LIBRARY COME TRUE FOR WALTON AND TIPTON TOWNSHIP."

THE ORIGINAL BUILDING WAS PLACED IN THE INDIANA HISTORIC REGISTER APRIL 12, 1998. A $1.2 MILLION DOLLAR, TWO STORY EXPANSION, WHICH WILL ENHANCE THE EXISTING APPEARANCE AND DOUBLE THE FLOOR SPACE, IS PLANNED IN THE NEAR FUTURE.

GIFT: $10,000; NOVEMBER 17, 1914
DEDICATION: DECEMBER 8, 1915
ARCHITECT: WILLIAM TURNER, WALTON
CONTRACTOR: WILLIAM TURNER, WALTON
STYLE: NEO CLASSICAL REVIVAL

"Warren Public Library, Interior, Original Shelving"

WARREN

WARREN PUBLIC LIBRARY

EXCERPTS FROM THE *WARREN TRIBUNE* NEWSPAPER ARTICLE, *"LIBRARY WAS DEDICATED SATURDAY,"* JUNE, 1920:

"THE WARREN PUBLIC LIBRARY WAS DEDICATED TO THE PUBLIC SATURDAY (JUNE 5, 1920). THE FIRST STEPS WERE TAKEN IN THE FALL OF 1914 DURING THE TIME THAT R. B. MCCRUM WAS SUPERINTENDENT OF THE LOCAL SCHOOLS. THE FIRST MEETING WAS HELD AT THE HIGH SCHOOL BUILDING ON OCTOBER 9, 1914 BUT EFFORTS TO LOCATE AT THE SCHOOL FAILED DUE TO OVER-CROWDING. IT WAS THEN DECIDED IN 1915 TO GET IN TOUCH WITH THE ANDREW CARNEGIE FOUNDATION TO SEE IF HELP COULD BE SECURED FROM THAT SOURCE.

THE REPLY FROM THE CARNEGIE FOUNDATION WAS FAVORABLE BUT IT WAS NOT UNTIL THE SPRING OF 1916 THAT ALL LEGAL STEPS HAD BEEN TAKEN. THE LIBRARY BOARD WAS ORGANIZED IN JUNE 1916. IN APRIL 1917 THE CARNEGIE FOUNDATION AGREED TO GIVE $10,000 WITH WHICH TO BUILD A LIBRARY IN WARREN, AND THE LOCAL BOARD BEGAN A CANVASS FOR SUITABLE LOCA-TION FOR THE SAME. OWNERS OF ADJOINING LIBRARY PROPERTY AT THIRD AND MAIN STREETS CON-TRIBUTED LIBERALLY TO THE FUND NEEDED TO PURCHASE THE LOT. CONTRACTS WERE CLOSED.

SOON AFTER BEGINNING WORK EVERYTHING HAD TO STOP FOR A TIME ON ACCOUNT OF WAR WORK. MATERIALS COULD NOT BE SHIPPED AND IN SOME INSTANCES COULD NOT BE SECURED FROM JOBBERS. IN 1918 TEMPORARY QUARTERS WERE SECURED FOR THE LIBRARY TO BE OPENED. THE CARNEGIE BUILDING WAS FINALLY DEDICATED ON JUNE 5, 1920."

GIFT: $10,000; APRIL 3, 1917
DEDICATION: JUNE 5, 1920
ARCHITECT: SAMUEL. A. CRAIG, HUNTINGTON
CONTRACTOR: AUGUST REUDLINGER
STYLE: NEO CLASSICAL REVIVAL

"Warsaw Community Public Library, Former Main Entrance"

WARSAW

WARSAW COMMUNITY PUBLIC LIBRARY

EXCERPTS FROM THE *"HISTORY OF LIBRARY: OPEN HOUSE DEDICATION"* BOOKLET, 2000:

"FROM THE TIME THE COUNTY WAS FORMED IN 1836, THE PIONEERS SHARED THE RESOURCES OF THEIR PRIVATE LIBRARIES. IN 1855, THE MCCLURE WORKINGMEN'S INSTITUTE CREATED A LIBRARY THAT SERVED THE WORKING MEN OF THE TOWN. IN 1858, THE COUNTY'S FIRST LIBRARY WAS ESTABLISHED IN A THREE-STORY BRICK HOUSE AT THE SOUTHWEST CORNER OF MARKET AND DETROIT STREETS. IN 1855, BOOKS FORMERLY BELONGING TO THE MCCLURE AND COUNTY LIBRARIES WERE TURNED OVER TO THE WARSAW PUBLIC LIBRARY AND WERE HOUSED IN THE OLD CENTER WARD SCHOOL BUILDING.

FOLLOWING THE STEPS NECESSARY TO OBTAIN A CARNEGIE GRANT, THE WARSAW CITY COUNCIL PASSED A RESOLUTION IN 1915, TO TAKE OVER THE LIBRARY IN CENTER WARD AND THE FIRST LIBRARY BOARD WAS APPOINTED. IN 1916, THE ORIGINAL CARNEGIE GRANT OF $15,000 WAS RECEIVED AND A BUILDING OF 6,134 SQUARE FEET WAS BUILT IN 1917. THIS EDIFICE CONTAINED 5,000 BOOKS AND SERVED 12,800 PEOPLE."

IN THE 1960S, IT BECAME APPARENT THAT THE LIBRARY NEEDED TO BE UPDATED. THE NAME WAS CHANGED TO THE WARSAW COMMUNITY PUBLIC LIBRARY, AND THERE WAS AN ADDITION OF 8,833 SQUARE FEET, DEDICATED IN 2000.

GIFT: $15,000; SEPTEMBER 29, 1915
DEDICATION: APRIL 26, 1917
ARCHITECT: SAMUEL A. CRAIG, HUNTINGTON
CONTRACTOR: EZRA FRANTZ, NORTH MANCHESTER
STYLE: ECLECTIC

"Warsaw Community Public Library, Façade, During Renovation"

"Warsaw Community Public Library, Façade, After Renovation"

"Washington Carnegie Public Library, Interior, Rotunda"

WASHINGTON

Washington Carnegie Public Library

Excerpts from the *"Programme for The Dedication of the Carnegie Public Library, A Historical Sketch,"* February 21, 1903:

"Washington was one of the beneficiaries of the generosities of William Maclure in 1855 and received one of the Workingmen's Libraries, which was maintained for forty years. The Maclure donated collection of books was scattered about the time the old township libraries went into their final repose.

The Carnegie Public Library of Washington, Indiana, originated in a suggestion made by the ladies of the Monday Afternoon Club. It was decided February 21, 1901, that a citizen committee be appointed to correspond with Mr. Carnegie. Carnegie responded promptly with an offer of $15,000, which was later increased by him to $20,000. The donation was accepted by the City Council and a annual income of $2,000 was guaranteed by the same body. On June 14, 1901, Mr. Joseph Cabel generously donated the square on which the building now stands. A library board of seven was appointed.

The building was completed and ready for occupancy by the later part of December, 1902. On January 7, 1903, Mrs. Annie Gibson was librarian in charge of over 2,300 volumes. On Saturday afternoon, February 21, 1903, dedication ceremonies were held at the First Christian Church and at the library. A public reception was held in the library from 6 to 7 p.m. that same evening."

During 1997-1998, the library underwent a major renovation, and there was also a 9,500 foot addition to the original building.

Gift: $20,000; March 8, 1901
Dedication: February 21, 1903
Architect: Patton & Miller, Chicago, Ill.
Contractor: Bulley & Andrews
Style: Neo Classical Revival

"Washington Carnegie Public Library, Children's Room, Reading Desk & Bench"

"Washington Carnegie Public Library, Fireplace, Entablature & Capital"

"Waterloo-Grant Township Public Library, Interior"

WATERLOO

WATERLOO-GRANT TOWNSHIP PUBLIC LIBRARY

EXCERPTS FROM THE *"HISTORY OF WATERLOO PUBLIC LIBRARY"* FILE:

"THE CLUBS OF WATERLOO WERE INSTRUMENTAL IN STARTING A LIBRARY CAMPAIGN IN THE TOWN. IN THE FALL OF 1912, A FREE LIBRARY WAS ORGANIZED IN WATERLOO, INDIANA, AND MAINTAINED BY PUBLIC SUBSCRIPTION UNTIL A LEVY FOR TAX MONEY COULD BE APPROPRIATED. IN JANUARY OF 1913, APPLICATION WAS MADE TO ANDREW CARNEGIE TO BUILD A LIBRARY BUILDING. THE CARNEGIE FOUNDATION RESPONDED WITH A GIFT OF $9,000.

ARCHITECT WILSON B. PARKER OF INDIANAPOLIS DESIGNED THE STRUCTURE, AND IT WAS CONSTRUCTED BY J. B. GOODALL AND SONS OF PERU, INDIANA. THE BUILDING WAS DEDICATED JANUARY 26, 1914, THE FIRST CARNEGIE LIBRARY IN DEKALB COUNTY.

JUDGE FRANK M. POWERS OF THE CIRCUIT COURT, DELIVERED THE DEDICATORY ADDRESS IN WHICH HE PAID HIGH TRIBUTE TO ANDREW CARNEGIE FOR HIS LIBRARY AND PEACE WORK. LETTERS WERE READ FROM A NUMBER OF FORMER CITIZENS, AMONG THEM ONE FROM JUDGE R. W. MCBRIDE OF INDIANAPOLIS, WHO SENT A COLLECTION OF 60 BOOKS AS A GIFT."

IN 1989, A $300,000 TWO-STORY ADDITION, DESIGNED BY HERMAN STRAUSS OF FORT WAYNE, WAS CONSTRUCTED. THIS MATCHING ADDITION DOUBLED THE SIZE OF THE ORIGINAL LIBRARY.

GIFT: $9,000; MARCH 14, 1913
DEDICATION: JANUARY 26, 1914
ARCHITECT: WILSON B. PARKER, INDIANAPOLIS
CONTRACTOR: J. B. GOODALL & SONS, PERU
STYLE: CRAFTSMAN-PRAIRIE TRADITION

"Waveland-Brown Township Public Library, Foyer, Historic Plaque"

WAVELAND

WAVELAND-BROWN TOWNSHIP PUBLIC LIBRARY

EXCERPTS FROM THE *"HISTORY OF WAVELAND LIBRARY,"* PAPER BY MRS. T. E. HUSTON, LIBRARIAN, 1931:

"IN 1889, THE PARMALEE CIRCULATING LIBRARY WAS STARTED IN WAVELAND AND PRIOR TO THAT WAS THE 1855 MACLURE WORKING MAN'S INSTITUTE COLLECTION AND THE TOWNSHIP LIBRARY. THIS WAS A SUBSCRIPTION LIBRARY AND BOOKS WERE SENT FROM INDIANAPOLIS, ABOUT FIFTY AT A TIME, CIRCULATED AND RETURNED; THE WHOLE LIBRARY WAS NEVER MORE THAN 500 VOLUMES. ANOTHER LIBRARY WAS OPERATED IN WAVELAND FOR A FEW YEARS BY THE FARMER'S INSTITUTE AND AUXILIARY. THE WAVELAND BOOK CLUB WAS FORMED IN 1900 AND CONTINUED UNTIL THE ESTABLISHMENT OF THE PUBLIC LIBRARY.

IN TIME, THE CARNEGIE CORPORATION, AFTER MUCH CORRESPONDENCE, DECIDED THAT WAVELAND MIGHT HAVE AS MUCH AS $10,000 FOR A LIBRARY BUILDING. THE GIFT OF THE PUBLIC LIBRARY BY ANDREW CARNEGIE IS AN OUTSTANDING SOURCE OF PLEASURE AND UPLIFT TO THE COMMUNITY.

THE PRISCILLA CIRCLE, A NEEDLEWORK ORGANIZATION, FINANCED THE LEGAL STEPS NECESSARY IN OBTAINING THE LIBRARY IN 1914. THE COMMUNITY IS DEEPLY INDEBTED TO MR. AND MRS. T. E. HUSTON WHO TOOK THE INITIATIVE IN SECURING THE LIBRARY, AFTER PURCHASE OF THE BUILDING LOT BY THE TOWN. THE LIBRARY WAS OPENED IN 1915, AFTER GENEROUS DONATIONS OF BOOKS BY CITIZENS AND ORGANIZATIONS HAD BROUGHT THE STOCK TO OVER 1,000. A GRAND OPENING WAS HELD WITH SPEECHES, SPECIAL MUSIC AND THE REGISTERING OF BORROWERS. THE MOST OUTSTANDING GIFT TO THE LIBRARY, IS A LARGE PAINTING OF A BROWN COUNTY RURAL SCENE GIVEN BY ARTIST, T. C. STEELE, WHO SPENT HIS BOYHOOD IN WAVELAND."

GIFT: $10,000; FEBRUARY 26, 1914
DEDICATION: APRIL 17, 1915
ARCHITECT: W. F. SHARPE, CRAWFORDSVILLE
CONTRACTOR: F. C. RICE, ROACHDALE
STYLE: CRAFTSMAN TRADITION

"West Lebanon-Pike Township Public Library, Façade"

WEST LEBANON

WEST LEBANON-PIKE TOWNSHIP PUBLIC LIBRARY

EXCERPTS FROM THE *"WEST LEBANON LIBRARY'S HISTORY," WEST LEBANON GAZETTE*, OCTOBER, 1916:

"PRIOR TO HAVING A LIBRARY, THE COMMUNITY HAD TO RELY UPON TRAVELING BOOKS. THEY WERE FREE FROM THE INDIANA STATE LIBRARY TO ANY GROUP OF FIVE OR MORE HAVING NO FREE PUBLIC LIBRARY, JUST PAYING POSTAGE. A MOVE TOWARDS SECURING A CARNEGIE LIBRARY BEGAN WITH A STATE-WINNING ESSAY BY EIGHTH GRADER PAUL BEEDLE ON *'WHY MY COMMUNITY SHOULD HAVE A PUBLIC LIBRARY,'* JUNE 6, 1914. ON SEPTEMBER 9, 1914, LEGAL STEPS WERE TAKEN AND ON OCTOBER 5, 1914, THE LIBRARY BOARD WAS ORGANIZED.

THE CARNEGIE BOARD APPROPRIATED $7,500 FOR THE NEW BUILDING ON MAY 16, 1915. MCCOY AND SKADDEN OF DANVILLE, ILLINOIS WERE THE CHOSEN ARCHITECTS. WM. H. GOODWINE AND HIS WIFE, DONATED A LOT ON THE CORNER OF HIGH AND WEST NORTH, JUST SOUTH OF THE LAMB HOTEL. E. S. MOORE OF DANVILLE, ILLINOIS RECEIVED THE BUILDING CONTRACT FOR THE LIBRARY, AND HIS BID WAS $7,000.

ON MARCH 23, 1916, CONSTRUCTION OF THE LIBRARY BEGAN, AND THE ROUGH RED SHALE BRICK WITH BEDFORD LIMESTONE TOOK ON A CRAFTSMAN-PRAIRIE TRADITIONAL STYLE. ON SEPTEMBER 12, 1916 THE LIBRARIAN BEGAN HER DUTIES. THE LIBRARY DEDICATION TOOK PLACE ON OCTOBER 14, 1916, SATURDAY AFTERNOON WHEN THE BUILDING WAS THROWN OPEN TO THE PUBLIC. A LARGE CROWD WAS PRESENT TO HEAR THE SPLENDID PROGRAM. OVER 1,000 BOOKS WERE CONTRIBUTED AND A CONSIDERABLE SUM IN CASH."

GIFT: $7,500; APRIL 19, 1915
DEDICATION: OCTOBER 14, 1916
ARCHITECT: MCCOY & SKADDEN, DANVILLE, ILL.
CONTRACTOR: E. S. MOORE, DANVILLE, ILL.
STYLE: CRAFTSMAN TRADITION

"West Lebanon-Pike Township Public Library, Original Furniture"

"West Lebanon-Pike Township Public Library, Bust, Andrew Carnegie"

"Westville-New Durham Township Public Library, Facade, 1915 Historic Photo"

PHOTO COURTESY OF THE WESTVILLE-NEW DURHAM PUBLIC LIBRARY

WESTVILLE

WESTVILLE-NEW DURHAM TOWNSHIP PUBLIC LIBRARY

EXCERPTS FROM THE *1951 WESTVILLE CENTENNIAL BOOKLET, "WESTVILLE PUBLIC LIBRARY"*:

"THE LADIES CALLIOPE SOCIETY WAS ORGANIZED FEBRUARY 6, 1875 FOR THE PURPOSE OF SOCIAL AND INTELLECTUAL IMPROVEMENT. THE LADIES CHOSE A CIRCULATING LIBRARY AS THEIR FIRST PROJECT AND DONATED SUCH BOOKS AS THEY THOUGHT WOULD BE BENEFICIAL TO THE UNREAD RURAL COMMUNITY.

IN 1876, THE SOCIETY REORGANIZED UNDER THE NAME OF LADIES HOME LIBRARY ASSOCIATION. THE DONATED GIFT OF A FORMER DOCTOR'S OFFICE BECAME THE FIRST LIBRARY BUILDING IN WESTVILLE. THE LIBRARY WAS ENTIRELY DEPENDENT UPON THE PERSONAL POCKETBOOKS OF A HANDFUL OF WOMEN TRUSTEES. THE LIBRARY WAS LATER SOLD AND $500 OF THE PROCEEDS WAS USED TO PURCHASE THE LOT WHERE THE NEW BUILDING NOW STANDS.

THE WESTVILLE PUBLIC LIBRARY WAS DEDICATED AUGUST 4, 1915. THE BUILDING IS A HANDSOME AND SUBSTANTIAL STRUCTURE, 50 x 48 FEET OF BROWN BRICK. TABLES, CHAIRS, AND BOOKCASES WERE FURNISHED BY THE CARNEGIE FOUNDATION. HUNDREDS VISITED THE LIBRARY ON ITS DEDICATION DAY. AT 1 P.M. A DINNER WAS SERVED IN THE BASEMENT BY THE BOARD OF DIRECTORS IN HONOR OF THE MEMBERS OF THE LADIES HOMES LIBRARY ASSOCIATION AND THE OLD CALLIOPE SOCIETY. THE PRESENT LIBRARY IS A FITTING TRIBUTE TO THAT LOYAL GROUP OF WESTVILLE WOMEN WHO PLANTED THE SEEDS FROM WHENCE GREW THE WESTVILLE PUBLIC LIBRARY."

A FRONT ADDITION WAS BUILT IN 1969 AND A REAR ADDITION WAS COMPLETED IN 1997.

GIFT: $8,000; DECEMBER 8, 1913
DEDICATION: AUGUST 4, 1915
ARCHITECT: WILSON B. PARKER, INDIANAPOLIS
CONTRACTOR: GROSS & GOODALL, LAPORTE
STYLE-CRAFTSMAN-PRAIRIE TRADITION

"Westville-New Durham Township Public Library, Façade, Original & Additions"

"Westville-New durham Towhship Public Library, Interior, Windows"

"Whiting Public Library, Façade"

WHITING

WHITING PUBLIC LIBRARY

EXCERPTS FROM *"THE HISTORY OF THE WHITING PUBLIC LIBRARY"* FILE:

"THE FIRST STEPS TOWARD A PUBLIC LIBRARY FOR WHITING WERE TAKEN DURING THE SUMMER OF 1904. MISS MERICA HOAGLAND OF THE INDIANA STATE LIBRARY COMMISSION SPOKE TO THE CITIZENS OF WHITING IN REGARDS TO THE PROPOSED LIBRARY AT A VERY ENTHUSIASTIC MEETING HELD IN GOEBEL'S OPERA HOUSE ON SEPTEMBER 30, 1904.

A LETTER WRITTEN TO ANDREW CARNEGIE, A PITTSBURGH STEEL TYCOON, RESULTED IN A $15,000 DONATION THAT WAS RECEIVED ON JANUARY 9, 1905. SOON THEREAFTER, THE STANDARD OIL COMPANY DONATED TWO LOTS AT THE NORTH END OF OLIVER STREET AND OHIO AVENUE, UPON WHICH, THE PERMANENT LIBRARY WOULD BE ERECTED. MEANWHILE, A TEMPORARY ROOM IN THE PEDERSEN BLOCK, AT THE CORNER OF SHERIDAN AND 119TH STREETS, WAS RENTED AND OPENED AS A LIBRARY IN MARCH, 1905.

ON OCTOBER 1, 1905, WORK ON THE NEW CARNEGIE BUILDING BEGAN. ON DECEMBER 2, 1905, THE CORNERSTONE, BEARING THE INSCRIPTION 'THE GIFT OF ANDREW CARNEGIE-A.D. 1905,' WAS LAID WITH CEREMONIES AND A PARADE. FINALLY ON JULY 31, 1906, THE WHITING PUBLIC LIBRARY OPENED ITS UNIQUE NEW BUILDING TO THE PUBLIC. THE ROMANESQUE RED BRICK EXTERIOR, THE POLYGONAL TURRET TOWER, THE SEMI CIRCULAR ARCHED ENTRY AND ARCHED PICTURE WINDOWS GIVES THE LIBRARY A FORTRESS LIKE APPEARANCE. THE TOTAL COST OF THE BUILDING WAS $20,000."

THE WHITING PUBLIC LIBRARY HAS GONE THROUGH SEVERAL EXPANSIVE TECHNOLOGICAL CHANGES SINCE IT FIRST OPENED ITS DOORS TO THE PUBLIC; HOWEVER, THE ORIGINAL CARNEGIE BUILDING HAS KEPT ITS HISTORICAL INTEGRITY.

GIFT: $15,000; JANUARY 9, 1905
DEDICATION: JULY 31, 1906
ARCHITECT: PAUL O. MORATZ, BLOOMINGTON, ILL.
CONTRACTOR: MR. REESE, BLOOMINGTON, ILL.
STYLE: ECLECTIC-ROMANESQUE REVIVAL

"Whiting Public Library, Interior, Indiana Room, Stained Glass"

"Whiting Public Library, Main Entrance, Arched Portal"

"Pulaski County Public Library, Winamac, Neoclassical Façade"

WINAMAC

PULASKI COUNTY PUBLIC LIBRARY

EXCERPTS FROM THE *"HISTORY OF THE PULASKI COUNTY PUBLIC LIBRARY"* FILE:

"PRIOR TO THE 20TH CENTURY, SEVERAL ATTEMPTS HAD BEEN MADE TO DEVELOP A SYSTEM-ATIC METHOD FOR CIRCULATING BOOKS IN WINAMAC. THE FIRST CIRCULATING LIBRARY IN WINAMAC WAS OPENED IN 1854. THE MACLURE WORKINGMAN'S INSTITUTE WAS ESTABLISHED IN 1857 AND THEN, THE TOWNSHIP LIBRARY FORMED. THROUGH THE EFFORTS OF WILLIAM H. KELLY OF THE WINAMAC SCHOOL AND THE WOMAN'S CLUB, THE READING ROOM IN THE YARNELL BLOCK WAS OPENED IN SEPTEMBER 1905, WITH MISS JOSIE O'CONNELL SERVING AS THE LIBRARIAN.

IN 1914, AS THE READING ROOM OUTGREW ITS FOUR WALLS, THE OFFICIALS OF THE WINAMAC LIBRARY REQUESTED, AND RECEIVED, FUNDS FROM THE CARNEGIE FOUNDATION AND CONSTRUCT-ED A PUBLIC LIBRARY ON RIVERSIDE DRIVE, NEXT TO THE THE 1892 WINAMAC PUBLIC SCHOOL. THE CARNEGIE PUBLIC LIBRARY WAS DEDICATED NOVEMBER 13, 1916.

ACCORDING TO THE *LIBRARY OCCURRENT* MAGAZINE, DECEMBER 1916 ISSUE, 'THE DEDICATION WAS HELD NOVEMBER 13, 1916, WITH A PUBLIC RECEPTION. A SHORT EVENING PROGRAM INCLUD-ED BRIEF TALKS BY MEMBERS OF THE LIBRARY BOARD AND BUILDING COMMITTEE. LIGHT REFRESH-MENTS WERE SERVED AND THE VARIOUS FEATURES OF THE LIBRARY WERE EXPLAINED TO VISI-TORS'."

A HALF CENTURY LATER, DESPITE LIMITED SPACE, THE LIBRARY STRENGTHENED ITS COLLEC-TION, EXTENDED SERVICES, OPENED A BRANCH IN MEDARYVILLE IN 1965, AND BECAME THE PULASKI COUNTY PUBLIC LIBRARY IN 1969. A NEW ADDITION WAS OPENED ON MARCH 28, 1983, FOLLOWED BY A RENOVATION OF THE CARNEGIE LIBRARY. DEDICATION CEREMONIES WERE HELD ON JULY 17, 1983.

GIFT: $10,000; JANUARY 6, 1911
DEDICATION: NOVEMBER 13, 1916
ARCHITECT: W. S. KAUFMAN & SON, RICHMOND
CONTRACTOR: YOUNG & HODSHIRE, MONTICELLO
STYLE: NEO CLASSICAL REVIVAL

"Winchester Community Public Library, Stairway, Wood Paneling"

WINCHESTER

WINCHESTER COMMUNITY PUBLIC LIBRARY

A CAMPAIGN FOR A PUBLIC LIBRARY WAS BEGUN IN NOVEMBER, 1906 BY THE WINCHESTER LIBRARY ASSOCIATION. AFTER A SERIES OF COMMITTEE MEETINGS, VISITS OF COMMISSION WORKERS, AND A PUBLIC MEETING ADDRESSED BY THE SECRETARY OF THE PUBLIC LIBRARY COMMISSION, THE IDEA WAS BROUGHT BEFORE THE CITY COUNCIL. THE COUNCIL REFUSED TO LEVY A TAX, SO THE SUBSCRIPTION PLAN WAS USED, AND IN 1912, A LIBRARY TAX WAS LEVIED AND A LIBRARY BOARD WAS APPOINTED. IN JULY, 1911 THE WOMEN OF WINCHESTER OPENED A SMALL READING ROOM IN A HOUSE ON FRANKLIN STREET, AND MANAGED A CIRCULATING LIBRARY, WHICH, IN TIME, WAS TURNED OVER TO THE PUBLIC LIBRARY BOARD.

EVENTUALLY THE SCHOOL BOARD TOOK UP THE MATTER OF A LIBRARY BUILDING. CARNEGIE FUNDS WERE REQUESTED AND GRANTED IN 1915, DESPITE SOME LOCAL OPPOSITION. A LOT AT NORTH AND EAST STREETS THAT BELONGED TO THE SCHOOL BOARD WAS SELECTED AS THE BUILDING SITE. ELMER E. DUNLAP WAS CHOSEN AS THE ARCHITECT AND THE GENERAL CONTRACT WENT TO OTIS W. WILLIAMS. THE ORIGINAL BUILDING COST $12,000. ON FEBRUARY 21, 1916 THE NEW CARNEGIE LIBRARY WAS OPENED. THE LIBRARY WAS DEDICATED ON MARCH 15, 1916 WITH AN OPEN HOUSE RECEPTION PRESIDED OVER BY MISS MARY DIGGS, LIBRARIAN.

THE CARNEGIE LIBRARY BUILDING WAS REMODELED IN 1977 AND 1993. A NEW ADJOINING BUILDING OF 16,000 SQUARE FEET WAS CONSTRUCTED IN THE EARLY 1990S. THE COLLECTION WAS MOVED TO THE NEW BUILDING, AND THE CARNEGIE STRUCTURE IS NOW USED AS PUBLIC MEETING ROOMS WITH STORAGE IN THE LOWER LEVEL.

GIFT: $12,000; APRIL 23, 1915
DEDICATION: MARCH 15, 1916
ARCHITECT: ELMER E. DUNLAP, INDIANAPOLIS
CONTRACTOR: OTIS W. WILLIAMS
STYLE: NEO CLASSICAL REVIVAL

"Worthington-Jefferson Township Public Library, Foyer, Fanlight"

WORTHINGTON

WORTHINGTON-JEFFERSON TOWNSHIP PUBLIC LIBRARY

EXCERPTS FROM THE *"HISTORY OF THE WORTHINGTON PUBLIC LIBRARY,"* PAPER BY ALICE WILLS, LIBRARIAN, 1931:

"THE WORTHINGTON PUBLIC LIBRARY WAS ORGANIZED IN 1912 BY POPULAR SUBSCRIPTION TO THOSE WHO LIVED IN TOWN AND JEFFERSON TOWNSHIP. THE LIBRARY CAMPAIGN BEGAN WITH A PUBLIC MEETING THAT WAS ADDRESSED BY THE SECRETARY OF THE PUBLIC LIBRARY COMMISSION. THE LIBRARY BOARD WAS ORGANIZED JULY 26, 1912 WITH SEVEN MEMBERS. THE FIRST WEEK IN JUNE, 1913 WAS SET ASIDE FOR A BOOK SHOWER TO BUILD THE COLLECTION AND BY JUNE, 1915 THERE WERE 926 BOOKS LOANED FROM A BRICK BUILDING DOWNTOWN.

ON OCTOBER 7, 1916 THE LIBRARY BOARD APPOINTED A COMMITTEE TO SOLICIT FUNDS TO PAY FOR THE LOT NEAR THE HADDEN HOTEL UPON WHICH THE CARNEGIE LIBRARY BUILDING WAS TO BE ERECTED. ON APRIL 10, 1917 CARNEGIE GRANTED $10,000 FOR THE BUILDING AND THE CONTRACT WAS LET SEPTEMBER 4, 1917 TO JAMES M. DYER AND SON OF WORTHINGTON. THE CORNERSTONE WAS LAID WITH CEREMONY OCTOBER 5, 1917. THE CONTRACTORS WORKED UNDER THE DISADVANTAGES OF A LATE START AND AN EARLY AND SEVERE WINTER.

IN THE SPRING OF 1918, WITH THE HELP OF THE TRAINING CLASS AND THE WOLF PATROL OF THE BOY SCOUTS, THE LIBRARY WAS MOVED INTO THE NEW BUILDING. THE FOLLOWING WAS SAID OF THE SCOUTS, IN A 1918 COPY OF THE *WORTHINGTON TIMES*, 'THE BOY SCOUTS CAME, WITH CARTS AND WHEELBARROWS, AND HAULED THE 3,000 VOLUMES. THEY DID THEIR WORK WITH PERFECT WILLINGNESS AND GREAT CARE'."

A RENOVATION OF THE CARNEGIE BUILDING AND A NEW ADDITION WERE COMPLETED IN 2002 AND DEDICATED IN 2003.

GIFT: $10,000; APRIL 3, 1917
DEDICATION: APRIL 1, 1918
ARCHITECT: WILSON B. PARKER, INDIANAPOLIS
CONTRACTOR: JAMES M. DYER & SON, WORTHINGTON
STYLE: CRAFTSMAN-PRAIRIE TRADITION

Carnegie Altered

Service In Another Capacity

"Noble County Government Annex, Exposed South Façade"

ALBION

NOBLE COUNTY GOVERNMENT ANNEX

EXCERPTS FROM *"A HISTORY OF THE NOBLE COUNTY PUBLIC LIBRARY"* FILE:

"ALBION'S QUEST FOR A LIBRARY BEGAN WITH TWO LADIES, A SUBSCRIPTION LIST, AND A CHICKEN PIE SUPPER. THE FIRST LIBRARY OPENED SEPTEMBER 2, 1914 IN THE LAW OFFICE OF JUDGE WRIGLEY. LATER THAT YEAR, THE LIBRARY WAS MOVED TWO MORE TIMES, FINALLY RESIDING IN ROOMS OVER THE ALBION NATIONAL BANK.

RECEIVING NOTICE FROM THE CARNEGIE CORPORATION IN FEBRUARY, 1916 THAT THEY WOULD BE AWARDED A $10,000 GRANT, THE LIBRARY BOARD PURCHASED LAND ON THE COURTHOUSE SQUARE FROM JUDGE WRIGLEY. THE CARNEGIE CORPORATION APPROVED THE ARCHITECT'S PLANS, AND IN JANUARY 1917, THE BOARD ACCEPTED THE BID OF $9,950 TO BUILD THE LIBRARY.

IN JUNE, 1917 THE LAYING OF THE CORNERSTONE WAS ACCOMPANIED BY IMPRESSIVE CERE-MONIES. A COPPER BOX CONTAINING A HISTORY OF THE ALBION LIBRARY AND OTHER MEMENTOS WAS PLACED INSIDE THE CORNERSTONE (REOPENED 1996 DURING ABANDONMENT AND RENOVA-TION). THE LIBRARY WAS DEDICATED IN MAY OF 1918. THE BOOKS WERE MOVED FROM THE ALBION NATIONAL BANK BUILDING AND A NEW LIBRARIAN, MISS LUTIE EARL, WAS HIRED."

THE 1918 ALBION PUBLIC LIBRARY THAT WAS BUILT WITH CARNEGIE MONIES WAS SOLD TO THE NOBLE COUNTY COMMISSIONERS IN 1995. THE CARNEGIE BUILDING WAS CONVERTED INTO A NOBLE COUNTY GOVERNMENT OFFICE ANNEX. THE BUILDING WAS NEARLY ENCLOSED BY ADDITION AND RENOVATION ON THE EAST AND WEST WALLS, LEAVING A SPACIOUS OPEN INTERIOR. THE MOD-ERN NOBLE COUNTY PUBLIC LIBRARY, LOCATED AT THE SUBURBAN EAST EDGE OF THE COMMUNI-TY, CURRENTLY SERVES ALBION AND AREAS OF NOBLE COUNTY.

GIFT: $10,000; JANUARY 28, 1916
DEDICATION: JUNE 2, 1918
ARCHITECT: GRANT C. MILLER, CHICAGO, ILL.
CONTRACTOR: JOHN & DON GATWOOD
STYLE: CRAFTSMAN-PRAIRIE TRADITION
CURRENT USE: NOBLE COUNTY GOVERNMENT ANNEX

"Anderson Fine Arts Center, Main Entrance, Relief Sculpture, Lion's Head"

ANDERSON

ANDERSON FINE ARTS CENTER

THE FIRST CIRCULATING LIBRARY IN ANDERSON WAS OPERATED BY A FEW PRIVATE CITIZENS AND WAS FOUNDED IN 1881. IN 1894, THE PUBLIC LIBRARY OF ANDERSON WAS OPENED WITH ABOUT 1,000 VOLUMES, OBTAINED MOSTLY FROM THE Y. M. C. A., AND THE SUBSCRIPTION LIBRARY. ONE ROOM OVER A STORE BUILDING WAS THE LIBRARY'S FIRST HOME; LATER TWO LARGER ROOMS WERE SECURED, AND THE MASONIC TEMPLE LATER FURNISHED QUARTERS.

CONSTRUCTION ON THE CARNEGIE BUILDING, WHICH SERVED ANDERSON UNTIL 1987, BEGAN IN 1902 AND WAS COMPLETED IN 1905. IN 1902, M. M. DUNLAP, THE MAYOR OF ANDERSON, HAD WRITTEN TO MR. CARNEGIE REQUESTING FUNDS FOR A LIBRARY. MR. CARNEGIE RESPONDED WITH A GRANT OF $50,000. THE COMMON COUNCIL GAVE ANDERSON A VALUABLE LOT IN THE HEART OF ANDERSON, UPON WHICH TO ERECT THE EDIFICE.

ARCHITECTS RICHARDS, MCCARTY, AND BULFORD DESIGNED A NEOCLASSICAL STYLED BUILDING THAT THE LOCAL CONTRACTORS, THOMPSON AND MILLSPAUGH, BUILT. THE MOST DYNAMIC FEATURE OF THE BUILDING IS THE 23-FOOT DIAMETER STAINED GLASS DOME THAT RISES 40 FEET ABOVE THE FLOOR. THE WREATH AND GARLAND DESIGNS INCLUDED IN THE STAINED GLASS DOME ARE REPEATED THROUGHOUT THE STRUCTURE.

FROM 1987 TO 1996, THE ANDERSON CARNEGIE LIBRARY SAT EMPTY AFTER THE LIBRARY MOVED TO ITS CURRENT LOCATION AT 12TH AND MAIN. THE ANDERSON FINE ARTS CENTER ACQUIRED THE BUILDING FROM THE CITY AND BEGAN FUND RAISING AND RESTORATION IN THE FALL OF 1996. A GRAND OPENING CELEBRATION AND DEDICATION FOR THE $2 MILLION DOLLAR RESTORATION WAS HELD IN MAY, 1998. THE CARNEGIE BUILDING WAS PLACED ON THE NATIONAL REGISTER OF HISTORIC PLACES IN 1985.

GIFT: $50,000; APRIL 11, 1902
DEDICATION: APRIL 20, 1905
ARCHITECT: RICHARDS, MCCARTY & BULFORD, COLUMBUS, OHIO
CONTRACTOR: THOMPSON & MILLSPAUGH, ANDERSON
STYLE: BEAUX ARTS-NEO CLASSICAL
CURRENT USE: FINE ARTS CENTER

"Monroe County Historical Society, Museum, Interior, Main Floor Gallery"

BLOOMINGTON

MONROE COUNTY HISTORICAL SOCIETY

EXCERPTS FROM *"NOTES ABOUT THE CARNEGIE IN THE YEAR 2000,"* PAPER BY THE LATE DAVID BUCOVE, FORMER DIRECTOR, MONROE COUNTY PUBLIC LIBRARY:

"THE MONROE COUNTY LIBRARY HAD ITS ORIGIN IN 1818. A ONE-STORY BRICK BUILDING, ERECTED DIRECTLY EAST OF THE COURTHOUSE DURING THE 1820S, WAS THE HOME OF THE COUNTY LIBRARY UNTIL 1894 WHEN, IT WAS COMBINED IN THE CENTRAL SCHOOL BUILDING WITH THE PUBLIC SCHOOL LIBRARY. FROM 1894 TO 1909, THE TWO LIBRARIES WERE KEPT IN A ROOM IN THE CENTRAL SCHOOL BUILDING. THE SOROSIS CLUB, A LOCAL WOMAN'S GROUP, HAD TRIED TO OBTAIN FUNDS FROM ANDREW CARNEGIE FOR A NEW LIBRARY BUILDING AS EARLY AS 1897. THE NINETEENTH CENTURY CLUB CONTINUED THE LIBRARY EFFORT AND HELPED REESTABLISH THE LIBRARY IN A ROOM IN THE NEW COURTHOUSE IN 1909.

ANDREW CARNEGIE PLEDGED $31,000 IN 1915. THE CARNEGIE LIBRARY WAS BUILT ON A LOT PURCHASED FROM THE CITY SCHOOLS FOR $12,000. THE BUILDING WAS COMPLETED AND DEDICATED ON FEBRUARY 1, 1918. CONSTRUCTED OF SOLID LIMESTONE, THE LIBRARY BUILDING IS A REMINDER OF THE REGIONAL IMPORTANCE OF INDIANA LIMESTONE AS A BUILDING MATERIAL.

IN 1970, THE LIBRARY WAS MOVED A BLOCK EAST TO A NEW BUILDING AND AFTER 52 YEARS OF USE, THE CARNEGIE BUILDING WAS NO LONGER A LIBRARY BUILDING. ON OCTOBER 10, 1973 THE CARNEGIE BUILDING WAS DETERMINED BY THE DEPARTMENT OF INTERIOR TO BE ELIGIBLE FOR THE NATIONAL REGISTER FOR HISTORIC PLACES. THE OWNERSHIP IS NOW IN THE HANDS OF THE MONROE COUNTY HISTORICAL SOCIETY. A MATCHING ADDITION OF BEDFORD LIMESTONE WAS CONSTRUCTED AND COMPLETED IN 2000."

GIFT: $31,000; OCTOBER 21, 1915
DEDICATION: FEBRUARY 1, 1918
ARCHITECT: WILSON B. PARKER, INDIANAPOLIS
CONTRACTOR: GEORGE A. WEAVER & SON, INDIANAPOLIS
STYLE: NEO CLASSICAL REVIVAL
CURRENT USE: MUSEUM, ARCHIVES, GIFT SHOP & OFFICES

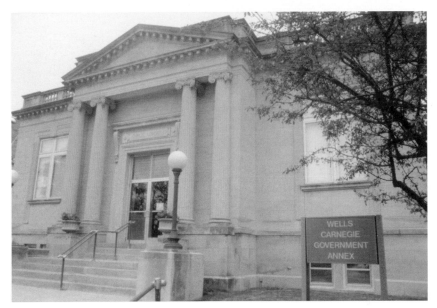

"Wells Carnegie Government Annex, Façade"

BLUFFTON

WELLS CARNEGIE GOVERNMENT ANNEX

BEFORE 1893, THERE WAS JUST THE SEMBLANCE OF A LIBRARY IN BLUFFTON, THE BOOKS HAV-ING BEEN DONATED BY CHILDREN AND A FEW ADULTS. A COUNTY LIBRARY FUND WAS ESTABLISHED IN 1817, THE YEAR WELLS COUNTY WAS FOUNDED. THE FIRST LIBRARY WAS ORGANIZED BY COUN-TY OFFICIALS IN BLUFFTON IN 1853. IN 1855, BLUFFTON RECEIVED FUNDS FROM THE ESTATE OF WILLIAM MACLURE OF NEW HARMONY TO PURCHASE BOOKS. FROM 1881 TO 1902, THE BLUFFTON PUBLIC LIBRARY WAS HOUSED IN THE BLUFFTON HIGH SCHOOL.

IN 1892, THE BLUFFTON COMMUNITY AUTHORIZED A SMALL LIBRARY TAX AND A SEVEN-MEM-BER BOARD WAS SELECTED. THE LIBRARY WAS MOVED FROM THE HIGH SCHOOL TO THE BASEMENT OF THE COUNTY COURTHOUSE. ANDREW CARNEGIE FUNDS WERE APPLIED FOR, AND IN JANUARY, 1903, $13,000 WAS GRANTED BY THE CARNEGIE FOUNDATION. THE CONSTRUCTION OF THE CARNEGIE LIBRARY BUILDING BEGAN EARLY IN MARCH, 1904. THE BUILDING WAS OPENED TO THE PUBLIC MAY 15, 1905.

DURING THE 1960S, A TWO-FLOOR ADDITION WAS MADE TO THE REAR OF THE ORIGINAL BUILD-ING, DOUBLING THE SIZE OF THE LIBRARY. THE BUILDING'S LAST DAY OF OPERATION AS A PUBLIC LIBRARY WAS SEPTEMBER 6, 1991. THE BUILDING WAS THEN RENOVATED AND REOPENED AS A WELLS COUNTY COURTHOUSE ANNEX. A NEW LIBRARY WAS CONSTRUCTED DIRECTLY SOUTH, ACROSS WASHINGTON STREET.

GIFT: $13,000; JANUARY 13, 1903
DEDICATION: MAY 15, 1905
ARCHITECT: CUNO KIBELE, BLUFFTON
CONTRACTOR: ILLINGSWORTH & COMPANY
STYLE: NEO CLASSICAL REVIVAL
CURRENT USE: WELLS COUNTY COURTHOUSE ANNEX

"Boonville City Police Headquarters, Facade"

BOONVILLE

BOONVILLE CITY POLICE HEADQUARTERS

IN 1911, THE FIRST ATTEMPT AT STARTING A LIBRARY IN BOONVILLE WAS MADE. THE WOMEN'S CLUB OF BOONVILLE, WHICH WAS NEWLY FOUNDED, DECIDED TO OPEN A MEETING ROOM IN THE MATTHEWSON OPERA HOUSE. THE BOONVILLE WOMEN'S CLUB ORGANIZED THE FUNDING FOR THE NEW LIBRARY AND RAISED $4,000. HOWEVER, THE AMOUNT RAISED WAS NOT ENOUGH AND THEY TURNED TO ANDREW CARNEGIE FOR ADDITIONAL FUNDING. ON NOVEMBER 3, 1913, THE COMMUNITY OF BOONVILLE RECEIVED $12,000 FROM THE CARNEGIE FOUNDATION.

THE T. D. SCALES CORNER LOT, LOCATED AT FOURTH AND LOCUST STREETS WAS SECURED AS A SITE FOR THE NEW LIBRARY BUILDING AT A COST OF $4,000. AFTER NEARLY TWO YEARS, THE LIBRARY WAS COMPLETED AND THE DEDICATION WAS HELD ON THE EVENING OF SEPTEMBER 14, 1915, A SPECIAL INVITATION BEING SENT OUT TO BOONVILLE'S CHILDREN. THE EXTERIOR OF THE COMMODIOUS 64' x 34' FOOT BUILDING WAS MADE OF DARK VITRIFIED BRICK WITH BEDFORD STONE TRIMMINGS. THE STRUCTURE REFLECTS THE ENGLISH TUDOR PERIOD OF THE LATE 15TH AND EARLY 16TH CENTURIES. THE INTERIOR WAS FURNISHED WITH LIBRARY BUREAU FURNITURE. MRS. ANNA ISLEY WAS THE FIRST LIBRARIAN.

THE CARNEGIE BUILDING SERVED AS A LIBRARY FROM 1915 UNTIL 1986 WHEN THE COLLECTION OUTGREW THE LIMITED SPACE AND THE NEW BOONVILLE-WARRICK COUNTY PUBLIC LIBRARY WAS BUILT. THE ORIGINAL CARNEGIE LIBRARY BUILDING NOW SERVES AS THE HEADQUARTERS FOR THE BOONVILLE CITY POLICE.

GIFT: $12,000; NOVEMBER 3, 1913
DEDICATION: SEPTEMBER 14, 1915
ARCHITECT: CLIFFORD SHOPBELL, EVANSVILLE
CONTRACTOR: ROTH CONSTRUCTION COMPANY
STYLE: TUDOR GOTHIC-JACOBEAN REVIVAL
CURRENT USE: BOONVILLE CITY POLICE HEADQUARTERS

"Brownsburg Chamber of Commerce, Façade"

BROWNSBURG

BROWNSBURG CHAMBER OF COMMERCE

EXCERPTS FROM *THE VILLAGE OF BROWNSBURG* BY PEG KENNEDY AND FRANKIE KONOVSEK, PAGES 149-150, LAMPLIGHT PUBLISHING, ROBINSON, ILLINOIS, 1979:

"SYLVESTER MOORE, BROWNSBURG SUPERINTENDENT OF SCHOOLS, AND HIS WIFE ANNA REALIZED THE NEED FOR A LOCAL PUBLIC LIBRARY IN 1916. A PLAN WAS CONCEIVED WITH HELP FROM THE STATE SECRETARY OF THE LIBRARY COMMISSION AND BY VISITING THE CARNEGIE-BUILT, COATESVILLE PUBLIC LIBRARY. A WRITTEN APPEAL WAS MADE TO ANDREW CARNEGIE TO FUND THE BROWNSBURG PUBLIC LIBRARY. ONCE THE LEGAL REQUIREMENTS WERE MET, THE CARNEGIE FOUNDATION MADE A GIFT OF $12,500 ON APRIL 12, 1917 THAT WAS ACCEPTED.

THE LOT AT 104 EAST MAIN WAS PURCHASED FROM S. S. TALBERT FOR $3,500. DESPITE THE WAR, THE BUILDING WENT UP QUICKLY. NORMAN HADEN HILL WAS SELECTED AS THE ARCHITECT IN MAY, 1917, AND J. F. HEINZMANN WAS GIVEN THE BUILDING CONTRACT. ON SEPTEMBER 18, 1917, SCHOOL WAS DISMISSED FOR THE LAYING OF THE CORNERSTONE. BY THE SPRING OF 1918 THE BUILDING WAS NEARING COMPLETION AND THE DEDICATION TOOK PLACE JUNE 14, 1918."

THE TOWN OUTGREW THE CARNEGIE LIBRARY AND A NEW BUILDING WAS CONSTRUCTED IN 1979 AT 450 SOUTH JEFFERSON STREET. IN 1983, THE CARNEGIE LIBRARY WAS UTILIZED BY THE BROWNSBURG POLICE DEPARTMENT BUT TODAY THE CHAMBER OF COMMERCE OCCUPIES THE BUILDING.

GIFT: $12,500; APRIL 12, 1917
DEDICATION: JUNE 14, 1918
ARCHITECT: NORMAN H. HILL, INDIANAPOLIS
CONTRACTOR: J. F. HEINZMANN
STYLE: CRAFTSMAN-PRAIRIE TRADITION
CURRENT USE: BROWNSBURG CHAMBER OF COMMERCE

"DeKalb County Historical Society, Butler, Front Entrance"

BUTLER

DeKalb County Historical Society

Excerpts from *"The History of the Butler Carnegie Public Library"* file:

"The Ladies Cultural Club of Butler first realized the need of a public library and undertook to organize one in the year 1905. To start the library, books and magazines were contributed by the people of Butler. The library board consisted of nearly 20 members instead of the usual seven members. For almost ten years the library struggled on in this way of little funding.

After Mrs. F. L. Kiplinger attended the laying of the cornerstone of a Carnegie Library in neighboring Waterloo, Indiana, she was asked to take steps to secure a Carnegie library for the city of Butler. After some correspondence with the Carnegie Corporation, matters progressed rapidly. The newly selected, seven member library board then presented their request to the Carnegie Corporation and in a short time received a check for $10,000. The site where the library was built was donated from the landlord as a memorial to his daughter. The building was erected in 1914-1915. The Butler Carnegie Public Library was dedicated May 31, 1915.

During the 1990s, the library board decided that due to the issues of an aging building, handicap accessibility, parking and a landlocked structure with no room to grow, the library building was to be abandoned and the library moved to the former Butler Fraternal Order of the Eagles building. Proceedings began to transfer ownership over to the DeKalb County Historical Society, Inc. with the provisions that no major changes be made, and that it become a county museum."

Gift: $10,000; December 8, 1913
Dedication: May 31, 1915
Architect: Cosmo Ellwood, Elkhart
Contractor: J. C. Bontranger, Elkhart
Style: Craftsman-Prairie Tradition
Current Use: Museum, Archives & Offices

"Ye Olde Library Restaurant & Woody's Place, Carmel, Facade"

CARMEL

YE OLDE LIBRARY RESTAURANT & WOODY'S PLACE

In 1896, the Wednesday Literary Club was formed to satisfy its members "thirst for knowledge and self improvement." The first Carmel library was located at the Carmel Telephone Exchange. The telephone operators, acting as librarians, kept track of checked out and returned books.

The Wednesday Literary Club applied for funding from the Carnegie Corporation but negotiations were slow. In March of 1913, a gift of $11,000 was received by the Carmel library board from the Carnegie Corporation. A site committee located the best possible land and bought the site at 40 East Main Street from Edgar and Orvilla Small. Notice to the contractors was published in the *Carmel Standard* newspaper on August 22, 1913. Contracts were let and the building duly started. The 45' x 60' foot building was made of yellow, tan, and brown brick on the exterior. The first board meeting in the new building took place on May 26, 1914, and the library was open to the public on June 6, 1914.

In 1971 the Carmel Carnegie Public Library was sold to the Town of Carmel for town hall offices and a new library was constructed. In 1980, the renovated building was added to the Indiana Register of Historic Sites and Structures and the National Register of Historic Places. In 1998, the building was sold again, this time for use as a commercial restaurant and bar.

Gift: $11,000; March 14, 1913
Dedication: June 6, 1914
Architect: Austin Bond, Carmel
Contractor: Red Masten, Carmel
Style: Craftsman-Prairie Tradition
Current Use: Commercial Restaurant & Bar

"Adams County Circuit Court, Decatur, Book Shelves & Column"

DECATUR

ADAMS COUNTY CIRCUIT COURT

EXCERPTS FROM THE *"DECATUR PUBLIC LIBRARY 1905-1980"* BOOKLET:

"THE DECATUR PUBLIC LIBRARY HAD ITS START IN JULY, 1904 WITH THE APPOINTMENT OF A LIBRARY BOARD. THE PRESIDENT OF THE LIBRARY BOARD WAS AUTHORIZED TO COMMUNICATE WITH ANDREW CARNEGIE TO NOTIFY HIM, 'THAT THE DECATUR PUBLIC LIBRARY BOARD HAD BEEN APPOINTED AND REGULARLY ORGANIZED AND THE INITIAL STEPS TAKEN AS REQUIRED IN MR. CARNEGIE'S PROPOSITION TO MAKE A DONATION TO THE ENTERPRISE.'

MR. CARNEGIE'S PROPOSED GIFT OF $10,000 WAS FOUND TO BE INADEQUATE, AND, ON PETITION, RAISED THIS TO $12,000 IF THE CITY COUNCIL WOULD PLEDGE $1,200 A YEAR. THIS WAS DONE AND THE PROJECT OF THE NEW BUILDING COULD PROCEED, WITH OSCAR HOFFMANN AS ARCHITECT.

LOT 97 ON THIRD STREET WAS PURCHASED BY DONATIONS AND MORTGAGE AND THE LAND CLEARED FOR A LIBRARY BUILDING. THE NEW BUILDING WAS BUILT IN 1905 AND DEDICATED JULY, 1906. THE TOTAL COST OF THE PROJECT AMOUNTED TO $15,490.03, AND MISS ANNETTA MOSES WAS HIRED AS THE FIRST LIBRARIAN AT $30 A MONTH.

THE LIBRARY WAS RENOVATED IN 1958 AND THE ENTIRE BUILDING WAS UTILIZED FOR LIBRARY SERVICES. SOON DEMAND AGAIN OUTSTRIPPED FACILITY AND IT WAS FINALLY DECIDED TO BUILD A NEW LIBRARY, ADJACENT TO THE SOUTH OF THE ORIGINAL CARNEGIE LIBRARY WHICH OPENED IN 1980."

GIFT: $12,000; MARCH 8, 1904
DEDICATION: JULY 19, 1906
ARCHITECT: OSCAR HOFFMANN
CONTRACTOR: MANN & CHRISTEN
STYLE: NEO CLASSICAL REVIVAL
CURRENT USE: ADAMS COUNTY CIRCUIT COURT

"Abandoned Indiana Harbor Branch, East Chicago, Facade"

EAST CHICAGO

EAST CHICAGO PUBLIC LIBRARY, INDIANA HARBOR BRANCH

ABANDONED, TRANSITION TO DANCE ACADEMY

EXCERPTS FROM THE *EAST CHICAGO, INDIANA* MAGAZINE, *"THE EAST CHICAGO PUBLIC LIBRARY: ITS HISTORY AND GROWTH,"* ARTICLE BY FRANK H. WHITMORE, MAIN LIBRARIAN, AUGUST, 1926, PAGES 213 & 257.

"THE MOVEMENT TO ESTABLISH A LIBRARY STARTED IN 1908 WITH THE EFFORTS OF MRS. JOHN KENNEDY, THEN PRESIDENT OF THE TUESDAY READING CLUB WHICH LATER BECAME THE EAST CHICAGO WOMAN'S CLUB. THE ORGANIZATION OF THE LIBRARY BOARD TOOK PLACE ON SEPTEMBER 16, 1909. THE LIBRARY IN THE INDIANA HARBOR SECTION WAS OPENED FOR CIRCULATION OVER THE FIRE STATION.

PLANS LOOKING TO THE CONSTRUCTION OF LIBRARY BUILDINGS WERE DISCUSSED ON DECEMBER 6, 1910. MR. ANDREW CARNEGIE GAVE A GENEROUS GIFT OF $40,000, JANUARY 31, 1911, THAT WAS EXPENDED FOR THE CONSTRUCTION OF THE INDIANA BRANCH AT THE CORNER OF 136TH STREET AND GRAPEVINE, NOW GRAND BOULEVARD, AND THE BARING AVENUE BRANCH [NOW CALLED THE PASTRICK BRANCH] AT THE INTERSECTION OF BARING AND CHICAGO AVENUES. BOTH LIBRARY BRANCHES WERE DEDICATED MAY, 1913."

THE INDIANA HARBOR BRANCH CLOSED ON OCTOBER 8, 1983 AND SUBSEQUENTLY WAS PUR-CHASED BY A PRIVATE PARTY. DUE TO THE BUILDING'S PHYSICAL DECLINE, IT WAS NEARLY DEMOL-ISHED; HOWEVER, A COMMUNITY DANCE ACADEMY IS IN THE PROCESS OF OCCUPYING THE SOON-TO-BE-RESTORED STRUCTURE.

GIFT: $20,000; JANUARY 31, 1911
DEDICATION: MAY 17, 1913
ARCHITECT: ARGYLE E. ROBINSON, CHICAGO, ILL.
CONTRACTOR: UNLOCATED
STYLE: CRAFTSMAN-PRAIRIE TRADITION
CURRENT USE: ABANDONED, TRANSITION TO COMMUNITY DANCE ACADEMY

"Privately Owned, Former Elwood Carnegie Library, Facade"

ELWOOD

PRIVATE OWNER

EXCERPTS FROM THE *"ELWOOD PUBLIC LIBRARY: ONE HUNDRED YEARS OF SERVICE 1898-1998,"* CENTENNIAL CELEBRATION, OCTOBER 17, 1998, COMPILED BY LORETTA DODD, INDIANA ROOM DIRECTOR:

"ON AUGUST 27, 1901 A REQUEST WAS SENT TO ANDREW CARNEGIE AT HIS SCOTTISH HOME, SKIBO CASTLE, SCOTLAND. A RESPONSE CAME FROM JAMES BERTRAM, CARNEGIE'S PERSONAL SECRETARY ON OCTOBER 4, 1901 REPORTING THAT MR. CARNEGIE WOULD PROVIDE $25,000 FOR A FREE PUBLIC LIBRARY FOR ELWOOD. IN SPITE OF SOME OPPOSITION FROM THE LABOR UNIONS, THE CARNEGIE OFFER WAS ACCEPTED.

A BUILDING SITE WAS LOCATED AT NORTH A AND 16TH STREET AND PURCHASED APRIL 17, 1902 AND CONSTRUCTION BEGAN IN 1903. IN JULY 1903, MRS. F. L. SAYLOR WAS INSTRUCTED TO MAKE AN APPEAL TO MR. CARNEGIE FOR AN EXTRA $5,000 TO COMPLETE THE BUILDING AND FUR-NISHINGS. CARNEGIE AGREED AGAIN PROVIDED THAT THE CITY OF ELWOOD WOULD INCREASE THE ANNUAL TAX LEVY TO $3,000. THE COUNCIL APPROVED. ON JUNE 1, 1904, THE NEW CARNEGIE BUILDING WAS DEDICATED FOR THE SO DESCRIBED, 'MARVEL OF BEAUTY.' THE ADDRESS WAS DELIVERED BY DR. WILLIAM LOWE BRYAN, PRESIDENT OF INDIANA UNIVERSITY.

THE CARNEGIE BUILDING HAD BECOME OBSOLETE OVER TIME. THE GROUNDBREAKING FOR THE NEW LIBRARY WAS HELD ON NOVEMBER 1, 1995 AT 1600 MAIN STREET, ACROSS FROM THE ELWOOD CARNEGIE LIBRARY BUILDING THAT WAS TO BE ABANDONED AND SOLD. ON JANUARY 12, 1997, THE NEW ELWOOD PUBLIC LIBRARY OPENED WITH A FORMAL DEDICATION."

RECENTLY THE CARNEGIE BUILDING WAS SOLD TO A PRIVATE PARTY.

GIFT: $30,000; OCTOBER 3, 1901
DEDICATION: JUNE 1, 1904
ARCHITECT: JAEKEL & LAYCOCK, INDIANAPOLIS
CONTRACTOR: UNLOCATED
STYLE: NEO CLASSICAL REVIVAL
CURRENT USE: PRIVATE OWNER

"Fortville Youth Center, Façade"

FORTVILLE

FORTVILLE YOUTH CENTER

IN 1914 A SMALL GROUP OF CITIZENS IN FORTVILLE HAD THE IDEA OF FORMING A PUBLIC LIBRARY. AFTER LEARNING ABOUT THE CARNEGIE FOUNDATION CORPORATION, IT WAS DECIDED TO COMMUNICATE WITH THE CORPORATION BEGINNING ON JANUARY 16, 1916. A LIBRARY BOARD WAS ORGANIZED IN SEPTEMBER, 1916. THE SELECTED SITE HAD HOUSES THAT HAD TO BE REMOVED TO ACCOMMODATE THE LIBRARY BUILDING. CONSTRUCTION OF THE BUILDING WAS STARTED SEPTEMBER 4, 1917. THE FORTVILLE CARNEGIE LIBRARY WAS OPENED TO THE PUBLIC ON JULY 3, 1918, AND THE DEDICATION WAS HELD SATURDAY AUGUST 10, 1918.

AFTER A NEW LIBRARY WAS BUILT IN THE LATE 1980S, THE CARNEGIE BUILDING WAS PURCHASE BY A PRIVATE PARTY WHO ESTABLISHED A PHOTOGRAPHY BUSINESS AND REMODELED INTO AN APARTMENT. THE BUILDING WAS PURCHASED IN THE MID-1990S AS A MEETING PLACE FOR A YOUTH GROUP FROM THE LOCAL METHODIST CHURCH AND ALSO AS A MEETING ROOM FOR THE CUB SCOUTS AND BOY SCOUTS.

GIFT: $10,000; MARCH 31, 1916
DEDICATION: AUGUST 10, 1918
ARCHITECT: ERNEST FAUSSETT, FORTVILLE
CONTRACTOR: MR. SIDES, INDIANAPOLIS
STYLE: CRAFTSMAN-PRAIRIE TRADITION
CURRENT USE: FORTVILLE YOUTH CENTER

"Franklin, Condominiums, Façade"

FRANKLIN

CONDOMINIUMS

EXCERPTS FROM THE PROGRAM DEDICATION, OPEN HOUSE ADDITION, *"BRIEF HISTORY OF THE LIBRARY,"* OCTOBER 25, 1964:

"BEFORE THE MIDDLE OF THE 19TH CENTURY, THE COUNTY LIBRARY HAD PASSED OUT OF EXISTENCE. TOWNSHIP LIBRARIES WERE ESTABLISHED AFTER 1852 AND FOR THE NEXT 50 YEARS AFFORDED THE COMMUNITY WITH THE BEST READING OPPORTUNITIES. IN 1882, FRANKLIN RECEIVED $500 FROM PHILANTHROPIST, ROBERT MACLURE, FOR THE PURCHASE OF BOOKS FOR A READING ROOM. THE YOUNG PEOPLE'S READING CIRCLE WAS INSTITUTED IN 1887.

IN 1911 THE CIVIC-MINDED, CLUB WOMEN OF FRANKLIN ORGANIZED THE FIRST FRANKLIN PUBLIC LIBRARY DESPITE TAXPAYER OPPOSITION. A LIBRARY BOARD WAS APPOINTED. A ROOM WAS OPENED IN THE HULSMAN BLOCK, DECEMBER 5, 1911. IN THE NEXT SEVERAL YEARS, SERVICE WAS EXTENDED TO THREE NEARBY TOWNSHIPS ON A CONTRACTUAL BASIS.

THE LIBRARY BOARD APPEALED TO THE CARNEGIE FOUNDATION FOR MONIES TO BUILD A NEW LIBRARY AND A GIFT OF $17,5000 WAS GRANTED APRIL 28, 1913. THE COST OF THE BUILDING SITE WAS $5,000. AFTER THREE YEARS TO THE DAY OF NOTIFICATION OF CARNEGIE'S GIFT AND A TOTAL COST OF $20,000, THE LIBRARY WAS DEDICATED ON APRIL 28, 1916."

A MAJOR ADDITION WAS DEDICATED OCTOBER 25, 1964. TOWNSHIP MERGERS RESULTED IN THE LIBRARY CHANGING ITS NAME FROM TO THE FRANKLIN-JOHNSON COUNTY PUBLIC LIBRARY IN 1977 AND EVENTUALLY TO THE JOHNSON COUNTY PUBLIC LIBRARY IN 1989. A NEW LIBRARY WAS CONSTRUCTED AND THE CARNEGIE ABANDONED. THE CARNEGIE BUILDING WAS SOLD IN 1988 TO A LOCAL DEVELOPER WHO SUBDIVIDED THE BUILDING INTO APARTMENTS.

GIFT: $17,500; APRIL 28, 1913
DEDICATION: APRIL 28, 1916
ARCHITECT: GRAHAM & HILL, INDIANAPOLIS
CONTRACTOR: ROY BRYANT
STYLE: PSEUDO-ITALIAN RENAISSANCE
CURRENT USE: PRIVATE CONDOMINIUMS

"Abandoned Louis J. Bailey Branch, Gary Public Library, Building rear"

GARY

GARY PUBLIC LIBRARY, LOUIS J. BAILEY BRANCH

ABANDONED, TO BE RAZED

THE LIBRARY BRANCH WAS ESTABLISHED IN 1913, BUT BY 1916 THE BRANCH HAD OUTGROWN ITS SCHOOL QUARTERS, THE FROEBEL SCHOOL WANTED TO USE THE SPACE FOR ITS OWN PURPOSES. THE GARY PUBLIC LIBRARY DECIDED TO BUILD ITS OWN BRANCH BUILDING. SOMETIMES CALLED THE FROEBEL SCHOOL BRANCH, AND LATER, WHEN THE CARNEGIE BUILDING WAS CONSTRUCTED ACROSS THE STREET FROM THE SCHOOL, IT WAS RENAMED THE BAILEY BRANCH IN HONOR OF THE GARY PUBLIC LIBRARY'S FIRST LIBRARIAN, LOUIS J. BAILEY.

FOUR LOTS AT 15TH AND MADISON WERE BOUGHT FOR $5,200 FOR THE BUILDING SITE. THE BUILDING WAS CONSTRUCTED OF TAPESTRY BRICK, A DUTCH BOND, AND A QUARRY-SLATE ROOF, AND FUMED OAK TRIM FINISH. IT WAS CONSTRUCTED WITH PALLADIAN WINDOWS ON ITS GABLED ENDS, AND HAD AN IRON FENCE OUT FRONT. INSIDE, THE BRANCH HAD A MAIN READING ROOM ON THE GROUND FLOOR, AND AN AUDITORIUM AND TWO CLUBROOMS IN THE BASEMENT.

THE LIBRARY WAS DEDICATED JANUARY 6, 1918, EVEN THOUGH A BLIZZARD SNOWSTORM CANCELED THE OPENING FESTIVITIES. ADDRESSES WERE SPOKEN IN HUNGARIAN, ITALIAN, AND SLAVIC, AS WELL AS ENGLISH. A COLLECTION SPECIALTY WAS FOREIGN LANGUAGE BOOKS: POLISH, HUNGARIAN, CROATIAN, LITHUANIAN AND ITALIAN. THE BAILEY BRANCH CONCENTRATED ITS ATTENTION ON ACTIVITIES FOR THE LARGE NUMBERS OF FOREIGN BORN IMMIGRANTS RESIDING IN THE SURROUNDING NEIGHBORHOODS DURING ITS EARLY YEARS.

THE BAILEY BRANCH CLOSED ITS DOORS FOR THE FINAL TIME IN 1977, AND, REMAINS ABANDONED TO DATE.

GIFT: $25,000; EARLY 1917
DEDICATION: JANUARY 13, 1918
ARCHITECT: A. F. WICKES, GARY
CONTRACTOR: MARCELLUS GEROMETTA, GARY
STYLE: NEO COLONIAL REVIVAL
CURRENT USE: ABANDONED, TO BE DEMOLISHED

"Goshen City Hall, Façade"

GOSHEN

GOSHEN CITY HALL

EXCERPTS FROM *"THE FIRST HALF CENTURY: GOSHEN CARNEGIE PUBLIC LIBRARY ,"* PAPER BY MERLE SHANKLIN, PRESIDENT OF THE GOSHEN CARNEGIE PUBLIC LIBRARY BOARD, 1951:

"THE IDEA FOR A GOSHEN FREE PUBLIC LIBRARY ORIGINATED WITH THE WOMEN OF THE CITY AND ACTIVELY PROMOTED BY THE WOMEN'S CLUBS, FOREMOST OF WHICH WAS THE BEACON LIGHT. ON FRIDAY, JANUARY 22, 1897, A MEETING WAS HELD IN THE LIBRARY OF THE HIGH SCHOOL FOR THE PURPOSE OF ORGANIZING A LIBRARY ASSOCIATION.

A COMMITTEE WAS SENT TO NEW YORK CITY ON DECEMBER 20, 1900 TO CONFER WITH MR. BERTRAM, SECRETARY TO MR. CARNEGIE. THE JOURNEY BROUGHT NEWS THAT ANDREW CARNEGIE HAD GIVEN GOSHEN $15,000 FOR A LIBRARY BUILDING, AND LATER SECURED AN ADDITIONAL $10,000 FOR A TOTAL OF $25,000. IN 1901, GOSHEN HAD THE DISTINCTION OF HAVING BEEN THE SMALLEST CITY IN THE UNITED STATES TO FIRST RECEIVE A GIFT FROM THE CARNEGIE CORPORATION AND THE FIRST CITY IN INDIANA TO RECEIVE A CARNEGIE GIFT. A LOT WAS PURCHASED FOR $3,200 ON MAY 8, 1901 AND THE LIBRARY WAS CONSTRUCTED IN 1902. THE DEDICATION OCCURRED TWO YEARS AFTER THE DATE OF MR. CARNEGIE'S GIFT TO GOSHEN.

AFTER 64 YEARS OF SERVICE, THE CARNEGIE LIBRARY WAS CONSIDERED INADEQUATE FOR THE GROWING POPULATION. A NEW GOSHEN PUBLIC LIBRARY AT MAIN AND PURL STREETS WAS CONSTRUCTED DURING 1967-1968 AND THE CARNEGIE WAS ABANDONED. THE CARNEGIE LIBRARY WAS RESTORED AND PLACED ON THE NATIONAL REGISTER OF HISTORIC PLACES. AFTER SEVERAL, CARING COMMERCIAL OWNERS, THE CARNEGIE LIBRARY WAS PURCHASED BY THE CITY AND HAS SERVED SINCE OCTOBER, 2001 AS THE GOSHEN CITY HALL."

GIFT: $25,000; JANUARY 15, 1901
DEDICATION: JANUARY 15, 1903
ARCHITECT: PATTON & MILLER, CHICAGO, ILL.
CONTRACTOR: WILLIAM H. MAXWELL, ANGOLA
STYLE: BEAU ARTS CLASSICISM
CURRENT USE: GOSHEN CITY HALL

"Carnegie's Restaurant, Bake House & Deli, Greenfield, Facade"

GREENFIELD

CARNEGIE'S RESTAURANT, BAKE HOUSE & DELI

EXCERPTS FROM THE *"GREENFIELD PUBLIC LIBRARY CELEBRATES 100 YEARS OF SERVICE"* BROCHURE, SUMMER 1998:

"IN 1878, W. H. SIMMS, WHO WAS THEN SUPERINTENDENT OF CITY SCHOOLS, ORGANIZED A LIBRARY. ON NOVEMBER 24, 1879, AN ASSOCIATION WAS FORMED, COMPOSED OF THE MEMBERS OF THE GREENFIELD HIGH SCHOOL. THE OBJECT OF THE ASSOCIATION WAS TO PROCURE MEANS TO ENLARGE THE NEW HIGH SCHOOL LIBRARY.

ON NOVEMBER 5, 1897, A MEETING WAS HELD AT THE NEW HIGH SCHOOL BUILDING FOR THE PURPOSE OF CONSIDERING WAYS AND MEANS OF ESTABLISHING A PUBLIC LIBRARY. IN THE FALL OF 1898, A COMMITTEE WAS APPOINTED TO SELECT BOOKS. THE DOORS WERE THROWN OPEN TO THE PUBLIC, JANUARY 5, 1898. BY 1900, THE HIGH SCHOOL LIBRARY HAD 2,030 BOOKS AND THEY WERE KEPT THERE UNTIL OCTOBER, 1909, WHEN IT WAS MOVED INTO THE NEW CARNEGIE BUILD-ING.

IN 1906 THE HIGH SCHOOL LIBRARY ROOM WAS BECOMING CROWDED. THE SCHOOL BOARD APPLIED TO THE CARNEGIE FOUNDATION FOR FUNDING FOR A NEW LIBRARY. THEY WERE ENTIRELY SUCCESSFUL IN THEIR ENDEAVOR. A GIFT OF $10,000 WAS GRANTED, MARCH 8, 1904. MRS. MELISSA COOPER DONATED THE GROUND FOR THE CARNEGIE BUILDING.

THE CARNEGIE BUILDING OPENED SEPTEMBER, 1909, AND REMAINED THE PUBLIC LIBRARY UNTIL APRIL 1, 1985, WHEN THE LIBRARY WAS MOVED TO THE PRESENT LOCATION AT 700 NORTH BROADWAY. THE BUILDING WAS SOLD TO COMMERCIAL INTERESTS WHO HAVE ESTABLISHED A RESTAURANT, BAKE HOUSE AND DELI KNOWN AS CARNEGIE'S."

GIFT: $10,000; MARCH 8, 1904
DEDICATION: SEPTEMBER, 1909
ARCHITECT: S. W. GORDON, GREENFIELD
CONTRACTOR: WOLF & EWING
STYLE: NEO CLASSICAL REVIVAL
CURRENT USE: COMMERCIAL RESTAURANT, BAKE HOUSE & DELI

"Greensburg City Hall, Facade"

GREENSBURG

GREENSBURG CITY HALL

EXCERPTS FROM THE *GREENSBURG DAILY NEWS*, SPECIAL SUPPLEMENT, *"LIBRARY'S ANNIVERSARY,"* ARTICLE BY NANCI HELLMICH, JANUARY 25, 1980:

"NEWSPAPER FILES FROM 1857, DISCLOSE THAT THERE WERE TWO LIBRARIES OPEN TO THE PUBLIC IN GREENSBURG. THE MACLURE LIBRARY WAS FREE TO MEMBERS OF THE WORKINGMEN'S INSTITUTE, ONE OF 144 WORKINGMEN'S INSTITUTES ESTABLISHED IN INDIANA. THE SECOND LIBRARY WAS THE TOWNSHIP LIBRARY, FOUNDED IN 1855 BY PROFESSOR LARRABEE. THE 1824 DECATUR COUNTY LIBRARY PRECEDED THE MACLURE AND TOWNSHIP LIBRARIES. THE DEMANDS OF THE CIVIL WAR ENDED THE GREENSBURG PUBLIC LIBRARIES.

IT WAS IN 1901 THAT MAYOR A. M. WILLOUGHBY WROTE A LETTER TO ANDREW CARNEGIE REQUESTING FINANCIAL ASSISTANCE. IN SPRING OF 1902, THE TOWN RECEIVED NEWS THAT CARNEGIE AGREED TO GIVE GREENSBURG $15,000 FOR A NEW LIBRARY. THE TRIANGULAR PLOT WAS PURCHASED FROM W. A. WATSON WHO DONATED $1,000 OF THE PRICE OF $6,000.

ON AUGUST 21, 1903, THE CORNERSTONE WAS LAID. THE ESTIMATED COST WAS $10,725. THE REMAINDER OF CARNEGIE'S $15,000 GIFT WAS USED FOR THE INTERIOR DECORATION AND FURNITURE FOR THE NEW BUILDING. ON JANUARY 24, 1905, THE BUILDING WAS PRESENTED TO THE CITIZENS OF GREENSBURG. THE FOLLOWING DAY THE LIBRARY WAS OPEN FOR THE CIRCULATION OF BOOKS."

AN ADDITION WAS BUILT IN 1965. LATER ON, THE BOOK COLLECTION OUTGREW THE CARNEGIE LIBRARY, AND A NEW LIBRARY WAS CONSTRUCTED ON THE EAST EDGE OF THE CITY AND OCCUPIED IN 1993. THE CARNEGIE LIBRARY BECAME THE NEW LOCATION FOR THE GREENSBURG CITY HALL.

GIFT: $15,000; MARCH 14, 1902
DEDICATION: JANUARY 24, 1905
ARCHITECT: HARRIS & SHOPBELL, EVANSVILLE
CONTRACTOR: PULSE & PORTER, GREENSBURG
STYLE: NEO CLASSICAL REVIVAL
CURRENT USE: GREENSBURG CITY HALL

"Hobart Historical Society, Facade"

HOBART

HOBART HISTORICAL SOCIETY

EXCERPTS FROM THE UNIVERSITY OF ILLINOIS LIBRARY SCHOOL, LIBRARY SCIENCE 92, *"LIBRARY SERVICE FOR THE HOBART COMMUNITY,"* TERM PAPER BY HELEN L. NORRIS, MAY, 1945:

"AS PART OF THE GARY PUBLIC LIBRARY'S EXTENSION OF SERVICE, A BRANCH OF THE GARY PUBLIC LIBRARY WAS ESTABLISHED IN HOBART IN 1914. MRS. FANNIE A. WERNER OF THE WOMEN'S READING CLUB OF HOBART LED THE WAY FOR ESTABLISHING A LIBRARY. HOBART TOWNSHIP VOTED A TAX FOR SERVICE AS PART OF THE GARY PUBLIC LIBRARY SYSTEM. THE FIRST BRANCH WAS LAUNCHED IN A HOUSE ACROSS FROM THE HIGH SCHOOL ON JANUARY 5, 1914.

THE LIBRARY BOARD SECURED A CARNEGIE GRANT OF $16,000 ON JANUARY 14, 1914. THE PUBLIC LIBRARY COMMISSION OVERSAW THE CARNEGIE LIBRARY DEVELOPMENT. THE WOMAN'S READING CLUB OF HOBART RAISED $1,250 TO PAY FOR THE LIBRARY LOT. THE LIBRARY BUILDING WAS CONSTRUCTED NEXT TO THE HIGH SCHOOL, 'A DEPARTURE FROM THE USUAL TYPE OF LIBRARY BUILDING, MORE DOMESTIC IN ARCHITECTURE AFTER THE MANNER OF THE ENGLISH RENAISSANCE.' THE DEDICATION OF THE HOBART PUBLIC LIBRARY BUILDING OCCURRED ON THE AFTERNOON OF JANUARY 10, 1915."

TOWNSHIP BRANCH SERVICE LASTED THROUGH 1958, WHEN HOBART TOWNSHIP SEPARATED FROM THE GARY PUBLIC LIBRARY, AND JOINED THE NEWLY FORMED LAKE COUNTY PUBLIC LIBRARY SYSTEM. THE COMMUNITY OF HOBART IS ONE OF THIRTEEN BRANCH LIBRARIES SERVICED BY THE LAKE COUNTY PUBLIC LIBRARY, MERRILLVILLE. THE HOBART CARNEGIE LIBRARY BUILDING AT 706 E. FOURTH STREET WAS SOLD TO THE HOBART HISTORICAL SOCIETY, INC. IN 1968 TO BE PRE-SERVED AS LANDMARK, AND A MUSEUM FOR HISTORICAL COLLECTIONS.

GIFT: $16,000; JANUARY 14, 1914
DEDICATION: JANUARY 10, 1915
ARCHITECT: A. F. WICKES, GARY
CONTRACTOR: INGWALD MOE, GARY
STYLE: TUDOR GOTHIC REVIVAL
CURRENT USE: MUSEUM, ARCHIVES & OFFICES

"Huntington Public Schools Administration, Cartouche & Festoon"

HUNTINGTON

HUNTINGTON PUBLIC SCHOOLS ADMINISTRATION

EXCERPTS FROM THE *"CITY FREE LIBRARY,"* HUNTINGTON, INDIANA BOOKLET, TENTH ANNIVERSARY, FEBRUARY 2, 1913:

"HUNTINGTON'S FIRST LIBRARY COLLECTION FOR PUBLIC USE WAS OWNED AND CIRCULATED BY MR. ROBERT CLARK. THE FIRST ORGANIZATION OF A LIBRARY FOR THE CITY OF HUNTINGTON OCCURRED IN THE YEAR 1874 AND WAS CALLED THE PUBLIC SCHOOL LIBRARY ASSOCIATION. DURING A SPECIAL MEETING OF THE SCHOOL BOARD APRIL 24, 1889, A FREE PUBLIC LIBRARY WAS ESTABLISHED, CONNECTED WITH THE CITY SCHOOLS. THE CENTRAL SCHOOL BUILDING GAVE SPACE FOR THE BOOKS, MANY OF WHICH HAD BELONGED TO THE FAMOUS MECHANICS AND WORKINGMEN'S LIBRARY, ESTABLISHED BY WILLIAM MCCLURE. IN 1899 THE LIBRARY WAS REORGANIZED UNDER STATE LAWS, MAKING IT A FREE LIBRARY, THUS REACHING MORE PEOPLE.

IN DECEMBER OF 1901 THE SCHOOL BOARD OF HUNTINGTON RECEIVED A LETTER FROM ANDREW CARNEGIE, OFFERING $25,000 FOR A LIBRARY BUILDING. IN JANUARY OF 1902, THE BOARD FORMALLY ACCEPTED MR. CARNEGIE'S OFFER AND DONATED A SUITABLE SITE. THE BUILDING WAS FIRST OPENED TO THE PUBLIC ON SATURDAY EVENING, FEBRUARY 21, 1903.

HUNTINGTON SHOULD FEEL PROUD OF ITS LIBRARY. THREE TIMES HAS THE BUILDING BEEN CHOSEN AS A MODEL ONE, FOR ITS SIZE, AND AS A TYPICAL ONE OF THE STATE. SOME THINGS THE BOARD HOPES TO ACCOMPLISH ARE TO CONVINCE EVERY PERSON OF THE JOY OF READING AND TO MAKE BETTER CITIZENS FOR HUNTINGTON."

THE CARNEGIE LIBRARY SERVED THE COMMUNITY UNTIL MAY 11, 1987, WHEN A NEW LIBRARY WAS ESTABLISHED AT 200 WEST MARKET STREET IN HUNTINGTON.

GIFT: $25,000; DECEMBER 21, 1901
DEDICATION: FEBRUARY 21, 1903
ARCHITECT: PATTON & MILLER, CHICAGO, ILL.
CONTRACTOR: WILLIAM H. MAXWELL, ANGOLA
STYLE: BEAUX ARTS CLASSICISM
CURRENT USE: HUNTINGTON PUBLIC SCHOOLS ADMINISTRATION

"Indianapolis Public Schools Administration, National Register Plaque"

INDIANAPOLIS

INDIANAPOLIS PUBLIC SCHOOLS ADMINISTRATION

THE HAWTHORNE BRANCH #2 AT OHIO AND MOUNT STREETS WAS ORIGINALLY ONE OF FIVE CARNEGIE FUNDED, INDIANAPOLIS PUBLIC LIBRARY BRANCHES LOCATED IN THE CITY AND THE ONLY ONE THAT IS PRESENTLY SERVING IN ANOTHER CAPACITY, OTHER THAN A LIBRARY. THE HAWTHORNE BRANCH SERVED FROM 1910 TO 1955 AND NOW SERVES AS ADMINISTRATIVE OFFICES FOR THE INDIANAPOLIS SCHOOL BOARD. THE STRUCTURE HAS BEEN PLACED ON THE NATIONAL REGISTER OF HISTORIC PLACES.

AFTER THE VIOLENT HOMESTEAD STRIKE OF 1892 AT THE CARNEGIE-OWNED HOMESTEAD STEEL WORKS, HOMESTEAD, PENNSYLVANIA, AMERICAN LABOR HARBORED ILL FEELINGS TOWARDS CARNEGIE AND THE "BLOOD MONEY" THAT HE GAVE FOR THE CONSTRUCTION OF LIBRARIES. AS A RESULT, DURING THE EARLY CONSTRUCTION OF THE HAWTHORNE BRANCH (1909-1910), THE STRUCTURE WAS BOMBED BY THE FORCES OF VINDICTIVE LABOR. EARLIER A LOCAL BANKER HAD WARNED THAT CARNEGIE'S GIFT "WOULD STUNT THE GROWTH OF CIVIC PRIDE."

THE CRAFTSMAN-NEOCLASSICAL STYLED BUILDING WAS DEDICATED NOVEMBER 18, 1911 AND NAMED FOR THE NEARBY NATHANIEL HAWTHORNE SCHOOL, WHICH IT MAINLY SERVED. CHARLES R. WILLIAMS, THE MAIN SPEAKER, SPOKE OF *"THE MINISTRY OF BOOKS."* THE DECLINE OF THE NEIGHBORHOOD AFTER WORLD WAR II RESULTED IN A SHARP DROP IN LIBRARY PATRONAGE AND MATERIAL CIRCULATION, THUS RESULTING IN ITS CLOSING IN 1955.

GIFT: $20,000; JANUARY 19, 1909
DEDICATION: NOVEMBER 25, 1910
ARCHITECT: DEITRICH A. BOHLEN, INDIANAPOLIS
CONTRACTOR: ALBERT VON SPRECKELSON, INDIANAPOLIS
STYLE: CRAFTSMAN-NEO CLASSIC REVIVAL
CURRENT USE: INDIANAPOLIS PUBLIC SCHOOLS ADMINISTRATION

"Abandoned Jeffersonville Library, Bull's Eye Window"

JEFFERSONVILLE

ABANDONED, FUTURE JEFFERSONVILLE ARTS COUNCIL

EXCERPTS FROM THE *"HISTORY OF THE JEFFERSONVILLE TOWNSHIP PUBLIC LIBRARY,"* PAPER BY BERTHA F. POINDEXTER, LIBRARIAN, 1931:

"EARLY IN THE ERA OF WOMEN'S LITERARY CLUBS, THE MEMBERS OF SEVERAL CLUBS IN JEFFERSONVILLE BECAME AROUSED TO THE NEED FOR A PUBLIC LIBRARY. ON DECEMBER 1, 1900, THE BOOKS OF THE OLD TOWNSHIP LIBRARY, MAINLY RELICS OF THE MACLURE WORKINGMEN'S LIBRARY, WERE TRANSFERRED TO THE NEW PUBLIC LIBRARY ASSOCIATION. THE CITIZENS NATIONAL BANK OFFERED A RENT-FREE ROOM. ON DECEMBER 17, 1900, THE LIBRARY OPENED.

EARLY IN THE SPRING OF 1901, MISS HANNAH ZULAUF, A LEADER IN CIVIC AFFAIRS, WITH THE ASSISTANCE OF MISS POINDEXTER, SENT A LETTER TO ANDREW CARNEGIE. AN ENCOURAGING LETTER CAME FROM MR. CARNEGIE'S SECRETARY IN DECEMBER OF 1901. THE LIBRARY BOARD WROTE TO MR. CARNEGIE AND ON FEBRUARY 17, 1902, A LETTER WAS RECEIVED FROM SECRETARY BERTRAM SAYING A GIFT OF $16,000 WAS AVAILABLE FOR A LIBRARY BUILDING.

ONCE THE PLANS MET THE REQUIREMENTS OF MR. CARNEGIE, WORK PROGRESSED RAPIDLY. IN DECEMBER OF 1902, THE CITY OF JEFFERSONVILLE DONATED WARDER PARK ON COURT AVENUE FOR THE LIBRARY SITE. THE CORNERSTONE WAS LAID ON SATURDAY, SEPTEMBER 19, 1903. AFTER FIFTEEN AND A HALF MONTHS MORE, THE BUILDING WAS COMPLETED ON JANUARY 1905. ON FEBRUARY 18, 1905, THE LIBRARY OPENED TO THE PUBLIC."

AFTER SERVING THE COMMUNITY FOR 65 YEARS, THE CARNEGIE LIBRARY WAS ABANDONED FOR A NEW BUILDING IN MAY 16, 1970. THE FUTURE USE OF THE BUILDING IS PLANNED FOR OFFICES AND MUSEUM SPACE FOR THE JEFFERSONVILLE ARTS COUNCIL.

GIFT: $16,000; FEBRUARY 15, 1902
DEDICATION: FEBRUARY 18, 1905
ARCHITECT: LOOMIS & CLARKE, JEFFERSONVILLE
CONTRACTOR: UNLOCATED
STYLE: BEAUX ARTS CLASSICISM-ITALIAN RENAISSANCE
CURRENT USE: ABANDONED, FUTURE JEFFERSONVILLE ARTS COUNCIL

"Law Offices, Kendallville, Façade"

KENDALLVILLE

LAW OFFICES

EXCERPTS FROM THE *"HISTORY OF THE LIBRARY"* FILE:

"EARLY IN THE YEAR 1900 THE PEOPLE OF KENDALLVILLE, ESPECIALLY THE MEMBERS OF THE LITERARY CLUBS, BEGAN TO FEEL THE NEED FOR A PUBLIC LIBRARY FOR THEMSELVES AND PARTICULARLY FOR THE YOUNG PEOPLE OF THE CITY. THE CIVIC CLUB OF KENDALLVILLE AND ITS PRESIDENT, MRS. C. W. KIMMEL SPEARHEADED THE DRIVE FOR A PUBLIC LIBRARY. A ROOM IN THE BASEMENT OF THE CENTRAL SCHOOL BUILDING WAS THE FIRST PUBLIC LIBRARY IN KENDALLVILLE, OPENED JANUARY, 1911. IN OCTOBER, 1911 A LIBRARY BOARD WAS FORMED AND A FUND RAISING CAMPAIGN BEGAN TO SECURE A TAX LEVY FOR THE OPERATION OF THE LIBRARY.

THE LIBRARY BOARD PREVAILED UPON THE CARNEGIE CORPORATION TO GRANT A BUILDING FUND OF $12,500 AND IT WAS GRANTED JULY 13, 1912. A BUILDING SITE WAS DONATED. GRANT C. MILLER OF CHICAGO WAS THE ARCHITECT AND GEORGE F. DIGGINS, A LOCAL CONTRACTOR, CARRIED OUT SPECIFICATIONS IN SO CONSCIENTIOUS A MANNER THAT THE LIBRARY BUILDING WILL ALWAYS BE A MONUMENT TO HIS EFFICIENCY AND PUBLIC SPIRIT. THE CORNERSTONE WAS LAID JULY 19, 1913. THE BUILDING PROGRESSED AS PLANNED AND THE DEDICATION EXERCISES WERE HELD MAY 21, 1914. THE COST OF THE LIBRARY BUILDING WAS $14,087.23, ADDITIONAL FURNITURE AND EQUIPMENT $871.95."

THE LIBRARY DISCONTINUED SERVICE IN THE CARNEGIE BUILDING AND MOVED TO A NEW BUILDING THREE BLOCKS WEST, ONE BLOCK WEST OF MAIN STREET, IN 1968.

GIFT: $12,500; JULY 13, 1912
DEDICATION: MAY 21, 1914
ARCHITECT: GRANT C. MILLER, CHICAGO, ILL.
CONTRACTOR: GEORGE F. DIGGINS, KENDALLVILLE
STYLE: CRAFTSMAN-PRAIRIE TRADITION
CURRENT USE: LAW OFFICES

"Lowell, Realty Office, Façade"

LOWELL

REALTY OFFICE

EXCERPTS FROM THE *"THREE CREEK BICENTENNIAL"* BOOKLET, 1976:

"IN 1904 THE LOWELL AREA HAD A SMALL SUBSCRIPTION LIBRARY OF 500 BOOKS. IN 1914, REV. SIMPSON CONTACTED THE SECRETARY OF THE LIBRARY COMMISSION TO FIND THE PROPER PROCEDURES AND LAWS FOR ESTABLISHING A PUBLIC LIBRARY. THE PUBLIC LIBRARY COMMISSION ADVISED 'A TOWN AND TOWNSHIP TAX LEVY OF TEN CENTS TO RAISE $2,000, THE AMOUNT REQUIRED FROM LOWELL.' IN 1915, REV. SIMPSON HELD MEETINGS TO DISCUSS LIBRARY ORGANIZATION, AND CIRCULATED TAX PETITIONS. A SUBSCRIPTION LIST WAS CIRCULATED AND THERE WERE PLENTY OF SUBSCRIBERS SIGNED UP.

IN 1917 THE LOWELL LIBRARY WAS ORGANIZED AND HOUSED ON THE SECOND FLOOR OF THE DAVIS STORE BUILDING. IN NOVEMBER, 1920, LOWELL, SCHNEIDER, CEDAR CREEK TOWNSHIP AND WEST CREEK TOWNSHIP OPENED A PUBLIC LIBRARY ON THE TOWN SQUARE WITH $12,500 SUPPLIED BY THE CARNEGIE CORPORATION OF NEW YORK AND $2,000 CONTRIBUTED BY THE TOWNS PEOPLE. THE CARNEGIE-BUILT LOWELL LIBRARY WAS THE LAST CARNEGIE-FUNDED LIBRARY IN INDIANA."

THE CARNEGIE LIBRARY SERVED THE AREA UNTIL DECEMBER OF 1969. A NEW LIBRARY BUILDING WAS OPENED IN 1993 AT 250 NORTH FREMONT ON THE EAST EDGE OF LOWELL IN A PLEASANT WOODED AREA. THE ORIGINAL CARNEGIE BUILDING WAS SOLD, AND NOW SERVES AS OFFICES FOR A LOCAL REALTY COMPANY.

GIFT: $12,500; MARCH 11, 1918
DEDICATION: NOVEMBER 15, 1920
ARCHITECT: CLIFFORD WILEY, CHICAGO, ILL.
CONTRACTOR: UNLOCATED
STYLE: CRAFTSMAN-PRAIRIE TRADITION
CURRENT USE: REALTY OFFICE

"Mishawaka, Private Residence, Façade"

MISHAWAKA

PRIVATE RESIDENCE

EXCERPTS FROM THE *SOUTH BEND NEWS TIMES*, *"COMPILED HISTORY OF THE LIBRARY,"* BASED ON THE *"BRIEF HISTORY OF THE MISHAWAKA PUBLIC LIBRARY,"* PAPER BY FLORA M. CASE, CITY LIBRARIAN, OCTOBER 15, 1929:

"THE MISHAWAKA PUBLIC LIBRARY WAS ESTABLISHED IN 1907. PRIOR TO THIS DATE THERE HAD BEEN SEVERAL LIBRARY MOVEMENTS. A DONATION OF $500 FROM THE ESTATE OF WILLIAM MACLURE OF NEW HARMONY WAS AWARDED FOR LIBRARY BOOKS. THE MACLURE LIBRARY AND A PENN TOWNSHIP LIBRARY WERE DESTROYED BY THE FIRE OF SEPTEMBER 5, 1872 AND NEVER REESTABLISHED. FOR SEVERAL YEARS A SUBSCRIPTION LIBRARY KNOWN AS THE LADIES' LIBRARY WAS ACTIVE AND WAS HOUSED FREE IN VARIOUS BUILDINGS. ON AUGUST 21, 1906 A TAX LEVY WAS PASSED FOR THE ORGANIZATION OF A PUBLIC LIBRARY.

THE MOVEMENT FOR A NEW LIBRARY BUILDING WAS GAINING STEAM AFTER THE ORGANIZATION OF THE MISHAWAKA WOMAN'S CLUB. LOTS WERE DONATED ON NORTH HILL AND FIRST STREETS. ON JANUARY 6, 1915, THE CARNEGIE CORPORATION PROMISED THE $30,000 NEEDED FOR THE BUILDING AND EQUIPMENT. COMPLETED MAY 1, 1916, THE LIBRARY WAS IMMEDIATELY OCCUPIED AND OPENED FOR PUBLIC INSPECTION ON THE EVENING OF MAY 5TH."

BY 1961, THE CARNEGIE LIBRARY BOARD RECOGNIZED THE NEED FOR ADDITIONAL SPACE AND EXPANDED FACILITIES FOR THE LIBRARY. CONSTRUCTION BEGAN AND THE PRESENT BUILDING ON LINCOLNWAY EAST WAS OPENED ON JULY 27, 1969. ANOTHER MAJOR EXPANSION WAS DEDICATED APRIL 18, 1999. THE ORIGINAL CARNEGIE LIBRARY IS CURRENTLY A PRIVATE HOME.

GIFT: $30,000; JANUARY 6, 1915
DEDICATION: MAY 5, 1916
ARCHITECT: A. F. WICKES, GARY
CONTRACTOR: INGWALD MOE, GARY
STYLE: GOTHIC REVIVAL
CURRENT USE: PRIVATE RESIDENCE

"White County Historical Society, Façade"

MONTICELLO

WHITE COUNTY HISTORICAL SOCIETY

EXCERPTS FROM *A STANDARD HISTORY OF WHITE COUNTY, INDIANA, "THE MONTICELLO PUBLIC LIBRARY,"* PAGES 313-318 BY W. H. HAMELLE, LEWIS PUBLISHING COMPANY, CHICAGO & NEW YORK, 1915:

"IN THE EARLY PART OF THE YEAR OF 1903, SOME AGITATION WAS STARTED WITH REFERENCE TO A PUBLIC LIBRARY. AS A RESULT, A SUBSCRIPTION WAS STARTED FOR THE PUBLIC LIBRARY. A BOARD OF TRUSTEES WAS APPOINTED ON APRIL 6, 1903. THE COUNTY COMMISSIONERS TENDERED THE USE OF TWO NORTHWEST ROOMS ON THE GROUND FLOOR OF THE COURTHOUSE FOR THE LIBRARY UNTIL PERMANENT QUARTERS WERE OBTAINED. ON THE AFTERNOON OF SEPTEMBER 1, 1903, THE MONTICELLO PUBLIC LIBRARY WAS OPENED TO THE PUBLIC.

THE QUESTION OF A DONATION FROM ANDREW CARNEGIE BEGAN TO BE AGITATED, AND ON DECEMBER 12, 1905, THE PRESIDENT OF THE BOARD WROTE TO MR. CARNEGIE AND ASCERTAINED WHAT STEPS SHOULD BE TAKEN. ON JANUARY 20, 1906, AN OFFER OF $10,000 FOR A BUILDING WAS TAKEN. THE LOT WAS PURCHASED IN 1906. MR. CARNEGIE'S GIFT WAS THEN ACCEPTED.

IN AUGUST OF 1907 THE LIBRARY WAS MOVED FROM THE COURTHOUSE TO ITS NEW HOME. THERE WAS NO FORMAL OPENING, BUT WHEN ALL WAS IN ORDER, THE DOORS WERE THROWN OPEN TO THE PUBLIC AND THUS BEGAN THE REAL LIFE OF THE MONTICELLO PUBLIC LIBRARY."

THERE HAS BEEN LITTLE CHANGE IN THE LIBRARY OVER ALMOST A CENTURY; HOWEVER, A SOUTH ADDITION TO THE ORIGINAL BUILDING WAS CONSTRUCTED IN 1957. THE LIBRARY MOVED TO A NEW LOCATION A FEW BLOCKS WEST IN 1992, AND THE CARNEGIE BUILDING BECAME THE WHITE COUNTY HISTORICAL SOCIETY HEADQUARTERS AND MUSEUM.

GIFT: $10,000; JANUARY 16, 1906
DEDICATION: AUGUST, 1907
ARCHITECT: CHARLES E. KENDRICK, ROCHESTER
CONTRACTOR: PETER LEVINDOUSKI, LAFAYETTE
STYLE: PSEUDO-RENAISSANCE REVIVAL
CURRENT USE: MUSEUM, ARCHIVES & OFFICES

"Commercial Bank, Mooresville, Façade"

MOORESVILLE

COMMERCIAL BANK

EXCERPTS FROM THE *"MOORESVILLE LIBRARY HISTORY"* FILE:

"AT A DECEMBER 8, 1911 MEETING, MEMBERS OF THE MISSIONARY SOCIETY OF THE FRIENDS CHURCH SHARED THEIR CONCERNS WITH JACOB P. DUNN, PRESIDENT OF THE PUBLIC LIBRARY COMMISSION, THAT MOORESVILLE NEEDED A PUBLIC LIBRARY. AFTER LOCAL LITERARY CLUBS, EDUCATIONAL ORGANIZATIONS AND RELIGIOUS SOCIETIES ENDORSED THE IDEA, A PUBLIC MEETING WAS CALLED TO DISCUSS THE PROPOSAL. A COMMITTEE BEGAN CIRCULATING A PETITION FOR A LIBRARY IN MOORESVILLE. PRACTICALLY NO ONE OPPOSED THE LIBRARY MOVEMENT.

IN MAY 1912, THE TOWN BOARD VOTED TO LEVY A TAX FOR A PUBLIC LIBRARY AND APPOINTED MEMBERS OF THE LIBRARY BOARD. THE NEWLY FORMED LIBRARY BOARD DECIDED IN JULY 1912 TO ASK FOR A MONETARY GIFT FROM THE CARNEGIE FOUNDATION, WHICH ANSWERED THE REQUEST WITH A $10,000 GRANT.

A TEMPORARY LIBRARY WAS SET UP IN A RENTED ROOM IN THE ODD FELLOWS BUILDING. THE LIBRARY BOARD SELECTED 32 WEST MAIN STREET AS THE SITE FOR THE CARNEGIE STRUCTURE. DONATIONS FROM THE COMMUNITY PAID FOR THE LAND, FURNISHINGS AND INITIAL EXPENSES. THE LIBRARY WAS DEDICATED ON JANUARY 27, 1916. A HISTORY OF THE MOORESVILLE LIBRARY MOVEMENT WAS GIVEN BY THE SECRETARY OF THE LIBRARY BOARD, MR. D. B. JOHNSON."

EXACTLY 72 YEARS LATER ON JANUARY 27, 1988, THE LIBRARY MOVED TO ITS NEW LOCATION AT 220 WEST HARRISON STREET. THE CARNEGIE BUILDING WAS PURCHASED BY AN ADJACENT BANK AND WAS RENOVATED AND EXPANDED, SERVING AS THE BANK'S HOME OFFICE AND CURRENTLY AS A BRANCH BANK.

GIFT: $10,000; JANUARY 2, 1913
DEDICATION: JANUARY 27, 1916
ARCHITECT: T. L. BROOKIE, INDIANAPOLIS
CONTRACTOR: CHARLES FERGUSON & FRANK MARKHE
STYLE: TUDOR GOTHIC REVIVAL
CURRENT USE: COMMERCIAL BANK

"Mount Vernon City Hall, Meeting Room"

MOUNT VERNON

MOUNT VERNON CITY HALL

EXCERPTS FROM *"THE MOUNT VERNON PUBLIC LIBRARY"* HISTORY FILE:

"THE BEGINNINGS OF MOUNT VERNON'S PUBLIC LIBRARY CENTERS AROUND ONE PRINCIPAL CHARACTER, MRS. MATILDA GREATHOUSE ALEXANDER (1842-1904). POSSESSED OF A SUPERIOR INTELLECTUAL ABILITY, MRS. ALEXANDER BECAME THE AUTHOR OF A NUMBER OF LITERARY EFFORTS, INCLUDING SEVERAL NOVELS (*HERE AND HEREAFTER, GOING WEST*), A NUMBER OF POEMS, AND A DRAMA. SHE WAS ALSO A CORRESPONDENT OF THE *INDIANAPOLIS TIMES*.

IN 1892 SHE TOOK THE FIRST STEP TOWARD ESTABLISHING A LIBRARY BY ORGANIZING A LIT-ERARY CLUB, OFFERING HER HOME AS A MEETING PLACE. SOON THE CITY COUNCIL GRANTED A ROOM UPSTAIRS IN CITY HALL FOR THE LIBRARY AND MRS. ALEXANDER STARTED THE BOOK COLLECTION BY GIVING HER ENTIRE PERSONAL LIBRARY OF OVER 1,000 VOLUMES. IN AUGUST 1895 IT WAS OPENED 'FOR THE BENEFIT AND CULTURE OF THE CITIZENS OF MOUNT VERNON.'

SOMETIME IN 1903 A SERIES OF MOVES WERE MADE WHICH RESULTED IN MOUNT VERNON'S OBTAINING THE LIBRARY. THE CARNEGIE CORPORATION ASKED FOR SUPPORT FROM THE CITY AND BLACK TOWNSHIP, AND THE ARTICLES OF INCORPORATION WERE AMENDED TO READ 'THE ALEXANDRIAN FREE PUBLIC LIBRARY.' MR. CARNEGIE DULY DONATED $12,500 FOR THE BUILDING AND LATER $1,400 FOR THE EQUIPMENT. THE BUILDING WAS DEDICATED ON SUNDAY, OCTOBER 15, 1905. THE NAME 'ALEXANDRIAN FREE PUBLIC LIBRARY' WAS PLACED OVER THE MAIN DOOR IN LASTING MEMORY OF MRS. ALEXANDER WHO HAD PASSED AWAY SEPTEMBER 28, 1904, NOT LIVING TO SEE THE CARNEGIE LIBRARY COMPLETED. IN DEATH, SHE WILLED ALL HER PROPERTIES TO THE LIBRARY."

GIFT: $14,000; DECEMBER 27, 1902
DEDICATION: OCTOBER 15, 1905
ARCHITECT: HARRIS & SHOPBELL, EVANSVILLE
CONTRACTOR: E. H. ROBERTS, EVANSVILLE
STYLE: NEO CLASSICAL REVIVAL
CURRENT USE: MOUNT VERNON CITY HALL

"Carnegie Center for Art & History, New Albany, Façade"

NEW ALBANY

CARNEGIE CENTER FOR ART & HISTORY

THE FOLLOWING EXCERPT IS FROM THE *NEW ALBANY EVENING TRIBUNE*, FEBRUARY 14, 1904:

"THE CARNEGIE PUBLIC LIBRARY AT BANK AND SPRING STREETS WAS OPENED THIS MORNING [FEBRUARY 14, 1904] TO PATRONS FOR THE FIRST TIME FOR THE DISTRIBUTION OF BOOKS. THE OPENING HAS BEEN DELAYED FOR SEVERAL DAYS ON ACCOUNT OF THE NON-ARRIVAL OF SOME OF THE EQUIPMENT. NO CEREMONIES ATTENDED THE OPENING THAT WAS INFORMAL IN CHARACTER.

WHAT IS KNOWN AS THE 'OPEN SHELF' SYSTEM WILL BE GIVEN A TRIAL IN THE LIBRARY AND PATRONS WILL BE GIVEN FREE ACCESS TO THE BOOKS AND CAN SELECT THOSE THEY DESIRE FROM THE SHELVES INSTEAD OF SELECTING BY CATALOGUE.

MR. CARNEGIE DURING 1903 ESTABLISHED 105 LIBRARIES, AN AVERAGE OF TWO A WEEK. AND, THOUGH THE IMPRESSION HAS GOT ABOUT THAT LIBRARIES ARE HIS SPECIALTIES, MR. CARNEGIE'S DONATION TO OTHER CAUSES AMOUNTED TO TWICE AS MUCH. [FOR EXAMPLE, ALTHOUGH] A MILLION AND A HALF OF THIS WENT TO PHILADELPHIA FOR BRANCH LIBRARIES, THE SAME AMOUNT WENT TO THE HAGUE TRIBUNAL, OR COMMISSION."

ALTHOUGH THE LIBRARY HAS LONG MOVED TO ITS NEW LOCATION, THE ORIGINAL RENOVATED CARNEGIE BUILDING, WHICH IS NOW THE CARNEGIE CENTER FOR ART & HISTORY IS STILL OWNED AND MANAGED BY THE NEW ALBANY—FLOYD COUNTY LIBRARY. A TOURISM BROCHURE STATES THAT THE CARNEGIE CENTER FOR ART & HISTORY, "OFFERS AN OPPORTUNITY TO ENJOY ART WORKS IN A VARIETY OF MEDIA, TO TAKE PART IN LECTURES AND WORKSHOPS BASED ON THOSE EXHIBITS, AND TO LEARN MORE ABOUT THE COLORFUL HISTORY OF FLOYD COUNTY, INDIANA."

GIFT: $40,000; MARCH 14, 1902
DEDICATION: FEBRUARY 5, 1904
ARCHITECT: ARTHUR LOOMIS, JEFFERSONVILLE
CONTRACTOR: PAUL MOOSEMILLER
STYLE: BEAUX ARTS CLASSICISM
CURRENT USE: ART & HISTORY MUSEUM & OFFICES

"New Carlisle Town Hall, Façade"

NEW CARLISLE

NEW CARLISLE TOWN HALL

EXCERPTS FROM *"A HISTORY OF THE NEW CARLISLE-OLIVE TOWNSHIP PUBLIC LIBRARY"* FILE:

"IN OCTOBER 1898, WAS ORGANIZED WHAT IS NOW KNOWN AS THE CARLISLE CLOVER CLUB OR CCC, AN ORGANIZATION OF YOUNG WOMEN, WHOSE PURPOSE WAS LITERARY WORK, SOCIAL ENTERTAINMENT FOR ITS MEMBERS AND A PLAN TO WORK FOR A PUBLIC LIBRARY FOR NEW CARLISLE. AFTER CONSIDERABLE FUND RAISING AND BOOK DONATIONS, A LIBRARY WAS FORMALLY OPENED FEBRUARY 21, 1902.

DURING WORLD WAR I, THE COMMUNITY LEADERS RECOGNIZED THE PUBLIC'S NEED FOR A NEW LIBRARY BUILDING. THE NEWLY ORGANIZED CHAMBER OF COMMERCE APPOINTED A LIBRARY COMMITTEE MARCH 2, 1917 TO INVESTIGATE THE LIBRARY SITUATION AND THE POSSIBILITY OF CARNEGIE FUNDING. LOTS WERE MADE AVAILABLE THROUGH DONATION ON MICHIGAN STREET IN THE BUSINESS DISTRICT APRIL 13, 1917. A TAX LEVY WAS APPROVED.

BY JULY 1918, PAPERS, BOOKS AND OTHER BELONGINGS OF THE FIRST LIBRARY BECAME THE PROPERTY OF THE NEW CARLISLE AND OLIVE TOWNSHIP PUBLIC LIBRARY. ALTHOUGH CONSTRUCTION WAS SLOWED BY WORLD WAR I, THE CARNEGIE BUILDING WAS DEDICATED JUNE 24, 1921 WITH AN OPEN HOUSE AND PROGRAM."

IN 1985, IN KEEPING WITH THE LIBRARY'S HERITAGE AND MISSION, AN ADDITION WAS BUILT TO THE EXISTING 1921 BUILDING. IN SPRING 2002, THE NEW CARLISLE-OLIVE TOWNSHIP PUBLIC LIBRARY MOVED TO A NEW BUILDING ON THE WEST SIDE OF THE COMMUNITY, AND THE CARNEGIE BUILDING IS NOW OCCUPIED AS THE NEW CARLISLE TOWN HALL.

GIFT: $9,000; SEPTEMBER 14, 1917
DEDICATION: JUNE 24, 1921
ARCHITECT: ERNEST W. YOUNG, SOUTH BEND
CONTRACTOR: MR. SAUDMIER
STYLE: TUDOR GOTHIC REVIVAL
CURRENT USE: NEW CARLISLE TOWN HALL

"Noblesville City Hall, Façade"

NOBLESVILLE

NOBLESVILLE CITY HALL

EXCERPTS FROM THE *"NOBLESVILLE PUBLIC LIBRARY AND ITS PREDECESSORS 1856-1956,"* CHAPTER II BY MARTHA LOU NICHOLSON, LIBRARY SCIENCE 500 TERM PAPER, INDIANA UNIVERSITY, AUGUST, 1957:

"THE STATE LIBRARY COMMISSION RECOMMENDED THAT AN EFFORT BE MADE TO PROCURE A GRANT FROM ANDREW CARNEGIE. ON FEBRUARY 3, 1911, WOMEN CONCERNED ABOUT THE LIBRARY MOVEMENT CALLED A MASS MEETING. THIS AROUSED THE CITY OFFICIALS TO ACTION, FOR ON FEBRUARY 7, 1911, THE MAYOR WROTE A LETTER TO ANDREW CARNEGIE AND RECEIVED A POSITIVE REPLY APRIL 3, 1911.

ON JUNE 1, 1911, THE CITY PURCHASED THE LOT ON THE SOUTHEAST CORNER OF TENTH AND CONNER STREETS FOR THE BUILDING OF THE CARNEGIE LIBRARY. THE LIBRARY BOARD WAS APPOINTED AND ORGANIZED JUNE 19, 1911. AFTER NEARLY TWO YEARS, THE BUILDING WAS DEDICATED MAY 7, 1913. ONE DEDICATION SPEAKER THOUGHT 'THE NEW LIBRARY WOULD BE A CENTER OF CULTURE, REFINEMENT, ART, LITERATURE AND ALL THINGS THAT WILL MAKE LIFE MORE ENJOYABLE AND WORTHWHILE'."

THE NOBLESVILLE PUBLIC LIBRARY WAS REMODELED IN 1971, DOUBLING THE SIZE OF THE ORIGINAL CARNEGIE BUILDING HOWEVER; THE POPULATION GROWTH FORCED THE LIBRARY TO MOVE TO A NEW BUILDING ON THE EAST SIDE OF THE COMMUNITY. THE CARNEGIE BUILDING WAS EXTENSIVELY REMODELED IN 1986, THE YEAR THE LIBRARY WAS TURNED OVER TO THE CITY OF NOBLESVILLE. TODAY THE CARNEGIE BUILDING SHELTERS THE NOBLESVILLE CITY HALL.

GIFT: $12,500; APRIL 3, 1911
DEDICATION: MAY 7, 1913
ARCHITECT: HERBERT FOLTZ, INDIANAPOLIS
CONTRACTOR: AARON SPANNUTH, NOBLESVILLE
STYLE: ECLECTIC-CRAFTSMAN-ITALIANATE
USE: NOBLESVILLE CITY HALL

"Law Offices, North Manchester, Façade"

NORTH MANCHESTER

LAW OFFICES

EXCERPTS FROM *"A BRIEF HISTORY OF THE NORTH MANCHESTER PUBLIC LIBRARY"* FILE:

"NORTH MANCHESTER'S FIRST PUBLIC LIBRARY WAS BEGUN IN 1908 BY THE NORTH MANCHESTER WOMAN'S CLUB AND WAS LOCATED IN THE TOWN HALL. AFTER A BOOK SHOWER WAS HELD FOR THE LIBRARY, MEMBERS OF THE CLUB TOOK TURNS SERVING AS LIBRARIAN. THE FIRST LIBRARY BOARD WAS APPOINTED IN 1909.

IN APRIL 1910, ANDREW CARNEGIE AGREED TO DONATE $10,000 FOR A LIBRARY BUILDING. PRIVATE CITIZENS RAISED $1,500 TO PURCHASE THE HARTER LOT ON MAIN STREET. CONSTRUCTION BEGAN IN APRIL 1911. SEVERAL SEPARATE CONTRACTS WERE AWARDED DIFFERENT BIDDERS FOR DIFFERENT PARTS OF THE JOB. THE CORNERSTONE WAS LAID JULY 18, 1911. THERE WAS CONSIDERABLE COMPANY ASSEMBLED, CONSIDERING THERE WAS NO EFFORT OF HAVING A CELEBRATION OF ANY MAGNITUDE.

THE NORTH MANCHESTER PUBLIC LIBRARY CARNEGIE BUILDING OPENED ON THURSDAY, APRIL 4, 1912. THE CARNEGIE BUILDING SERVED AS A LIBRARY THROUGH SEPTEMBER, 1995, BASICALLY UNCHANGED. THE CARNEGIE BUILDING BECAME INADEQUATE FOR THE COMMUNITY BY THE END OF THE 20TH CENTURY AND IN 1995-1996, THE LIBRARY BOARD PLACED A PROTECTIVE EASEMENT ON THE BUILDING THROUGH THE HISTORIC LANDMARKS FOUNDATION OF INDIANA. THE BUILDING WAS ABANDONED FOR USE AS A LIBRARY AND WAS SOLD TO PRIVATE PARTIES AND RENOVATED FOR LAW OFFICES.

THE NEW NORTH MANCHESTER PUBLIC LIBRARY, A GIFT FROM THE MARY K. PEABODY FOUNDATION OPENED ON MONDAY, OCTOBER 9, 1995."

GIFT: $10,000; APRIL 8, 1910
DEDICATION: APRIL 4, 1912
ARCHITECT: PATTON & MILLER, CHICAGO, ILL.
CONTRACTOR: EZRA FRANTZ, NORTH MANCHESTER
STYLE: GOTHIC REVIVAL
CURRENT USE: LAW OFFICES

"Youth Center, North Vernon, Inscribed Freize"

NORTH VERNON

YOUTH CENTER

EXCERPTS FROM THE *"HISTORY OF THE JENNINGS COUNTY PUBLIC LIBRARY"* FILE:

"JENNINGS COUNTY HOLDS THE DISTINCTION OF BEING THE FIRST COUNTY IN THE UNITED STATES TO LEGISLATE FOR FREE COUNTY LIBRARY SERVICE. IN 1813, COLONEL JOHN VAWTER, WHO PLOTTED THE TOWN OF VERNON, PROVIDED THAT 10 PERCENT OF THE SALES FROM ALL TOWN LOTS BE SET ASIDE FOR THE MAINTENANCE OF A FREE LIBRARY FOR THE COUNTY OF JENNINGS. THE FIRST WRITTEN RECORD OF LIBRARY SERVICE IN JENNINGS COUNTY RECORDED THAT THERE WERE EIGHT TRAVELING LIBRARIES.

ON AUGUST 17, 1917, THE FIRST LEGALLY AUTHORIZED LIBRARY BOARD CONVENED AND SET ABOUT TO ACQUIRE A CARNEGIE LIBRARY BUILDING. IN LESS THAN THREE YEARS THE BOARD WAS ABLE TO OPEN THE DOORS OF THE LIBRARY TO THE PUBLIC. THE CARNEGIE FOUNDATION GAVE THE COUNTY $20,000 FOR THE BUILDING AND ITS EQUIPMENT, WITH THE UNDERSTANDING THAT THE COUNTY WOULD PROVIDE FUNDS FOR THE BOOK COLLECTION AND STAFF.

THE SITE CHOSEN WAS ON WALNUT STREET BETWEEN JENNINGS AND JACKSON STREETS PUR-CHASED FOR $5,000. THE *NORTH VERNON PLAIN DEALER* NEWSPAPER KEPT THE CITIZENS OF THE COUNTY INFORMED OF ITS PROGRESS. THE LIBRARY OPENED IT DOORS IN FEBRUARY OF 1920 BUT THE OFFICIAL DEDICATION WAS HELD APRIL 10, 1920."

AN ADDITION WAS COMPLETED IN 1975, WHICH FEATURED A STREET LEVEL ENTRANCE. IN TIME, THE LIBRARY ABANDONED THE ORIGINAL CARNEGIE BUILDING AND MOVED TO A NEW BUILDING THAT WAS DEDICATED ON APRIL 20, 1997. THE CARNEGIE BUILDING IS CURRENTLY SERVING AS A YOUTH CENTER FOR THE COMMUNITY.

GIFT: $20,000; FEBRUARY 8, 1918
DEDICATION: APRIL 10, 1920
ARCHITECT: WILSON B. PARKER, INDIANAPOLIS
CONTRACTOR: STATE CONSTRUCTION COMPANY, INDIANAPOLIS
STYLE: PSEUDO GEORGIAN REVIVAL
CURRENT USE: YOUTH CENTER

"South Madison Community School District, Pendleton, Façade"

PENDLETON

SOUTH MADISON COMMUNITY SCHOOL DISTRICT ADMINISTRATION

EXCERPTS FROM *"A BRIEF HISTORY OF PENDELTON COMMUNITY LIBRARY"* FILE:

"THE EARLIEST LIBRARY ASSOCIATION IN PENDLETON WAS FORMED IN 1877, AND A LIBRARY WAS ESTABLISHED IN WHAT WAS KNOWN AS THE RED RIBBON READING ROOM, LOCATED IN THE COMMERCIAL BLOCK. IN 1909, THE INDEPENDENT SOCIAL CLUB PURCHASED BOOKS AND MAINTAINED A CIRCULATING LIBRARY.

A MASS MEETING EARLY IN 1910 RESULTED IN A REQUEST TO BENEFACTOR ANDREW CARNEGIE. A GRANT OF $8,000 WAS RECEIVED. THE LIBRARY BOARD MET FOR THE FIRST TIME ON JULY 10, 1910. THE GROUND WAS DONATED BY THOMAS M. HARDY ON EAST STATE STREET. THE PENDLETON-FALL CREEK TOWNSHIP PUBLIC LIBRARY WAS FORMALLY DEDICATED ON MARCH 1, 1912. MR. JACOB P. DUNN, PRESIDENT OF THE INDIANA PUBLIC LIBRARY COMMISSION, MADE AN ADDRESS. ACCORDING TO THE MARCH 1912 ISSUE OF THE *LIBRARY OCCURRENT*, THE OCCASION 'WAS ONE OF GENERAL REJOICING AND ENTHUSIASM, AND AUGURS WELL FOR THE SUCCESS OF THE LIBRARY'."

AN ADDITION TO THE PENDLETON CARNEGIE LIBRARY WAS DEDICATED ON OCTOBER 3, 1964 THAT MORE THAN DOUBLED THE FLOOR SPACE. GROUND WAS BROKEN FOR A NEW LIBRARY ON NOVEMBER 21, 1990. THE ORIGINAL CARNEGIE LIBRARY BUILDING BECAME THE PROPERTY OF THE SOUTH MADISON COMMUNITY SCHOOL CORPORATION.

GIFT: $8,000; APRIL 25, 1911
DEDICATION: MARCH 1, 1912
ARCHITECT: WILSON B. PARKER, INDIANAPOLIS
CONTRACTOR: CHARLES SAVAGE
STYLE: TUDOR GOTHIC REVIVAL
CURRENT USE: SCHOOL BOARD OFFICES & STORAGE

"Triangle Fraternity National Headquarters, Plainfield, Foyer, Historic Plaque"

PLAINFIELD

FRATERNITY HEADQUARTERS

EXCERPTS FROM *"A HISTORY OF THE PLAINFIELD PUBLIC LIBRARY, 1901-1968,"* PAPER BY IDA MAE GOOD MILLER, LIBRARIAN, OCTOBER 15, 1968:

"IN 1893 A GROUP OF PLAINFIELD LADIES FORMED THE WOMAN'S READING CLUB TO STUDY GREAT AUTHORS AND THEIR LITERATURE. DURING THE FALL 1900 MEETING OF THE WOMAN'S READING CLUB, A MEMBER PROPOSED A FREE READING ROOM OPENED TO THE PUBLIC. ADDITIONAL LOCAL CLUBS SUCH AS THE W. C. T. U. AND THE FRIDAY CLUB GOT BEHIND THE LIBRARY MOVEMENT IN PLAINFIELD, FORMING THE NUCLEUS OF THE PLAINFIELD LIBRARY ASSOCIATION.

AFTER A DECADE OF HARD WORK, AN APPEAL TO THE CARNEGIE CORPORATION PAID OFF WITH A $9,000 GIFT ON NOVEMBER 21, 1911. THE BOARD DISCUSSED THE BEST SITE FOR THE NEW LIBRARY BUILDING. THE HANNA SITE WAS SELECTED AND PURCHASED FOR $2,500. THE BOARD THEN CHOSE MR. WILSON B. PARKER, AN INDIANAPOLIS ARCHITECT, TO PLAN THE BUILDING. THE CORNERSTONE WAS LAID, WITH MASONIC CEREMONIES, ON FRIDAY, AUGUST 30, 1912. THE NEW CARNEGIE LIBRARY BUILDING WAS FINALLY OPENED TO THE PUBLIC ON MONDAY EVENING, JANUARY 27, 1913."

THE PUBLIC LIBRARY VACATED THE CARNEGIE BUILDING IN 1968 AND MOVED SOUTHEAST TO 1120 STAFFORD ROAD IN PLAINFIELD. THE CURRENT OCCUPANT OF THE CARNEGIE BUILDING AT 120 SOUTH CENTER STREET IS TRIANGLE FRATERNITY AND THEIR OFFICES.

GIFT: $9,000; NOVEMBER 21, 1911
DEDICATION: JANUARY 27, 1913
ARCHITECT: WILSON B. PARKER, INDIANAPOLIS
CONTRACTOR: SHELTON BARISON
STYLE: CRAFTSMAN-PRAIRIE TRADITION
CURRENT USE: FRATERNITY HEADQUARTERS

"Carnegie Center, Rensselaer, Façade"

RENSSELAER

CARNEGIE CENTER

RENSSELAER WAS ONE OF THE MANY INDIANA COMMUNITIES THAT BENEFITED FROM THE MACLURE BOOK DISTRIBUTION OF THE MID-1800S, LATER ABSORBED BY THE TOWNSHIP LIBRARY. THE LOCAL PUBLIC SCHOOL PURCHASED THE IROQUOIS LIBRARY COLLECTION IN 1889, BECOMING A NUCLEUS FOR THE SCHOOL LIBRARY. IN 1899, A NEW UNION STOCKHOLDER LIBRARY WAS ORGANIZED AND WAS GIVEN A NEW HOME IN THE NEW COURTHOUSE. TAXES WERE LEVIED AND THE JASPER PUBLIC LIBRARY WAS FORMED.

IN A 1903 LETTER FROM THE RENSSELAER LIBRARY BOARD ADDRESSED TO ANDREW CARNEGIE, AN URGENT REQUEST WAS MADE TO SECURE AN ADDITIONAL $2,000 GIFT ABOVE PLEDGE. APPROPRIATIONS WERE BASED ON COMMUNITY POPULATION SIZE, SO COMMUNITIES THE SIZE OF EARLY TWENTIETH CENTURY RENSSELAER, THE JASPER COUNTY SEAT, WERE TO RECEIVE THE MONETARY GIFT OF $10,000. THE BUILDING WOULD COST NEARLY $12,000.

IN RESPONSE, ANDREW CARNEGIE AGREED TO GRANT THE NEEDED $2,000 TO CONSTRUCT THE LIBRARY. DURING THIS TIME, MONEY WAS COLLECTED FOR BUILDING SITE, THE MAXIMUM RATE OF TAXATION WAS FIXED, AN ARCHITECT WAS HIRED, BIDS WERE RECEIVED, AND A BUILDING CONTRACT WAS LET. THE CORNERSTONE, A SOLID CUBE OF BLUE BEDFORD LIMESTONE, WAS LAID JULY 13, 1904. THE CARNEGIE BUILDING WAS DEDICATED ON SEPTEMBER 4, 1905.

TODAY, THE FORMER RENSSELAER PUBLIC LIBRARY IS PROVIDING SPACE AS THE CARNEGIE CENTER, THAT INCLUDES OFFICES FOR THE JASPER COUNTY FOUNDATION, CHAMBER OF COMMERCE, AND THE PRAIRIE ARTS COMMISSION PLUS AN ART GALLERY. THE MODERN JASPER COUNTY PUBLIC LIBRARY, ESTABLISHED IN 1992, NOW SERVES THE COMMUNITY AND MOST OF THE COUNTY AT 208 WEST SUSAN STREET IN RENSSELAER.

GIFT: $12,000; JANUARY 13, 1903
DEDICATION: SEPTEMBER 4, 1905
ARCHITECT: CHARLES WEATHERHOGG, FORT WAYNE
CONTRACTOR: RUSH & WARREN, RENSSELAER
STYLE: NEO CLASSICAL REVIVAL
CURRENT USE: OFFICES & ART GALLERY

"Private Residence, Rochester, Façade"

ROCHESTER

PRIVATE RESIDENCE

ON JANUARY 29, 1904, THE LOCAL WOMEN'S CLUB AND THE UNIVERSITY EXTENSION CLUB RAISED FUNDS TO START A LIBRARY COLLECTION THAT WAS HOUSED IN THE COURTHOUSE. IN MARCH OF 1904, THE WOMEN'S CLUB AND THE LIBRARY BOARD CONTACTED ANDREW CARNEGIE. ONCE THE COMMUNITY HAD MET ALL THE LEGAL REQUIREMENTS FOR SUPPORTING THE LIBRARY AND BUILDING, THE CARNEGIE FOUNDATION GRANTED $15,000 AT THE END OF 1904. THE LIBRARY WAS CONSTRUCTED OVER THE NEXT TWO YEARS AND WAS DEDICATED ON SEPTEMBER 4, 1907. THE FOLLOWING EXCERPTS ABOUT THE FORMAL DEDICATION ARE FROM THE *THE EVENING SENTINEL*, SEPTEMBER 6, 1907:

"THE NEW CARNEGIE LIBRARY, CORNER OF JEFFERSON AND 8TH STREETS, WAS OPENED TO THE PUBLIC WITH A SHORT AND PRETTY PROGRAM WEDNESDAY EVENING. WHILE THE CROWD GATHERED WILLIAMSON'S ORCHESTRA FURNISHED EXCELLENT MUSIC FOR THEIR ENTERTAINMENT AS THEY STROLLED ABOUT THE BUILDING DRINKING IN THE BEAUTY OF THE SURROUNDINGS AND THE GENERAL MAKEUP OF THE ENTIRE LIBRARY. THERE HAS BEEN MUCH HARD WORK AND THOSE WHO HAVE TOILED INCESSANTLY THAT THE END MIGHT BE ACCOMPLISHED CERTAINLY DESERVE THE FEELING OF CONTENTMENT THEY SURELY ENTERTAIN."

THE LANDLOCKED, RESIDENTIAL CARNEGIE LIBRARY BUILDING WAS ABANDONED MARCH 19, 1984, AND THE NEW LIBRARY WAS DEDICATED ON APRIL 2, 1984. THE FORMER LIBRARY WAS CONVERTED INTO A FULTON COUNTY GOVERNMENT ANNEX FOR A FEW YEARS AFTER ABANDONMENT. CURRENTLY THE CARNEGIE BUILDING IS A PRIVATE RESIDENCE.

GIFT: $15,000; DECEMBER 20, 1904
DEDICATION: SEPTEMBER 4, 1907
ARCHITECT: JOSPEH T. HUTTON, HAMMOND
CONTRACTOR: W. H. COOPER & J. J. HILL
STYLE: NEO CLASSICAL REVIVAL
CURRENT USE: PRIVATE RESIDENCE

"Owen County Government Annex, Spencer, Façade"

SPENCER

OWEN COUNTY GOVERNMENT ANNEX

EXCERPTS FROM THE *"OWEN COUNTY PUBLIC LIBRARY HISTORY,"* PAPER BY TAMMY CARNEY, GENEALOGY DEPARTMENT, OWEN COUNTY PUBLIC LIBRARY, 2000:

"APRIL 2, 1906 JOHN N. SLOAN, CLERK OF THE OWEN CIRCUIT COURT, FILED NOTICE WITH THE TOWN BOARD THAT A SUBSCRIPTION LIST IN THE AMOUNT OF $385.05 HAD BEEN FILED WITH HIM FOR THE PURPOSE OF ESTABLISHING A PUBLIC LIBRARY IN THE TOWN OF SPENCER. THE TWO BACK ROOMS ON THE SECOND FLOOR OF THE TOWN HALL WERE ASSIGNED TO THE SPENCER PUBLIC LIBRARY. THREE YEARS AFTER THE LIBRARY WAS STARTED, WASHINGTON TOWNSHIP WAS ALLOWED TO USE THE FACILITIES AT THE MINIMUM TAX ASSESSED. AS SHELF SPACE AND FLOOR SPACE BECAME NECESSARY, A NEW LIBRARY WAS IN ORDER.

ABOUT THIS TIME, ANDREW CARNEGIE WAS HELPING SMALL PUBLIC LIBRARIES BY PROVIDING FUNDS TO BUILD. IN 1911 A DONATION OF $10,000 FROM THE ANDREW CARNEGIE FOUNDATION MADE IT POSSIBLE TO ERECT A LIBRARY BUILDING IN SPENCER. ON JULY 29, 1911 THE CONTRACT FOR CONSTRUCTION WAS LET TO A. E. KEMMER OF LAFAYETTE FOR $7,930. THE BUILDING WAS COMPLETED AND THE DEDICATION WAS HELD JANUARY 1, 1912. THE OPENING RECEPTION WAS ATTENDED BY ABOUT 1,000 RESIDENTS. THE SPENCER ORCHESTRA PLAYED ALL DAY AND INTO THE NIGHT AND EACH GUEST WAS GIVEN A POSTCARD OF THE CARNEGIE LIBRARY."

IN JULY 1997 THE CARNEGIE LIBRARY BUILDING WAS CLOSED AND THE PUBLIC LIBRARY MOVED A FEW BLOCKS WEST OF THE COURTHOUSE SQUARE, THE FORMER HOME OF THE OWEN COUNTY STATE BANK. THE CARNEGIE BUILDING IS CURRENTLY AN OWEN COUNTY GOVERNMENT ANNEX THAT HOUSES THE COUNTY ARCHIVES AND THE PROBATION DEPARTMENT.

GIFT: $10,000; JANUARY 6, 1911
DEDICATION: JANUARY 1, 1912
ARCHITECT: WILSON B. PARKER, INDIANAPOLIS
CONTRACTOR: A. E. KEMMER, LAFAYETTE
STYLE: CRAFTSMAN-RENAISSANCE REVIVAL
CURRENT USE: OWEN COUNTY ARCHIVES & PROBATION DEPARTMENT

"Vevay Town Hall, Façade"

VEVAY

VEVAY TOWN HALL

EXCERPTS FROM THE *"HISTORY OF THE SWITZERLAND COUNTY LIBRARY,"* PAPER BY MISS AMY JOHNSON, LIBRARIAN, 1931:

"THE VEVAY RESIDENTS EARLY ORGANIZED A LIBRARY ASSOCIATION KNOWN AS THE VEVAY LITERARY SOCIETY. EIGHT TOWN LOTS WERE RESERVED FOR THE SOCIETY, AND THE STATE LEGIS-LATURE, IN 1816, PASSED AN ACT INCORPORATING THE LITERARY SOCIETY OF VEVAY. UNDER THE AUSPICES OF THE WILLIAM MACLURE FUND, THE LIBRARY IN VEVAY WAS CALLED THE SWITZERLAND COUNTY WORKING MAN'S INSTITUTE. TOWNSHIP LIBRARIES ALSO HAD THEIR DAY IN THE MID-TO-LATE 19TH CENTURY, AND VEVAY WAS NO EXCEPTION. THE METHODIST LYCEUM IN VEVAY WAS ORGANIZED IN 1888, AND A PUBLIC SCHOOL LIBRARY WAS FORMED; EACH LIBRARY BORE INFLUENCE ON THE COMMUNITY.

INTEREST IN A FREE CARNEGIE PUBLIC LIBRARY BEGAN IN 1913. A LIBRARY BOARD WAS APPOINTED DURING THE JULY 1, 1915 MEETING. AN APPEAL FOR ASSISTANCE TO HENRY N. SANBORN OF THE INDIANA PUBLIC LIBRARY COMMISSION WENT OUT. BY 1917, THE SMALL LIBRARY HAD OUTGROWN ITS QUARTERS.

THROUGH THE INITIATIVE OF MR. A. B. SHAW, THE CARNEGIE GIFT OF $12,500 WAS SECURED. A VACANT LOT ON FERRY STREET WAS BOUGHT FROM MRS. A. P. DUFOUR FOR $1,000. THE NEW CARNEGIE BUILDING WAS COMPLETED AND DEDICATED ON JANUARY 27, 1919."

THE CARNEGIE BUILDING WAS ABANDONED BY THE LIBRARY IN 1992 AND WAS MOVED TO THE NEW BUILDING ACROSS THE STREET AT 205 FERRY. CURRENTLY THE CARNEGIE BUILDING IS SERV-ING AS THE VEVAY TOWN HALL.

GIFT: $12,500; NOVEMBER 7, 1917
DEDICATION: JANUARY 27, 1919
ARCHITECT: WILSON B. PARKER, INDIANAPOLIS
CONTRACTOR: DUNLAP COMPANY
STYLE: NEO CLASSICAL REVIVAL
CURRENT USE: VEVAY TOWN HALL

"Cave Printing Company, Westfield, Façade"

WESTFIELD

COMMERCIAL PRINTING COMPANY

EXCERPTS FROM THE *"HISTORY OF THE WESTFIELD PUBLIC LIBRARY"* FILE:

"IN 1856 WESTFIELD RECEIVED A LIBRARY GRANT FROM THE WILLIAM MCCLURE FAMILY. TO RECEIVE THE GRANT A COMMUNITY HAD TO HAVE AT LEAST 100 BOOKS, A READING ROOM AND A LECTURE ROOM. THE LIBRARY DIED OUT DURING THE CIVIL WAR, BUT RETURNED TO LIFE IN 1883. IN 1901 IT WAS HOUSED IN A SMALL STOREROOM.

THE WESTFIELD PUBLIC LIBRARY OWES ITS INCEPTION TO TWO WOMAN'S CLUBS, THE MEMBERS OF WHICH IN JUNE, 1900, CAME TO THE LIBRARY'S ASSISTANCE AND WORKED DILIGENTLY FOR ITS SUCCESS. ON JANUARY 11, 1901, THE LIBRARY WAS OPENED. IN APRIL 1902, THE LIBRARY WAS REORGANIZED UNDER THE STATE LIBRARY THAT MADE IT A TOWNSHIP LIBRARY.

IN 1910, THE LIBRARY BOARD CONTACTED MR. ANDREW CARNEGIE AND WAS SENT AN APPLICATION FOR A LIBRARY DONATION. IN 1911, THROUGH A CARNEGIE GRANT, THE LIBRARY BUILDING WAS OPENED AT 104 WEST MAIN STREET. ON JULY 1, 1911, CALLERS INSPECTED THE BRICK AND STONED TRIMMED BUILDING AND SHOWED GREAT ENTHUSIASM AND APPRECIATION FOR THE GIFT OF ANDREW CARNEGIE TO WESTFIELD AND WASHINGTON TOWNSHIP."

IN 1978 LIBRARY OFFICIALS ELECTED TO ACQUIRE A SITE AND CONSTRUCT A NEW LIBRARY. IN 1983 THE NEW LIBRARY WAS OPENED IN OCTOBER AT 333 WEST HOOVER STREET AND THE CARNEGIE BUILDING WAS VACATED. IN 1995 A NEW ADDITION TO THE 'NEW' 1978 LIBRARY WAS UNDERTAKEN IN ONE OF THE FASTEST DEVELOPING AREAS IN INDIANA. THE CARNEGIE BUILDING IS CURRENTLY 'EMPLOYED' AS A COMMERCIAL PRINTING COMPANY.

GIFT: $9,000; APRIL 8, 1910
DEDICATION: JULY 1, 1911
ARCHITECT: ROBERT F. DAGGETT & COMPANY, INDIANAPOLIS
CONTRACTOR: L. L. COX & N. A. EARL
STYLE: NEO CLASSICAL REVIVAL
CURRENT USE: COMMERCIAL PRINTING COMPANY

"Former Williamsport Carnegie Library, Future Museum Site"

WILLIAMSPORT

PRIVATELY OWNED, FUTURE MUSEUM SITE

EXCERPTS FROM THE *"WILLIAMSPORT-WASHINGTON TOWNSHIP PUBLIC LIBRARY OBSERVES 75 YEARS,"* HISTORY FILE BY FLORENCE CRIPE, APRIL, 1992.

"IN DECEMBER, 1915, THE SEEDS OF A GRAND PLAN WERE SOWN FOR THE ERECTION OF A CARNEGIE PUBLIC LIBRARY IN WILLIAMSPORT. THE PETITION FOR THE LIBRARY WAS LED BY JANE BRODIE. IN JANUARY, 1916 THE LIBRARY BOARD SET OUT TO FIND A SUITABLE READING ROOM TO SERVE AS A "LIBRARY" UNTIL AN APPLICATION TO THE CARNEGIE CORPORATION COULD BE PROCESSED AND APPROVED.

THE FIRST WILLIAMSPORT-WASHINGTON TOWNSHIP PUBLIC LIBRARY WAS LOCATED IN A POR-TION OF THE TOWN HALL IN EARLY 1916. THE BOARD, IN MARCH, 1916, ACCEPTED THE OFFER OF PETER W. FLEMING TO PURCHASE HIS VACANT LOT ON FALLS STREET AS THE SITE FOR THE PER-MANENT LIBRARY. PURCHASE PRICE WAS $525.

IN MAY, 1916, ARCHITECT WILSON B. PARKER OF INDIANAPOLIS WAS HIRED TO PROCEED WITH THE BUILDING PLANS. BIDS WERE OPENED ON JULY 22, 1916. THE GENERAL CONTRACT FOR CON-STRUCTION WAS AWARDED TO JAMES L. BROWN OF SHOALS FOR $5,948. WORK WAS BEGUN IN THE LATE SUMMER OF 1916. THE LIBRARY OFFICIALLY OPENED MID-JUNE, 1917."

IN JANUARY OF 1999, THE LIBRARY PURCHASED LAND TO BUILD A NEW LIBRARY THAT WAS COM-PLETED JULY, 2002. THE ABANDONED CARNEGIE BUILDING WAS PURCHASED BY A PRIVATE PARTY IN MARCH, 2003 AND PLANS CALL FOR A FUTURE MUSEUM SITE. THE MAINTAINED BUILDING HAS RETAINED ITS ORIGINAL EARLY 19TH CENTURY FLAVOR, FOR THERE HAVE BEEN NO RENOVATIONS.

GIFT: $8,000; MARCH 31, 1916
DEDICATION: JUNE 15, 1917
ARCHITECT: WILSON B. PARKER, INDIANAPOLIS
CONTRACTOR: JAMES L. BROWN, SHOALS
STYLE: NEO CLASSIC REVIVAL
CURRENT USE: PRIVATE OWNERSHIP, FUTURE MUSEUM SITE

"DePauw University, Greencastle, Emison Art Center, West Façade"

DEPAUW UNIVERSITY

EMISON HALL, SCHOOL OF FINE ARTS
GREENCASTLE, INDIANA

EXCERPTS FROM *DEPAUW: A PICTORIAL HISTORY* BY CLIFTON J. PHILLIPS AND JOHN J. BAUGHMAN, ET.AL., DEPAUW UNIVERSITY, 1987:

THE DEPAUW UNIVERSITY LIBRARY HAD ITS ORIGINS IN 1840. GROWING STEADILY, THE COLLECTION DID NOT REQUIRE THE SERVICES OF A LIBRARIAN UNTIL 1854. IN 1879, A FIRE ALMOST DESTROYED WEST COLLEGE AND THE LIBRARY. FROM 1870, THE LIBRARY BECAME MORE SIGNIFICANT AND ASSUMED A MORE IMPORTANT ROLE. AFTER THE TURN OF THE 20TH CENTURY, ANDREW CARNEGIE WAS APPEALED TO FOR FUNDING TO HELP BUILD A NEW LIBRARY:

"THROUGH THE UNTIRING EFFORTS OF PRESIDENT HUGHES AND DR. SALEM TOWN, TOGETHER WITH THE LIBERALITY OF ANDREW CARNEGIE AND DEPAUW'S MANY STAUNCH FRIENDS, THE NECESSARY FUNDS WERE PROVIDED TO BUILD A CAMPUS LIBRARY. IN 1908 THE ANDREW CARNEGIE LIBRARY WAS BUILT WITH A GRANT FROM THE INDUSTRIALIST OF $50,000, PLUS A SUBSCRIPTION FROM DONORS OF $57,000 FOR MAINTENANCE. AFTER NEARLY 50 YEARS AS THE DEPAUW MAIN LIBRARY, IT WAS CONVERTED INTO THE EMISON ART CENTER. THE CARNEGIE LIBRARY WAS DESCRIBED IN 1908 AS THE 'MOST BEAUTIFUL BUILDING ON CAMPUS.'

THE NEW ROY O. WEST LIBRARY OPENED IN 1956 ON THE SITE OF THE FORMER WEST COLLEGE. IN 1958 THE FORMER CARNEGIE LIBRARY WAS CONVERTED TO THE UNIVERSITY ART CENTER. A NEW SOUTH ENTRANCE WAS CREATED AND THE REMODELED LIBRARY WAS DEDICATED ON OLD GOLD DAY 1958. IN 1986 IT WAS NAMED THE EMISON ART CENTER."

GIFT: $50,000; MARCH 21, 1905
DEDICATION: OCTOBER 30, 1908
ARCHITECT: DEITRICH A. BOHLEN, INDIANAPOLIS
CONTRACTOR: WM. P. JUNGCLAUS, INDIANAPOLIS
STYLE: BEAUX ARTS CLASSICISM
CURRENT USE: UNIVERSITY ART CENTER

"DePauw University, Greencastle, Emison Art Center, Endowment Cornerstone"

"DePauw University, Greencastle, Emison Art Center, Dedication Cornerstone"

"Earlham College, Richmond, Tyler Hall, West Façade"

EARLHAM COLLEGE

TYLER HALL, SOCIAL STUDIES
RICHMOND, INDIANA

WHILE THE EARLHAM COLLEGE LIBRARY HAD ITS BEGINNING IN 1847 WHEN THE COLLEGE OPENED, IT WAS SLOW TO GROW. IN 1872, THE FIRST SALARIED LIBRARIAN WAS APPOINTED. EARLHAM COLLEGE PRESIDENT KELLY SUGGESTED THE IMPORTANCE OF A NEW LIBRARY BUILDING IN HIS FIRST ANNUAL COLLEGE REPORT. LINDLEY HALL HOUSED THE EARLHAM COLLEGE LIBRARY OF 10,000 VOLUMES PRIOR TO THE CONSTRUCTION OF THE CARNEGIE FUNDED LIBRARY, BUT BY 1905, THE SECOND FLOOR ROOMS IN LINDLEY HALL WERE TOO CROWDED.

EARLHAM COLLEGE RECEIVED AN OFFER FROM ANDREW CARNEGIE IN 1905 FOR $30,000 FOR THE BUILDING IF THE COLLEGE WOULD RAISE AN EQUAL AMOUNT IN ENDOWMENT. IT WAS AGREED. FOR THE NEXT YEAR AND A HALF, A SUCCESSFUL SUBSCRIPTION CAMPAIGN WAS CARRIED OUT TO RAISE MONIES FOR THE ENDOWMENT TO HELP BUILD A COLLEGE LIBRARY "AS NEARLY PERFECT AS HUMANLY POSSIBLE."

THE NEW CAMPUS LIBRARY OPENED IN 1907. THE TOTAL COST OF THE BRICK BUILDING WAS $38,329. IT WAS CONSIDERED A MODEL LIBRARY. THE INDIANA PUBLIC LIBRARY COMMISSION SELECTED THE LIBRARY AS AN IDEAL PLACE TO HOLD ITS SUMMER LIBRARY SCHOOL FROM 1908 TO 1913, FORMERLY HELD AT WINONA LAKE.

DURING THE EARLY 1960S, PRESIDENT BOLLING DECIDED THAT THE COLLEGE NEEDED A NEW LIBRARY FACILITY SINCE THE CARNEGIE BUILDING HAD PASSED ITS CAPACITY AND WAS OUTDATED. THE NEW LILLY LIBRARY WAS CONSTRUCTED ON THE WEST SIDE OF CAMPUS DURING THE MID 1960S, AND THE CARNEGIE LIBRARY BUILDING WAS TRANSFORMED INTO CLASSROOMS AND THE SOCIAL SCIENCE DEPARTMENT. A FUTURE PLAN FOR THE BUILDING'S USE IS UNDERWAY.

GIFT: $30,000; MARCH 15, 1905
DEDICATION: DECEMBER 2, 1908
ARCHITECT: PATTON & MILLER, CHICAGO, ILL.
CONTRACTOR: UNLOCATED
STYLE: GEORGIAN REVIVAL
CURRENT USE: SOCIAL SCIENCE DEPARTMENT OFFICES & CLASSROOMS

"Earlham College, Richmond, Tyler Hall, Window & Grille"

Tyler Hall

Tyler Hall was built in 1907 as the college library and named in honor of Leon and Minnie Tyler of the Class of 1906. Funds for the building came from Andrew Carnegie, who required the College to raise a matching amount for library endowment. Since 1963 and the completion of Lilly Library, Tyler Hall has served as a home for some of the social sciences and related multidisciplinary programs.

Robert Lincoln Kelly - President

"Earlham College, Richmond, Tyler Hall, Historic Plaque"

"Moores Hill Community Center, Main Entrance, Fanlight, Quatrefoil Tracery"

MOORES HILL COLLEGE (1854-1917)

CARNEGIE HALL COMMUNITY CENTER, MOORES HILL, INDIANA

EXCERPTS FROM *MOORES HILL COLLEGE—AN INTIMATE HISTORY* BY JOHN W. WINKLEY, THE METHODIST PRINTING HOUSE, NASHVILLE, TENNESSEE, 1954:

"AS MOORES HILL COLLEGE (EST. 1854) GREW UNDER THE AUSPICES OF THE METHODIST EPISCOPAL CHURCH, THE NEED FOR AN ADDITIONAL BUILDING BECAME OBVIOUS. IT WAS DECIDED TO ASK ANDREW CARNEGIE TO DONATE HALF THE COST. MR. CARNEGIE AGREED ON THE CONDITION THAT THE COLLEGE RAISE THEIR HALF FIRST.

THE COLLEGE WAS SUCCESSFUL IN THEIR FUND RAISING AND CONSTRUCTION BEGAN. THE CORNERSTONE WAS LAID JUNE 12, 1907 AND THE BUILDING DEDICATED ON JUNE 18, 1908. TO HONOR ITS CHIEF BENEFACTOR, THE BUILDING WAS NAMED 'CARNEGIE HALL'; ONE OF FOUR WORLDWIDE. IN 1909, MOST OF THE COLLEGE CLASSES WERE MOVED TO THE NEW BUILDING AND USE OF CARNEGIE HALL BEGAN. THE COLLEGE LIBRARY WAS LOCATED ON THE FIRST FLOOR.

AFTER A FIRE THAT DESTROYED SEVERAL OTHER CAMPUS BUILDINGS IN 1915, THE COLLEGE HIT HARD ECONOMIC TIMES AND WAS RELOCATED TO EVANSVILLE [TO BECOME THE UNIVERSITY OF EVANSVILLE]. THE LAST COLLEGE COMMENCEMENT HELD AT CARNEGIE HALL WAS IN 1917. THE BUILDING WAS GIVEN TO THE TOWN OF MOORES HILL FOR USE AS A PUBLIC SCHOOL TO SOMEHOW EASE THE PAIN OF LOSING THE COLLEGE."

CARNEGIE HALL WAS USED AS THE PUBLIC SCHOOL BUILDING UNTIL 1978 WHEN SCHOOL CONSOLIDATION ABSORBED MOORES HILL INTO THE SOUTH DEARBORN SCHOOL CORPORATION. IN 1987, THE CARNEGIE HISTORIC LANDMARKS PRESERVATION SOCIETY WAS FORMED. THE ORGANIZATION CONTINUES TO PRESERVE THE UNIQUE BUILDING TODAY AS A COMMUNITY CENTER.

GIFT: $18,500; EARLY 1907
DEDICATION: JUNE 18, 1908
ARCHITECT: CRAPSEY & LAMM, CINCINNATI, OHIO
CONTRACTOR: UNKEFER & COMPANY, DAYTON, OHIO
STYLE: LATE GOTHIC REVIVAL
CURRENT USE: COMMUNITY CENTER

CARNEGIE RAZED

GONE WITH THE WIND, FIRE, & BULLDOZER

"Carlisle-Haddon Township Public Library, "After 1965 Fire"
PHOTO COURTESY SULLIVAN COUNTY PUBLIC LIBRARY, LOCAL HISTORY COLLECTION

CARLISLE

DEMOLISHED BY FIRE

EXCERPTS FROM *"THE CARLISLE, INDIANA SESQUICENTENNIAL 1815-1965,"* PAGE 61:

"AS EARLY AS 1818 THE STATE CONSTITUTION SET UP COUNTY LIBRARIES, AND SAMUEL JUDAH WAS THE FIRST PRESIDENT OF THE BOARD OF SULLIVAN COUNTY. IN 1852 TOWNSHIP LIBRARIES WERE ESTABLISHED, AND HADDON TOWNSHIP RECEIVED 108 BOOKS. IN 1856 CARLISLE HAD A MCCLURE MECHANICS INSTITUTE AND LIBRARY, THROUGH THE GENEROSITY OF WILLIAM MCCLURE, A PHILANTHROPIST OF NEW HARMONY.

THE HONOR OF ESTABLISHING THE PUBLIC LIBRARY MOVEMENT SHOULD GO TO THE WOMEN'S COOPERATIVE LEAGUE, AND ESPECIALLY TO MRS. JIM MCCONNELL. THESE WOMEN WORKED TIRE-LESSLY TO COLLECT BOOKS, AND ON JANUARY 1, 1915, THE LIBRARY WAS OPENED IN A ROOM IN THE NEW HIGH SCHOOL BUILDING.

IN OCTOBER, 1915, A CARNEGIE LIBRARY FOR CARLISLE-HADDON TOWNSHIP BECAME ASSURED WHEN THE CARNEGIE CORPORATION AGREED TO ERECT A $10,000 BUILDING, AND THE CARLISLE TOWN BOARD VOTED TO GIVE THE LIBRARY BOARD ONE FOURTH OF THE SCHOOL LOT AS A BUILD-ING SITE. ON OCTOBER 2, 1916 THE CORNERSTONE OF THE BUILDING WAS LAID WITH CEREMONY. THE DEDICATION DATE WAS APRIL 12, 1917.

ON FRIDAY MORNING, MARCH 19, 1965 THE CARNEGIE LIBRARY WAS IN FLAMES DUE TO DEFEC-TIVE WIRING, AND FIRE SO FAR ADVANCED THAT NOTHING COULD BE SAVED. ON MAY 1, 1968 THE CARLISLE LIBRARY JOINED THE SULLIVAN COUNTY PUBLIC LIBRARY SYSTEM. A NEW LIBRARY WAS BUILT ON THE SAME SITE AS THE ORIGINAL CARNEGIE BUILDING."

GIFT: $10,000: OCTOBER 6, 1915
DEDICATION: APRIL 12, 1917
ARCHITECT: JOHN B. BAYARD, VINCENNES
CONTRACTOR: C. B. WILLIS & SON, VINCENNES
STYLE: CRAFTSMAN-PRAIRIE TRADITION
DEMOLISHED: FIRE, 1965

"Coatesville-Clay Township Public Library"
PHOTO COURTESY COATESVILLE-CLAY TOWNSHIP PUBLIC LIBRARY

COATESVILLE

DEMOLISHED BY TORNADO

EXCERPTS FROM THE *LIBRARY OCCURRENT* MAGAZINE, OCTOBER 1916, PAGES 140-141:

"THE DEDICATION OF THE NEW LIBRARY BUILDING AT COATESVILLE WAS A FEATURE OF THE FOURTH OF JULY CELEBRATION [JULY 4, 1916]. THE MORNING HOURS WERE DEVOTED TO STORY TELLING TO THE CHILDREN. IN THE AFTERNOON, THERE WAS RECEPTION AND BOOK SHOWER AND AN INSPECTION OF THE LIBRARY. IN THE EVENING, AN OVERFLOW CROWD FILLED THE ASSEMBLY ROOM TO LISTEN TO THE PROGRAM. THE PUBLIC LIBRARY CAMPAIGN WAS STARTED BY THE COMMERCIAL CLUB OF COATESVILLE.

THE BUILDING, WHICH MEASURES 50 BY 32 FEET, IS LOCATED ON A LOT 60 BY 120 FEET ABOUT ONE BLOCK NORTH OF THE PUBLIC SQUARE. IT IS BUILT OF HYTEX BRICK OF THE SARABOND PATTERN. THE FURNITURE AND WOODWORK ARE OF FUMED OAK. THE LOWER LEVEL IS OF CONCRETE AND IS DIVIDED INTO FOUR ROOMS AND ENTRY. THE BUILDING WILL BE HEATED BY STEAM FROM ITS OWN PLANT, AND LIGHTED BY AN INDIRECT LIGHTING SYSTEM. THE BUILDING WAS CONSTRUCTED AT A COST OF $8,000, THE GIFT OF THE CARNEGIE CORPORATION TO THE PEOPLE OF COATESVILE AND CLAY TOWNSHIP."

THE LIBRARY WAS DESTROYED ON MARCH 26, 1948 BY A LATE AFTERNOON TORNADO THAT RIPPED THROUGH THE COMMUNITY. A PREFABRICATED BUILDING WAS SET UP WITH EMERGENCY GOVERNMENT FUNDING. THE PUBLIC LIBRARY WAS LATER REBUILT WITH DONATED MONIES.

GIFT: $8,000; APRIL 13, 1914
DEDICATION: JULY 4, 1916
ARCHITECT: GRAHAM & HILL, INDIANAPOLIS
CONTRACTOR: MASTEN LUMBER COMPANY, COATESVILLE
STYLE: CRAFTSMAN-NEO CLASSICAL REVIVAL
DEMOLISHED: TORNADO, MARCH 26, 1948

"Columbus Public Library, Facade"
POSTCARD COURTESY BARTHOLOMEW COUNTY PUBLIC LIBRARY

COLUMBUS

DEMOLISHED BY BULLDOZER

FROM THE *"HISTORY OF THE BARTHOLOMEW COUNTY PUBLIC LIBRARY"* TIME LINE FILE:

DECEMBER, 1901—FUNDING FOR A LIBRARY BUILDING WAS SOUGHT FROM ANDREW CARNEGIE
    WHO REPLIED ON DECEMBER 30, 1901 WITH A DONATION OF $15,000.
JANUARY, 1902—THE COMMERCIAL CLUB ASSISTS THE SCHOOL BOARD IN SECURING A LIBRARY
    SITE. THE CORNER OF FIFTH AT MECHANIC, NOW LAFAYETTE AVENUE WAS CHOSEN.
JUNE 1, 1903—DEDICATION OF THE CARNEGIE LIBRARY.

    THE FOLLOWING EXCERPTS ARE FROM THE *COLUMBUS EVENING REPUBLIC,* JUNE 2, 1903:
    "LOVERS OF LITERATURE, ART AND THE BETTER THINGS OF LIFE BRAVED THE STORMY WEATH-
ER. STATE LIBRARIAN, WILLIAM. E. HENRY GAVE THE DEDICATORY ADDRESS, *'THE PUBLIC LIBRARY
AS A SOURCE OF LIFE.'* MR. HENRY SAID 'THE LIBRARY SERVES THE INDIVIDUAL THROUGHOUT LIFE,
THE TRUE UNIVERSITY OF THE COMMON PEOPLE; THE PEOPLE'S COLLEGE. THE PUBLIC LIBRARY
SAYS UNTO EVERYONE: ' SEEK AND YE SHALL FIND, KNOCK AND IT SHALL BE OPENED UNTO YOU,
ASK AND YE SHALL RECEIVE.' GO OFTEN TO THIS BEAUTIFUL LIBRARY TEMPLE AND DRINK DEEP AT
ITS FOUNTAINS OF KNOWLEDGE, SCIENCE, ART AND LITERATURE."

1922—LIBRARY SERVICE EXTENDED TO ALL BARTHOLOMEW COUNTY RESIDENTS..
1923—THE LIBRARY WAS RENAMED THE COLUMBUS-BARTHOLOMEW COUNTY LIBRARYY
OCTOBER, 1969—THE NEW CLEO ROGERS MEMORIAL COUNTY LIBRARY OPENS.
1969-1970—THE ORIGINAL CARNEGIE BUILDING DEMOLISHED.

GIFT: $15,000; DECEMBER 30, 1901
DEDICATION: JUNE 1, 1903
ARCHITECT: J. W. GADDIS, VINCENNES
CONTRACTORS: COATES & PERKINSON
STYLE: PSEUDO BEAUX ARTS
DEMOLISHED: RAZED, 1969-1970

"Laying the Cornerstone, Carnegie Library at Connersville"
PHOTO COURTESY FAYETTE COUNTY PUBLIC LIBRARY

CONNERSVILLE

DEMOLISHED BY BULLDOZER

EXCERPTS FROM THE *"HISTORY OF THE LIBRARY"* FILE:

"ON NOVEMBER 18, 1893, A PETITION WAS PRESENTED TO THE CONNERSVILLE CITY COUNCIL FOR THE ESTABLISHMENT OF A PUBLIC LIBRARY. A TAX WAS LEVIED BY THE COUNCIL FOR THE NEW LIBRARY. THE NEW LIBRARY WAS FIRST OPENED TO THE PUBLIC MARCH 1894. BEFORE LONG, AFTER SEEING THE NEIGHBORING COMMUNITIES OF SHELBYVILLE, GREENSBURG, AND MUNCIE GENEROUSLY RECEIVE A CARNEGIE LIBRARY BUILDING, CONNERSVILLE WANTED THEIR OWN.

SIX LADIES REPRESENTING THE LITERARY CLUBS OF CONNERSVILLE MET ON FEBRUARY 15, 1907 AND FORMED THE LIBRARY SITE ASSOCIATION. TWO LOTS WERE BOUGHT AT A COST OF $6,210 AT 9TH AND GRAND STREETS AND WERE DEEDED TO THE CITY ON DECEMBER 19, 1909. NEGOTIATIONS WERE OPENED WITH ANDREW CARNEGIE IN HOPE OF SECURING A DONATION WITH WHICH TO BUILD. MR. CARNEGIE GAVE $20,000 FOR THE BUILDING. IN A SHORT TIME, ALBERT C. MOFFETT, THE BUILDING CONTRACTOR, AND HIS CREW STARTED WORK.

THE CORNER STONE WAS LAID SEPTEMBER 22, 1908. THE NEW CARNEGIE LIBRARY BUILDING WAS DEDICATED MARCH 22, 1909. JACOB P. DUNN, PRESIDENT OF THE INDIANA LIBRARY ASSOCIATION SPOKE ON, *'THE LIBRARY, A DEMOCRATIC INSTITUTION'*. THE FIRST CONNERSVILLE LIBRARY BOARD WAS FORMED MAY 21, 1918."

THE PRESENT BUILDING OF 21,522 SQUARE FEET, CONSTRUCTED ON THE SAME SITE, WAS OPENED FOR SERVICE APRIL 3, 1981, THE DEDICATION TAKING PLACE ON MAY 3, 1981.

GIFT: $20,000; DECEMBER 13, 1907
DEDICATION: MARCH 25, 1909
ARCHITECT: DUNLAP & GROSSUP, INDIANAPOLIS
CONTRACTOR: ALBERT C. MOFFETT
STYLE: RENAISSANCE REVIVAL
DEMOLISHED: RAZED, JANUARY 1980

"Elkhart Public Library, Facade"
POSTCARD COURTESY ELKHART PUBLIC LIBRARY

ELKHART

DEMOLISHED BY BULLDOZER

FROM THE *"ELKHART LIBRARY HISTORY"* TIME LINE:

APRIL 17, 1901---ANDREW HUBBLE BEARDSLEY AND GEORGE BYINGTON PRATT SECURED FROM
    ANDREW CARNEGIE THE GIFT OF $30,000 FOR THE BUILDING.
MAY 18, 1901---WING & MAHURIN, ARCHITECTS, SUBMITTED THE APPROVED BUILDING PLAN.
SEPTEMBER, 1901---CONSTRUCTION BEGINS ON CARNEGIE LIBRARY BUILDING.
OCTOBER 1, 1903---THE LIBRARY BOARD PRESENTED THE COMPLETED STRUCTURE TO THE CITY,
    A 'PUBLIC GIFT TO THE PUBLIC.'

    THE FOLLOWING ARTICLE APPEARED IN *LIBRARY JOURNAL* MAGAZINE IN DECEMBER 1903:
    "THE NEW ELKHART-CARNEGIE LIBRARY OF ELKHART, IND., OPENED ON OCTOBER 1, AND IS A
HANDSOME ADDITION TO THE LIBRARIES OF THE STATE. THE BUILDING, OF INDIANA DRESSED
STONE, IS DIGNIFIED AND SUBSTANTIAL IN APPEARANCE, AND ARTISTIC IN ALL DETAILS OF FIN-
ISHING AND DECORATION. THE VIEW ON ENTERING IS MOST ATTRACTIVE, WITH A TESSELLATED
FLOOR, 14 LARGE GREEK COLUMNS OF HIGHLY POLISHED VENEERED ITALIAN MARBLE, ARCHES,
CENTER DOME OF BEAUTIFUL COLORINGS, CEILING OF ART GLASS AND A FREE VISTA OF ALL PARTS
OF THE BUILDING."

MARCH, 1963---THE CARNEGIE LIBRARY BUILDING IS CLOSED. NEW LIBRARY OPENS.
OCTOBER, 1970--- CARNEGIE BUILDING DEMOLISHED. THE LOT WAS SOLD FOR A PARKING LOT.

GIFT: $35,000; MARCH 6, 1901
DEDICATION: OCTOBER 1, 1903
ARCHITECT: WING & MAHURIN, FORT WAYNE
CONTRACTOR: W. H. MAXWELL, ANGOLA
STYLE: NEO CLASSICAL REVIVAL
DEMOLISHED: RAZED, OCTOBER, 1970

"Cherry Street Branch, Evansville Public Library, Facade"
PHOTO COURTESY EVANSVILLE-VANDERBURGH PUBLIC LIBRARY

EVANSVILLE, CHERRY STREET BRANCH

DEMOLISHED BY BULLDOZER

EXCERPTS FROM *THE FIRST FIFTY YEARS OF THE EVANSVILLE-VANDERBURGH COUNTY PUBLIC LIBRARY,* BY HERBERT GOLDHOR, 1962:

"MISS MCCOLLOUGH, LIBRARIAN OF THE EVANSVILLE PUBLIC LIBRARY, HAD PROPOSED TO THE LIBRARY BOARD THAT A SEPARATE BRANCH BE ESTABLISHED FOR NEGROES. IN TIME THIS PROPOSAL WAS MADE TO MR. CARNEGIE AND IN 1913 HE GAVE $10,000 FOR WHAT WAS CALLED THE CHERRY BRANCH LIBRARY BUILDING LOCATED AT 515 CHERRY STREET. IT WAS OPENED ON NOVEMBER 24, 1914. IT WAS THE ONLY BRANCH PUBLIC LIBRARY EXCLUSIVELY FOR NEGROES, NORTH OF THE OHIO RIVER."

THE FOLLOWING EXCERPTS REGARDING THE DEDICATION APPEARED IN THE *LIBRARY CCURENT,* APRIL, 1915 ISSUE, PAGE 28:

"THE BUILDING FRONTS 56 FEET ON CHERRY STREET AND RUNS 40 FEET ON CHURCH STREET. THE MAIN ENTRANCE AND VESTIBULE ARE OF WHITE STONE. THE BALANCE OF THE EXTERIOR, IS OF A BROWN PRESSED BRICK. THE DEDICATORY EXERCISES WERE HELD IN THE MCFARLAND CHAPEL AND THE RECEPTION GIVEN IN THE NEW BUILDING."

IN 1955, THE CHERRY BRANCH LIBRARY WAS SOLD FOR $15,000 TO THE BOY SCOUTS. IN 1969, THE CARNEGIE BUILDING WAS RESOLD TO THE WELBORN MEMORIAL BAPTIST HOSPITAL. THE CHERRY BRANCH WAS DEMOLISHED DURING THE EARLY 1970s.

GIFT: $10,000; JANUARY 6, 1911
DEDICATION: NOVEMBER 24, 1914
ARCHITECT: CLIFFORD SHOPBELL, EVANSVILLE
CONTRACTOR: GEORGE GRAUL
STYLE: CRAFTSMAN-ECLECTIC
DEMOLISHED: RAZED, EARLY 1970s

"Fort Wayne Public Library, Demolition"
PHOTO COURTESY, ALLEN COUNTY PUBLIC LIBRARY

FORT WAYNE

Demolished by Bulldozer

EXCERPTS FROM *BEYOND BOOKS: ALLEN COUNTY'S PUBLIC LIBRARY HISTORY, 1895-1995*, BY DAWNE SLATER-PUTT. ALLEN COUNTY PUBLIC LIBRARY, FORT WAYNE, IND., PAGES 4-17, 1995:

"LIKE MANY OF OTHER INDIANA CITIES, FORT WAYNE WAS HOME TO A WORKING MEN'S INSTITUTE LIBRARY (1855-1869). THE CATHOLIC LIBRARY ASSOCIATION IN FORT WAYNE WAS ESTABLISHED IN 1871. IT COULD BE ARGUED THAT FORT WAYNE'S FIRST TRUE PUBLIC LIBRARY WAS THE FREE READING ROOM ESTABLISHED BY EMERINE J. HAMILTON AND HER DAUGHTERS.

THE IDEA OF A PUBLIC LIBRARY IN FORT WAYNE WAS CONCEIVED BY DAVID N. FOSTER IN THE LATE 1870S. FOSTER INTRODUCED THE RESOLUTION THAT THE WOMAN'S CLUB LEAGUE TAKE STEPS TO SECURE A PUBLIC LIBRARY. THE FREE PUBLIC LIBRARY OF FORT WAYNE WAS LOCATED IN CITY HALL, JANUARY 28, 1895.

IN 1901, THE WOMAN'S CLUB LEAGUE MOVED BACK INTO ACTION BY APPROACHING ANDREW CARNEGIE REGARDING A PUBLIC LIBRARY BUILDING GIFT. THE GIFT TOTALED $90,000, THE LARGEST SINGLE DONATION IN INDIANA BY CARNEGIE FOR A PUBLIC LIBRARY. CONSTRUCTION OF FORT WAYNE'S LIBRARY BUILDING WAS COMPLETE BY JANUARY OF 1904. THE $110,700 BUILDING COST WAS PAID WITH CARNEGIE'S $90,000 GIFT AND A BOARD OF SCHOOL TRUSTEES CONTRIBU-TION. THE DEDICATION OF THE CARNEGIE BUILDING TOOK PLACE JANUARY 7, 1904.

THE DOORS TO THE 1904 CARNEGIE LIBRARY BUILDING CLOSED FOR THE LAST TIME AUGUST 23, 1965. THE CARNEGIE BUILDING WAS RAZED IN THE FALL OF 1965 DUE TO INFERIOR CON-STRUCTION AND THE NEW LIBRARY WAS DEDICATED MAY 21, 1968."

GIFT: $90,000; MARCH 14, 1901
DEDICATION: JANUARY 7, 1904
ARCHITECT: ALFRED GRINDLE, FT. WAYNE
CONTRACTOR: WILLIAM GEAKE & SONS
STYLE: BEAUX ARTS CLASSICISM
DEMOLISHED: RAZED, FALL,1965

"Gary Public Library, Facade"
Photo Courtesy Allen County Public Library

GARY, MAIN

DEMOLISHED BY BULLDOZER

ORA L. WILDERMUTH, SCHOOLTEACHER, WAS CREDITED FOR THE FIRST PUBLIC LIBRARY SERVICE IN GARY HOWEVER, HE CLAIMED THE CREDIT SHOULD HAVE GONE TO A SMALL GROUP OF WOMEN PIONEER RESIDENTS. WILDERMUTH BECAME CUSTODIAN OF THE BOOKS, AND HIS TINY SCHOOLHOUSE BECAME THE TOWN LIBRARY UNTIL TRAMPS BROKE IN ONE COLD NIGHT AND USED SEVERAL VOLUMES TO FIRE THE STOVE. THE FIRST REGULAR LIBRARY WAS OPENED AT THE SOUTHEAST CORNER OF 7TH AND WASHINGTON IN MID-SEPTEMBER, 1908.

THE FIRST LIBRARY BOARD WAS FORMED MARCH 30, 1908. AFTER ORGANIZING THE LIBRARY IN A VACANT STOREROOM, LOUIS J. BAILEY OPENED IT ON DECEMBER 1, 1908, THE FIRST GARY PUBLIC LIBRARY. THE FIRST LIBRARY WAS TURNED OVER TO THE COMMUNITY FROM THE SCHOOLS ON JULY 10, 1911, A NEW LIBRARY BOARD HAVING BEEN ORGANIZED AT THAT TIME.

A $65,000 GIFT WAS OBTAINED FROM THE CARNEGIE FOUNDATION APRIL 28, 1910. THE CENTRAL LIBRARY WAS PUT UNDER CONSTRUCTION AT 5TH AND ADAMS ON A SITE CONSISTING OF TEN LOTS DONATED BY THE GARY LAND COMPANY. CONSTRUCTED OUT OF BEDFORD STONE, ITS SOUTHERN ENTRANCE HAD A SERIES OF SEVEN PAIRED, ENGAGED COLUMNS SUPPORTING A MASSIVE ENTABLATURE. THE DEDICATION WAS HELD FROM NOVEMBER 17TH TO 20TH, 1912.

THE QUESTION OVER WHETHER GARY PUBLIC LIBRARY SHOULD ENLARGE OR BUILD A NEW LIBRARY CAME IN 1955. A BUILDING FIRM DECIDED THAT THE ORIGINAL CARNEGIE STRUCTURE WAS BEYOND REPAIR AND RECOMMENDED A NEW LIBRARY BE BUILT. IN MAY 1962, THE LIBRARY WAS MOVED TO 739 WASHINGTON STREET. THE 50 YEAR OLD CARNEGE LIBRARY WAS RAZED, AND A NEW LIBRARY WAS BUILT AT THE SAME LOCATION, OPENING MAY 4, 1964.

GIFT: $65,000; APRIL 28, 1910
DEDICATION: NOVEMBER 17-19, 1912
ARCHITECT: HENRY D. WHITFIELD, NEW YORK CITY, NY
CONTRACTOR: JAMES I. BARNES, LOGANSPORT
STYLE: BEAUX ARTS CLASSICISM
DEMOLISHED: RAZED, 1962

"Hammond Public Library, Facade"
PHOTO COURTESY HAMMOND PUBLIC LIBRARY, CALUMET ROOM

HAMMOND

Demolished by Bulldozer

The city of Hammond had a need of a public library and reading room, but nothing was done until the Shakespeare Club, an organization of schoolteachers, took the matter into its hands. The Club sold membership cards to all those who wanted to read books, and bought new books with the monies raised.

In June 1903, the Club turned the books over to the city and a Public Library was organized according to the laws of Indiana. Its first home was in Miss Bloomhoff's millinery parlors. In January 1904, the library was moved to the Chicago Telephone Building on Rimback Avenue.

An appeal was mailed out to the Carnegie Corporation for the funding of a new library building. A reply was soon sent and funding of $27,000 was pledged. Local architect, Joseph T. Hutton designed the Beau Arts styled building and J. W. Reed was the general contractor. The Hammond Public Library was dedicated Saturday, July 8, 1905.

After 63 years of public service, the Carnegie library was leveled by bulldozer in 1968 and a new library was established. The new Hammond Public Library at 564 State Street has recently been renovated.

Gift: $27,000; January 14, 1904
Dedication: July 8, 1905
Architect: Joseph T. Hutton, Hammond
Contractor: J. W. Reed
Style: Beau Arts Classicism
Demolished: Razed, 1968

Indianapolis, Madison Avenue Branch

DEMOLISHED BY BULLDOZER

THE MADISON AVENUE BRANCH OF THE INDIANAPOLIS PUBLIC LIBRARY WAS DEDICATED APRIL 26, 1914, AND WAS THE LAST OF FIVE CARNEGIE BRANCH LIBRARIES CONSTRUCTED IN INDIANAPOLIS. THE HYBRID, NEOCLASSIC-CRAFTSMAN STYLED BUILDING SERVED THE SURROUNDING ETHNIC NEIGHBORHOODS, WHICH IN TIME BECAME OVERWHELMINGLY COMMERCIAL; ITS PEAK YEARS WERE THE GREAT DEPRESSION AND THE WORLD WAR II YEARS, (1929-1945). THE COLUMN ENTRANCE AND ARCHING WINDOWS REFLECTED A NEOCLASSIC STYLE, WHILE THE RECTANGULAR BUILDING, HIPPED ROOF, AND OVERHANGING EAVES ARE SIMPLE AND ECONOMICAL ELEMENTS OF THE CRAFTSMAN-PRAIRIE TRADITION.

AFTER 54 YEARS OF PATRONAGE, THE LIBRARY BRANCH WAS SOLD TO THE INDIANA STATE HIGHWAY COMMISSION IN 1968 FOR $55,000 AND LATER DEMOLISHED TO MAKE WAY FOR INTERSTATE 70. THE MADISON AVENUE BRANCH MERGED WITH THE PROSPECT BRANCH AT 1831 PROSPECT STREET.

GIFT: $20,000; JANUARY 19, 1909
DEDICATION: APRIL 26, 1914
ARCHITECT: E. G. GRAVES & R. F. DAGGETT, INDIANAPOLIS
CONTRACTOR: UNLOCATED
STYLE: NEO CLASSIC-CRAFTSMAN
DEMOLISHED: RAZED, 1968

INDIANAPOLIS, WEST INDIANAPOLIS BRANCH

DEMOLISHED BY BULLDOZER

THIS CARNEGIE BRANCH LIBRARY WAS DEDICATED JANUARY 12, 1912 ON HIGH GROUND NEAR THE WHITE RIVER WEST FORK. THE "HIGH GROUND" PROVED TO BE JUST HIGH ENOUGH DURING THE GREAT FLOOD OF 1913, WHEN FLOODWATERS CAME WITHIN A HALF-INCH OF THE BOOKSHELVES.

SURVIVING THE DISASTROUS FLOOD OF 1913, THE WEST INDIANAPOLIS BRANCH SERVED PATRONS FAITHFULLY FOR 74 YEARS; ITS BEST YEARS OF SERVICE WERE DURING THE GREAT DEPRESSION (1929-1940). OVER THE YEARS, INDUSTRIAL GROWTH, RAILROADS, AND HIGHWAYS MOVED IN AND SHRUNK THE RESIDENTIAL NEIGHBORHOOD. BY THE MID-1950S, PATRONAGE HAD DWINDLED AND THE LIBRARY WAS ABANDONED.

WHEN THE SCHOOL DISTRICT OPERATED THE PUBLIC LIBRARIES, A COVENANT ALLOWED THE LIBRARY TO RETURN TO THE INDIANAPOLIS SCHOOL SYSTEM. A NEW WEST INDIANAPOLIS BRANCH LIBRARY WAS CONSTRUCTED AND DEDICATED IN 1986 AT THE INTERSECTION OF MORRIS AND KAPPES STREETS. THE CARNEGIE BRANCH BUILDING WAS DEMOLISHED IN 2000.

GIFT: $20,000; JANUARY 19, 1909
DEDICATION: JANUARY 12, 1911
ARCHITECT: ROBERT F. DAGGETT, INDIANAPOLIS
CONTRACTOR: UNLOCATED
STYLE: BEAUX ARTS CLASSICISM
DEMOLISHED: RAZED, AUGUST 9, 1994

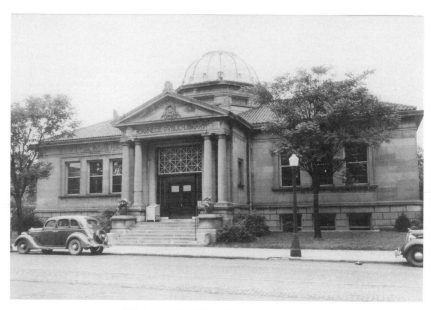

"Kokomo Public Library, Facade"
Photo Courtesy Kokomo-Howard County Public Library

KOKOMO

Demolished by Bulldozer

Excerpts from *Books Along The Wildcat* by Leonard B. Felkey, Kokomo-Howard County Public Library, 1990:

"For the first half of the 19th century, county libraries existed but poor roads prevented their use. A McClure Workingmen's Institute provided reading materials between 1855-1865. The Indiana School Law of 1852 provided for the establishment of township libraries. In 1854, Howard County was divided into six township library districts. The Civil War (1861-1865) depressed township library growth. Kokomo's first public library threw open its doors on January 7, 1886.

Eva M. Fitzgerald, librarian (1900-1906), led the way to its first own building, the Carnegie building. A letter was mailed to Andrew Carnegie December 2, 1901 and again on February 24, 1902 requesting funding for the library building. On March 14, 1902 word was received that Kokomo had a gift of $25,000. A lot was purchased for the building site. Groundbreaking took place May 12, 1903. On Monday morning, January 30, 1905, the library formally opened and a reception continued until 10:00 p.m.

On May 12, 1958 the name Carnegie Public Library changed to Kokomo Public Library. The Carnegie building was permanently closed on September 30, 1965. On November 25, 1965 the Carnegie building was demolished and the new library was opened to the public January 23, 1967."

Gift: $25,000: March 14, 1902
Dedication: January 30, 1905
Architect: James F. Bruff
Contractor: Feaster & Davis, Shelbyville
Style: Neo Classical Revival
Demolished: Razed, 1965

"Logansport Public Library, After the 1941 Fire"
PHOTO COURTESY LOGANSPORT-CASS COUNTY PUBLIC LIBRARY

LOGANSPORT

DEMOLISHED BY FIRE

FROM THE *"HISTORY OF THE LOGANSPORT PUBLIC LIBRARY,"* PAPER BY EDNA M. HOLDEN, COUNTY LIBRARIAN 1920-1967:

"LOGANSPORT HAD A LIBRARY PRIVATELY OWNED AND OPERATED BY MR. CHAUNEKY CARTER AS EARLY AS 1837. ANOTHER, KNOWN AS MCCLURE'S LIBRARY, EXISTED UNTIL 1867, THEN MERGED WITH TOWNSHIP LIBRARIES. UNDER THE AUSPICES OF THE WOMEN'S CHRISTIAN TEMPERANCE UNION, W.C.T.U., A CITIZENS FREE READING ROOM WAS OPENED IN JUNE OF 1890. THE FIRST LIBRARY WAS OPENED IN A REMODELED HOME ON THE PRESENT LIBRARY SITE ON NOVEMBER 1, 1894.

WITHIN A FEW YEARS LARGER FACILITIES WERE NEEDED, SO THE OLD BUILDING WAS RAZED AND WITH THE HELP OF ANDREW CARNEGIE, A NEW BEDFORD BUFF LIMESTONE, "FIREPROOF" LIBRARY WAS BUILT, OPENING ON SEPTEMBER 24, 1904. THE ACQUISITION OF THE CARNEGIE BUILDING IS LARGELY DUE TO THE EFFORTS OF MR. Q. A. MYERS AND THE BOARD OF TRUSTEES. THE CITY LIBRARY BECAME A COUNTY LIBRARY IN 1918, SERVING ALL OF CASS COUNTY EXCEPT FOR WALTON AND ROYAL CENTER THAT ALREADY HAD CARNEGIE LIBRARIES.

LIBRARY SERVICE WAS INTERRUPTED FOR ABOUT TWO WEEKS AFTER THE DISASTROUS FIRE OF MARCH 17, 1941. THE FIRE WAS DISCOVERED AFTER MIDNIGHT ON A SUNDAY IN FREEZING WEATHER. TWO LOCATIONS ON FIFTH STREET SERVED UNTIL THE LIBRARY WAS REBUILT AND OPENED IN 1942."

GIFT: $35,000; APRIL 26, 1902
DEDICATION: SEPTEMBER 24, 1904
ARCHITECT: ALFRED GRINDLE, FORT WAYNE
CONTRACTOR: JOHN E. BARNES & SON, LOGANSPORT
STYLE: NEO CLASSICAL REVIVAL
DEMOLISHED: FIRE, MARCH 17, 1941

"Plymouth Public Library, Facade"
PHOTO COURTESY PLYMOUTH PUBLIC LIBRARY

PLYMOUTH

DEMOLISHED BY BULLDOZER

EXCERPTS FROM THE *"HISTORY OF THE PLYMOUTH PUBLIC LIBRARY,"* PAPER BY MRS. STELLA BINKELE, LIBRARIAN, 1964:

"MRS. S. E. BOYS AND MRS. WINNIE HUMRICHOUSER LED THE CAMPAIGN TO START A PUBLIC LIBRARY IN PLYMOUTH AROUND 1908. A LIBRARY BOARD WAS APPOINTED, SUBSCRIPTION SOLICITED, FUNDRAISERS HELD AND ADVICE WAS SOUGHT FROM THE STATE LIBRARY.

LETTERS WERE WRITTEN TO ANDREW CARNEGIE BY THE LIBRARY BOARD PRESIDENT IN 1910. MR. CARNEGIE FINALLY AGREED TO $15,000. THE CLEVELAND LOT AT GARRO AND CENTER STREETS WAS PURCHASED FOR $1,000, THE OWNERS DONATING $500.

THE LAYING OF THE CORNERSTONE OCCURRED ON JULY 7, 1913. THE EXTERIOR WAS BUILT OF BUFF BRICK WITH STONE TRIMMINGS WHILE THE INTERIOR WAS CONVENIENTLY ARRANGED AND FURNISHED IN PLAIN LIGHT OAK. THE LIBRARY WAS FORMALLY DEDICATED ON TUESDAY EVENING, JANUARY 20, 1914 AND WAS OPEN TO THE PUBLIC A FEW DAYS LATER. THE FINAL COST WAS $17,000."

THE PRIDE OF PLYMOUTH'S CARNEGIE LIBRARY WAS SHOWING ITS AGE IN THE LATTER PART OF THE 20TH CENTURY AND A NEW BUILDING WAS DECIDED UPON DESPITE OPPOSITION. ON OCTOBER 15, 1976 THE CARNEGIE BUILDING WAS CLOSED AND DEMOLISHED. THE NEW PLYMOUTH PUBLIC LIBRARY WAS BUILT ON THE FORMER CARNEGIE BUILDING SITE AND WAS OPENED DECEMBER 1977 AND DEDICATED MARCH, 1978. THE ADJACENT *PLYMOUTH PILOT* NEWSPAPER BUILDING WAS ADDED ON AND DEDICATED 2002.

GIFT: $15,000; JANUARY 6, 1911
DEDICATION: JANUARY 20, 1914
ARCHITECT: W. S. KAUFMAN & SON, RICHMOND
CONTRACTOR: ARTHUR O'KEEFE, PLYMOUTH
STYLE: NEO CLASSIC REVIVAL
DEMOLISHED: RAZED, FALL,1976

"Portland Public Library, Facade"
PHOTO COURTESY JAY COUNTY HISTORICAL SOCIETY

PORTLAND

Demolished by Bulldozer

EXCERPTS FROM *"100 YEARS OF PUBLIC LIBRARY SERVICE,"* PAPER BY ROSALIE CLAMME, DIRECTOR, JAY COUNTY PUBLIC LIBRARY, 2002:

"IN 1897, THE PORTLAND ALUMNI ASSOCIATION AND CITY SCHOOL TEACHERS STARTED A MOVEMENT FOR A PUBLIC LIBRARY. THEY HELD A BOOK SHOWER AND PROVIDED A READING ROOM IN THE BIMEL BUILDING AT THE SOUTHEAST CORNER OF MAIN AND MERIDIAN STREETS.

ON MARCH 4, 1901, FRANK WHITE WROTE ANDREW CARNEGIE ON BEHALF OF THE LOCAL BOARD, ASKING FOR A GIFT OF $15,000 TO $20,000 FOR THE CONSTRUCTION OF A LIBRARY BUILDING. N. B. HAWKINS OF THE CITIZENS BANK FORWARDED WHITE'S LETTER TO U. S. SENATOR CHARLES FAIRBANKS, WHO IN TURN FORWARDED THE LETTER TO THE CARNEGIE CORPORATION ON MARCH 7, 1901. ONE WEEK LATER, A GIFT OF $15,000 WAS OFFERED.

IN EARLY MAY, 1901, THE TIPTON AND MCARTHUR LOTS WERE SELECTED ON EAST WALNUT STREET AND PURCHASED FOR $3,400 FROM DONATIONS FROM THE COMMUNITY. THE ARCHITECTURAL FIRM OF PATTON & MILLER OF CHICAGO, WHICH DESIGNED MANY CARNEGIE BUILDINGS, WAS RETAINED. THE LIBRARY WAS DEDICATED SEPTEMBER 10, 1902, AND SENATOR CHARLES FAIRBANKS WAS THE GUEST SPEAKER. LOCAL DONATIONS PROVIDED THE FURNISHINGS.

DURING THE MID-1970S A MODERN TWO-STORY ADDITION WAS BUILT TO THE FRONT CREATING FOUR FLOORS IN ALL. EVENTUALLY THE BUILDING WAS VACATED AS THE LIBRARY IN 1996 WHEN IT WAS MOVED TO A NEW, MUCH LARGER BUILDING. THE CARNEGIE BUILDING WAS DEMOLISHED IN 2000 AND THE JAY COUNTY CENTER FOR THE ARTS WAS BUILT IN ITS PLACE."

GIFT: $15,000; MARCH 12, 1901
DEDICATION: SEPTEMBER 10, 1902
ARCHITECT: PATTON & MILLER, CHICAGO, ILL.
CONTRACTOR: BULLEY & ANDREWS
STYLE: PSEUDO RENAISSANCE REVIVAL
DEMOLISHED: RAZED, 2000

"Remington-Carpenter Township Public Library, Facade"
PHOTO COURTESY JASPER COUNTY HISTORICAL SOCIETY

REMINGTON

DEMOLISHED BY FIRE

THE MOVEMENT FOR A PUBLIC LIBRARY BEGAN WITH THE FEDERATION OF CLUBS, AN ASSOCIA-
TION COMPOSED OF FIVE SOCIAL AND STUDY CLUBS IN REMINGTON. THE PUBLIC LIBRARY
COMMISSION HELPED TO GUIDE THE FEDERATION IN THE DIRECTION OF A FREE PUBLIC LIBRARY. A
LIBRARY WAS ESTABLISHED UPTOWN IN A NORTH ROOM ON OHIO STREET.

A SIGNIFICANT NUMBER OF BOOKS WERE OBTAINED FROM THE SCHOOL LIBRARY FOR THE
LIBRARY ROOM, AND BOOKS WERE BORROWED FROM THE STATE TRAVELING LIBRARY. THE FIRST
MEETING OF THE LEGALLY APPOINTED LIBRARY BOARD WAS MAY 14, 1913. THE FIRST LIBRARIAN
WAS MISS LOUISE HARTMAN, AND THE LIBRARY WAS OPENED TO THE PUBLIC ON JUNE 1, 1913.
LIBRARY PRIVILEGES WERE OFFERED TO THE RESIDENTS OF CARPENTER TOWNSHIP AND ACCEPTED
BY THE TOWNSHIP ADVISORY BOARD IN SEPTEMBER, 1914.

IN FEBRUARY, 1915, THE LIBRARY BOARD MOVED AHEAD IN THE MATTER OF SECURING A
CARNEGIE GIFT. A GIFT OF $10,000 WAS RECEIVED ON MARCH 16, 1915. A SITE FOR A NEW
LIBRARY ON OHIO STREET WAS OBTAINED, AND THE ARCHITECT'S PLANS WERE ACCEPTED BY THE
CARNEGIE CORPORATION. CONTRACTS FOR THE BUILDING WERE LET IN SEPTEMBER OF 1915. THE
CARNEGIE LIBRARY BUILDING WAS FORMALLY DEDICATED ON MAY 30, 1916.

AN EARLY MORNING FIRE DUE TO FAULTY ELECTRICAL WIRING DESTROYED THE BUILDING ON
APRIL 24, 1961. FROM 1961 TO 1964, A VACANT BUILDING SERVED AS THE PUBLIC LIBRARY WITH
A DONATED COLLECTION FROM THE STATE OF INDIANA. A NEW LIBRARY WAS REBUILT ON THE SAME
SITE OF THE BURNED CARNEGIE STRUCTURE, AND WAS OPENED IN 1964. A NEW 9,500 FOOT ADDI-
TION WAS CONSTRUCTED AND COMPLETED AND OPENED TO THE PUBLIC IN JUNE, 2002.

GIFT: $10,000; MARCH 16, 1915
DEDICATION: MAY 30, 1916
ARCHITECT: UNLOCATED
CONTRACTOR: UNLOCATED
STYLE: NEO CLASSICAL REVIVAL
DEMOLISHED: FIRE, APRIL 24, 1961

"Tipton Public Library, Facade"
PHOTO COURTESY TIPTON COUNTY PUBLIC LIBRARY

TIPTON

DEMOLISHED BY BULLDOZER

EXCERPTS FROM THE *"TIPTON COUNTY PUBLIC LIBRARY HISTORY"* FILE:

"THE FIRST LIBRARY IN TIPTON COUNTY WAS IN A CORNER OF THE COUNTY SUPERINTENDENT'S OFFICE IN THE LOG COURT HOUSE IN 1846, AND LATER THERE WAS A COUNTY LIBRARY WHICH WAS FUNDED FROM 10 PERCENT OF THE PROCEEDS OF THE SALE OF COUNTY LOTS.

IN MARCH, 1901, MRS. IDA MATTHEWS LED A DISCUSSION AT THE LITERARY AND SUFFRAGE CLUB IN TIPTON ON THE NEED FOR A LIBRARY. TIPTON WAS THE FIRST INDIANA CITY TO EMPLOY THE NEW STATE LAW ALLOWING CITIZENS TO TAX AND ORGANIZE THEIR OWN LIBRARY. THE LIBRARY OFFICIALLY OPENED ON THE THIRD FLOOR OF THE COURTHOUSE, MARCH 11, 1902.

AT ABOUT THIS TIME, ANDREW CARNEGIE DONATED $10,000 TO BUILD A LIBRARY IN TIPTON. THE BUILDING SITE CHOSEN WAS CONSIDERED A 'BEAUTY SPOT' ON THE SOUTHEAST COURTHOUSE-SQUARE. THE CONSTRUCTION WAS BEGUN THE SUMMER OF 1902. ON OCTOBER 14, 1902, THE CORNERSTONE WAS LAID. MRS. MATTHEWS CEREMONIOUSLY LAID THE FIRST BRICK OF THE NEW CARNEGIE LIBRARY AND IT OPENED ON MARCH 22, 1903. FURNITURE WAS STILL NEEDED AND MRS. MATTHEWS SUCCESSFULLY APPEALED TO CARNEGIE FOR $3,000 ADDITIONAL.

THE CARNEGIE BUILDING SERVED THE LIBRARY UNTIL 1981. DURING ITS LATTER YEARS THE BUILDING SUFFERED STRUCTURAL DAMAGE, AND HAD TO BE RAZED. THE PRESENT LIBRARY WAS COMPLETED AND OPENED ON MARCH 14, 1981. THE BUILDING INCORPORATED PARTS OF THE CARNEGIE BUILDING, INCLUDING TABLES, WOODWORK AND COLUMNS FROM THE CHILDREN'S ROOM, AND STAINED GLASS WINDOWS FRAMED AND HUNG AS ARTWORK."

GIFT: $13,000; MARCH 14, 1902
DEDICATION: NOVEMBER 24, 1903
ARCHITECT: J. F. ALEXANDER & SON
CONTRACTOR: EDWARD HENRY
STYLE: NEO CLASSICAL REVIVAL
DEMOLISHED: RAZED, 1981

"Valparaiso Public Library, Facade"
Photo Courtesy Porter County Public Library

VALPARAISIO

Demolished by Bulldozer

Excerpts from the Valparaiso Public Library booklet, *"Yesterday & Today,"* 2002:

"The Valparaiso Public Library was organized in accordance with an act of the State Legislature in February, 1838. The first public library building came into existence with the gift by the late Hubbart and Finnette Hunt of their residence on North Washington Street. When the library outgrew the Hunt Building it was evident that larger quarters nearer the center of the city must be acquired.

On April 22, 1906, the library board of trustees announced that the Andrew Carnegie Corporation would allow the City a grant of $20,000 for a new library building, provided the city council would guarantee to raise yearly a maintenance fund equal to ten percent of the grant and agree to provide a suitable lot for the building. The modern styled building, designed by Edward Tilton, a New York City architect, featured a street level entrance, little ornamentation, and open interiors without walls. Mr. Tilton was considered the leading American library architect during the early 20th century. The Carnegie Library was completed and opened to the public on May 26, 1916. Professor B. F. Williams gave the dedicatory address and the Kendrie Orchestra furnished the music."

In 1980, the new Porter County Public Library opened to the public. The Carnegie building was razed in 1994 to make way for a new building. The completed new Valparaiso Library at 103 Jefferson Street opened May 7, 1996.

Gift: $20,000; February 19, 1911
Dedication: May 26, 1916
Architect: E. L. Tilton, New York City
Contractor: Charles Lembke
Style: Modern
Demolished: Razed, 1994

APPENDIX A: MACLURE LIBRARIES IN INDIANA

ADAMS-DECATUR
ALLEN-FORT WAYNE
BARTHOLOMEW-COLUMBUS
BENTON-OXFORD
BLACKFORD-HARTFORD CITY
BOONE-LEBANON, THORNTOWN
BROWN-NASHVILLE
CARROLL-DELPHI
CASS-LOGANSPORT
CLARK-CHARLESTOWN, JEFFERSONVILLE
CLAY-BOWLING GREEN, BRAZIL
CLINTON-FRANKFORT
CRAWFORD-ALTON, LEAVENWORTH
DAVIESS-WASHINGTON
DEARBORN-AURORA, LAWRENCEBURG
DECATUR-GREENSBURG
DEKALB-AUBURN, VIENNA
DELAWARE-MUNCIE
ELKHART-ELKHART, GOSHEN
FAYETTE-CONNERSVILLE, WATERLOO
FLOYD-NEW ALBANY
FOUNTAIN-ATTICA, COVINGTON
FRANKLIN-BROOKVILLE, SPRINGFIELD
FULTON-ROCHESTER
GIBSON-BARREN, BLACK RIVER, MARSH CREEK, PATOKA,
    PRINCETON, SNAKE RUN
GRANT-MARION
GREENE-BLOOMFIELD, LINTON, WORTHINGTON
HAMILTON-NOBLESVILLE, WESTFIELD
HANCOCK-GREENFIELD
HARRISON-CORYDON
HENDRICKS-DANVILLE
HENRY-KNIGHTSTOWN, NEW CASTLE
HOWARD-KOKOMO, POLAR GROVE
HUNTINGTON-HUNTINGTON
JACKSON-SEYMOUR, UNIONTOWN, MARLING
JASPER-RENSSELAER
JAY-PORTLAND
JEFFERSON-NORTH MADISON, SOUTH HANOVER
JENNINGS-VERNON
JOHNSON-EDINBURGH, FRANKLIN, GREENWOOD
KNOX-VINCENNES
KOSCIUSKO-WARSAW
LAGRANGE-LAGRANGE, LIMA
LAKE-CROWN POINT
LAPORTE-LAPORTE, MICHIGAN CITY
LAWRENCE-BEDFORD
MADISON-ANDERSON
MARSHALL-PLYMOUTH
MARTIN-DOVER HILL, MOUNT PLEASANT
MIAMI-PERU
MONROE-BLOOMINGTON
MONTGOMERY-CRAWFORDSVILLE, WAVELAND
MORGAN-MARTINSVILLE, MOORESVILLE
NOBLE-ALBION
OHIO-RISING SUN
ORANGE-LOST RIVER, PAOLI
OWEN-GOSPORT, SPENCER
PARKE-ANNAPOLIS, BLOOMINGDALE, ROCKVILLE
PERRY-CANNELTON
PIKE-PETERSBURG, CLAY TOWNSHIP
PORTER-VALPARAISO
POSEY-CYNTHIANA, FARMERSVILLE, MT.VERNON, POSEYVILLE, SMITH TOWNSHIP,
    STEWARTSVILLE, WADESVILLE, NEW HARMONY
PULASKI-WINAMAC
PUTNAM-BAINBRIDGE, GREENCASTLE, PORTLAND MILLS

Randolph-Winchester
Ripley-Versailles
Rush-Rushville
St. Joseph-Mishawaka, South Bend
Scott-Lexington
Shelby-Shelbyville
Spencer-Liberty, Rockport
Starke-Knox
Steuben-Angola
Sullivan-Carlisle, New Lebanon, Sullivan, Merom
Switzerland-Vevay
Tippecanoe-Farmers, Lafayette
Tipton-Tipton
Union-Liberty, Cottage Grove
Vanderburgh-Evansville
Vermillion-Clinton, Eugene, Newport
Vigo-Terre Haute
Wabash-Wabash
Warren-Williamsport
Warrick-Boonville
Washington-Salem
Wayne-Cambridge City, Centerville, Richmond, Dublin
Wells-Bluffton
White-Monticello
Whitley-Columbia City

Appendix B: Chronological Order of Carnegie Gifts (1901-1918)

1901

01-15-1901   Goshen
02-18-1901   Marion
03-06-1901   Elkhart
03-07-1901   Wabash
03-08-1901   Crawfordsville
03-08-1901   Muncie
03-08-1901   Peru
03-08-1901   Washington
03-12-1901   Portland
03-14-1901   Fort Wayne
10-03-1901   Elwood
12-21-1901   Huntington
12-30-1901   Columbus
12-30-1901   Shelbyville

1902

01-09-1902   Bedford
01-22-1902   Greencastle
01-22-1902   Hartford City
02-15-1902   Jeffersonville
03-14-1902   Brazil
03-14-1902   Danville
03-14-1902   Greensburg
03-14-1902   Kokomo
03-14-1902   New Albany
03-14-1902   Tipton
04-11-1902   Anderson
04-26-1902   Alexandria
04-26-1902   Logansport
12-27-1902   Mount Vernon

1903

01-13-1903   Rensselaer
01-13-1903   Attica
01-13-1903   Bluffton
01-13-1903   Sullivan

```
01-22-1903  PRINCETON
02-02-1903  SEYMOUR
04-23-1903  LEBANON
11-25-1903  UNION CITY
```

1904

```
01-02-1904  POSEYVILLE
01-14-1904  HAMMOND
02-20-1904  SALEM
03-08-1904  DECATUR
03-08-1904  GREENFIELD
12-20-1904  ROCHESTER
12-30-1904  DELPHI
12-30-1904  WHITING
```

1905

```
03-15-1905  EARLHAM COLLEGE AT RICHMOND
03-21-1905  DEPAUW UNIVERSITY AT GREENCASTLE
11-24-1905  FRANKFORT
```

1906

```
01-16-1906  MONTICELLO
02-13-1906  MARTINSVILLE
04-11-1906  FOWLER
04-22-1906  VALPARAISO
04-23-1906  WINCHESTER
12-28-1906  CROWN POINT
```

1907

```
02-01-1907  MOORES HILL COLLEGE, DEARBORN COUNTY
02-21-1907  MONTPELIER
04-08-1907  LIGONIER
12-13-1907  CONNERSVILLE
12-24-1907  LINTON
```

1908

```
02-25-1908  CLINTON
07-22-1908  BLOOMFIELD
```

1909

```
01-19-1909  INDIANAPOLIS (5 BRANCHES)
03-27-1909  ANGOLA
12-02-1909  KENTLAND
```

1910

```
03-21-1910  VINCENNES
04-08-1910  NORTH MANCHESTER
04-08-1910  WESTFIELD
04-28-1910  GARY, MAIN
11-30-1910  BOSWELL
11-30-1910  BROOKVILLE
```

1911

```
01-06-1911  EVANSVILLE (3 BRANCHES)
01-06-1911  PLYMOUTH
01-06-1911  SPENCER
01-06-1911  WINAMAC
01-13-1911  EAST CHICAGO (2 BRANCHES)
02-19-1911  VALPARAISO
04-03-1911  NOBLESVILLE
```

227

04-25-1911 Knightstown
04-25-1911 Pendleton
11-21-1911 Earl Park
11-21-1911 Plainfield
12-07-1911 Sheridan

1912

07-13-1912 Kendallville
09-27-1912 Corydon
09-27-1912 Thorntown

1913

01-02-1913 Gas City
01-02-1913 Mooresville
01-09-1913 Osgood
01-31-1913 Paoli
01-31-1913 Roachdale
03-14-1913 Carmel
03-14-1913 Covington
03-14-1913 Garrett
03-14-1913 Shoals
03-14-1913 Waterloo
04-28-1913 Franklin
05-21-1913 Akron
05-21-1913 Brook
05-21-1913 Kewanna
07-09-1913 Kingman
07-09-1913 New Castle
11-03-1913 Boonville
12-08-1913 Butler
12-08-1913 Westville

1914

01-14-1914 Hobart
01-14-1914 Oxford
02-26-1914 Waveland
04-13-1914 Coatesville
04-13-1914 Lawrenceburg
04-13-1914 Rockville
05-08-1914 Kirklin
05-08-1914 Mitchell
06-11-1914 Roann
09-25-1914 Royal Center
11-17-1914 Walton
12-11-1914 Monon

1915

01-06-1915 Culver
01-06-1915 Liberty
01-06-1915 Mishawaka
01-06-1915 Orleans
02-06-1915 Darlington
03-16-1915 Remington
04-19-1915 Francesville
04-19-1915 West Lebanon
04-23-1915 Winchester
09-29-1915 Brookston
09-29-1915 Colfax
09-29-1915 Warsaw
10-06-1915 Carlisle
10-21-1915 Bloomington
12-03-1915 Milford
12-03-1915 Owensville
12-03-1915 Pierceton

12-03-1915 Rising Sun

1916

01-05-1916 Rockport
01-28-1916 Albion
01-28-1916 Linden
03-15-1916 Newburgh
03-31-1916 Fortville
03-31-1916 LaPorte
03-31-1916 Tell City
03-31-1916 Williamsport
05-15-1916 Atlanta
05-15-1916 Fort Branch
11-09-1916 Converse
11-09-1916 LaGrange
11-09-1916 Merom

1917

01-06-1917 Gary, Bailey Branch
02-03-1917 Flora
02-03-1917 Syracuse
04-03-1917 Monterey
04-03-1917 Warren
04-03-1917 Worthington
04-12-1917 Brownsburg
05-03-1917 Van Buren
09-14-1917 Grandview
09-14-1917 Hebron
09-14-1917 New Carlisle
09-14-1917 North Judson
11-07-1917 Vevay
11-22-1917 Scottsburg

1918

02-08-1918 North Vernon
03-11-1918 Lowell

On November 7, 1917, the Carnegie Corporation temporarily suspended its considerations of new applications for Carnegie gifts due to wartime demands on labor and building materials. The program was eventually shelved altogether, but all pledges prior to America's entry into World War I were honored.

Appendix C: Carnegie Gifts Listed by Dollar Amount & Recipients

$5,000= Monterey

$5,500=Poseyville

$7,000= Brook

$7,500= Corydon, Earl Park, Fowler, Kirklin, Linden, West Lebanon

$8,000= Boswell, Coatesville, Grandview, Kewanna, Kingman, Oxford, Paoli, Pendleton, Westville, Williamsport

$9,000= Colfax, Converse, Francesville, New Carlisle, Osgood, Plainfield, Waterloo, Westfield

$10,000= Albion, Angola, Atlanta, Attica, Brookston, Brookville, Butler, Carlisle,

Covington, Culver, Danville, Darlington, Delphi, Flora, Fort Branch, Fortville, Garrett, Greenfield, Hebron, Kentland, Knightstown, Liberty, Ligonier, Merom, Milford, Monon, Monticello, Montpelier, Mooresville, Newburgh, North Judson, North Manchester, Orleans, Pierceton, Remington, Rising Sun, Roachdale, Roann, Royal Center, Seymour, Shoals, Spencer, Syracuse, Tell City, Thorntown, Union City, Van Buren, Walton, Warren, Waveland, Winamac, Worthington

$11,000= Carmel, Lawrenceburg, Sullivan
$12,000= Bloomfield, Boonville, Crown Point, Decatur, Rensselaer, Winchester
$12,500= Akron, Brownsburg, Clinton, Gas City, Kendallville, LaGrange, Lowell, Martinsville, Noblesville, Owensville, Rockville, Scottsburg, Sheridan, Vevay
$13,000= Bluffton, Tipton
$14,000= Alexandria, Mount Vernon
$15,000= Columbus, Greensburg, Lebanon, Linton, Mitchell, Plymouth, Portland, Princeton, Rochester, Warsaw, Whiting
$16,000= Hartford City, Hobart (Gary branch), Jeffersonville, Salem
$17,000= Rockport
$17,500= Franklin
$18,500= Carnegie Hall at Moores Hill College, Dearborn County
$20,000= Bedford, Brazil, Connersville, Greencastle, New Castle, North Vernon, Shelbyville, Valparaiso, Wabash, Washington
$22,500= Frankfort
$25,000= Crawfordsville, Goshen, Huntington, Kokomo, Peru
$27,000= Hammond
$27,500= LaPorte
$30,000= Earlham College at Richmond, Elwood, Mishawaka
$31,000= Bloomington
$35,000= Elkhart, Logansport, Vincennes
$40,000= East Chicago (2 branches), New Albany
$50,000= Anderson, DePauw University at Greencastle, Marion
$55,000= Muncie
$60,000= Evansville (3 branches)
$90,000= Fort Wayne, Gary, Main & Bailey Branch (see also, former branch, Hobart)
$100,000= Indianapolis (5 branches)

Appendix D: Indiana Carnegie Libraries
Unaccepted Carnegie Gift Offers By Communities

Location, Promise Date & Amount	Reasons for Non Receipt
Auburn, Jan., 1909, $12,500	Carneige offer supplanted by local philanthropist
Batesville, July, 1905, $8,000.	Failure to meet requirements, local opposition
Bicknell, Feb., 1908, $6,500.	Failure to meet requirements, Local opposition
Cannelton, 1904	Unlocated
Goodland, Nov., 1911, $8,000.	Failure to meet requirements, Local opposition
Greenwood, May, 1916, $10,000.	Disagreement over library building site.
Hagerstown, April, 1918	World War One
Madison, Jan., 1916, $20,000.	Architectural problems, timetable delays
Oakland City, July, 1912, $7,500.	Local disagreement of site and 10% tax
Pennville, April, 1917	Unlocated
South Whitley, Aug., 1913, $10,000.	Inadequate tax base. No 10% tax.

Beaux Arts Classicism

Anderson-Beau Arts Neoclassical-fine art center
Columbus-Pseudo-Beaux Arts-demolished
Fort Wayne-demolished
Gary, Main Library-demolished
Goshen-city hall
Greencastle-DePauw University-Emison Art Center
Hammond-demolished
Huntington-school administration
Indianapolis-West Indianapolis Branch-demolished
Jeffersonville-future fine art center
Marion
New Albany-art and history center
Peru
Shelbyville

Colonial Revival

Gary Public Library, Louis J. Bailey Branch-abandoned, to be razed

Craftsman-Prairie Tradition

Albion-Noble County government annex
Angola
Atlanta
Bloomfield-Pseudo-Craftsman
Brownsburg-Chamber of Commerce
Butler-Dekalb County Historical Society
Carlisle-destroyed by fire
Carmel-restaurant & bar
Coatesville-destroyed by tornado-Craftsman-Neoclassical Revival
Colfax
Converse
East Chicago: Pastrick Branch-Indiana Harbor Branch-future dance center
Evansville-Cherry Branch-Craftsman-Eclectic-demolished
Flora
Fort Branch
Fortville-youth center
Francesville-Craftsman-Eclectic
Gas City-Craftsman-Neoclassical Revival
Hebron
Indianapolis, Hawthorne Branch-Craftsman-Neoclassical-school administration
Kendallville-law offices
Kentland-Craftsman-Gothic Revival
Kewanna
Kingman
Kirklin
LaGrange
Liberty-Craftsman-Renaissance Revival
Linden
Lowell-realty office
Merom
Monon-Craftsman-Renaissance Revival
Newburgh
Orleans
Paoli
Pierceton
Plainfield-fraternity headquarters
Rising Sun
Roachdale
Roann
Royal Center
Sheridan
Shoals

SPENCER-CRAFTSMAN-RENAISSANCE REVIVAL-OWEN COUNTY GOVT. ANNEX
SYRACUSE
THORNTOWN
WATERLOO
WAVELAND-CRAFTSMAN TRADITION
WEST LEBANON-CRAFTSMAN TRADITION
WESTVILLE
WORTHINGTON

ECLECTIC

BROOK-ECLECTIC-CRAFTSMAN-NEOCLASSICAL REVIVAL
BROOKSTON-ECLECTIC-CRAFTSMAN-NEOCLASSICAL REVIVAL
DARLINGTON-ECLECTIC-CRAFTSMAN-ITALIANATE
GARRETT-ECLECTIC-CRAFTSMAN-RENAISSANCE REVIVAL
NOBLESVILLE-ECLECTIC-CRAFTSMAN-ITALIANATE
WARSAW-ECLECTIC

TUDOR GOTHIC REVIVAL

BOONVILLE-JACOBEAN REVIVAL-CITY POLICE STATION
BOSWELL-PSEUDO-TUDOR GOTHIC
HOBART
INDIANAPOLIS-EAST WASHINGTON BRANCH
LINTON
MISHAWAKA-PRIVATE RESIDENCE
MOORES HILL-CARNEGIE HALL COMMUNITY CENTER-LATE GOTHIC REVIVAL
MOORESVILLE-COMMERCIAL BANK
NEW CARLISLE-TOWN HALL
NEW CASTLE
NORTH MANCHESTER-GOTHIC REVIVAL-LAW OFFICE
OSGOOD-GOTHIC MILITARY
PENDLETON
TELL CITY
VINCENNES-COLLEGIATE GOTHIC REVIVAL

ITALIANESQUE

FRANKLIN-PSEUDO-ITALIAN RENAISSANCE-APARTMENTS
INDIANAPOLIS-SPADES PARK BRANCH

MANNERIST REVIVAL

SULLIVAN-PSEUDO MANNERIST

MODERN

VALPARAISO-DEMOLISHED

NEO CLASSICAL REVIVAL

AKRON
ALEXANDRIA
BEDFORD
BLOOMINGTON-MONROE COUNTY HISTORICAL SOCIETY
BLUFFTON-WELLS COUNTY GOVERNMENT ANNEX
BRAZIL
CLINTON
CORYDON
COVINGTON
CRAWFORDSVILLE
CROWN POINT
DANVILLE
DECATUR-ADAMS COUNTY CIRCUIT COURT
DELPHI
ELKHART-DEMOLISHED
ELWOOD-PRIVATE OWNER

Fowler
Greencastle
Greenfield-restaurant
Greensburg-city hall
Hartford City
Indianapolis-Madison Avenue Branch-Neoclassic-Craftsman
Kokomo-demolished
LaPorte
Lawrenceburg
Lebanon
Ligonier
Logansport-destroyed by fire
Martinsville
Monterey
Mount Vernon-city hall
Muncie
Owensville
Oxford
Plymouth-demolished
Poseyville
Princeton
Remington-destroyed by fire
Rensselaer-cultural center
Rochester-private home
Salem
Seymour
Tipton-demolished
Union City
Van Buren
Vevay-City Hall
Wabash
Walton
Warren
Washington
Westfield-commercial printing shop
Williamsport-abandoned, for sale
Winamac
Winchester

Neo Georgian Revival

Earl Park-Pseudo-Georgian Revival
Grandview-Pseudo-Georgian Revival
Milford
North Judson
North Vernon-youth center-Pseudo-Georgian Revival
Richmond-Earlham College-Tyler Hall
Rockville-Pseudo-Georgian Revival

Renaissance Revival

Attica
Brookville
Connersville-demolished
Culver
Evansville-Chandler East Branch & Franklin Park West Branch
Frankfort
Knightstown
Mitchell-Pseudo-Renaissance Revival
Monticello-White County Hist. Society-Pseudo-Renaissance Revival
Montpelier
Portland-Pseudo-Renaissance Revival-demolished
Rockport
Scottsburg
Romanesque Revival
Whiting-Eclectic Romanesque Revival

Appendix F: Indiana Carnegie Libraries by County

ADAMS (1) DECATUR
ALLEN (1) FORT WAYNE
BARTHOLOMEW (1) COLUMBUS
BENTON (4) BOSWELL, EARL PARK, FOWLER, OXFORD
BLACKFORD (2) HARTFORD CITY, MONTPELIER
BOONE (2) LEBANON, THORNTOWN
BROWN (0)
CARROLL (2) DELPHI, FLORA
CASS (3) LOGANSPORT, ROYAL CENTER, WALTON
CLARK (1) JEFFERSONVILLE
CLAY (1) BRAZIL
CLINTON (3) COLFAX, FRANKFORT, KIRKLIN
CRAWFORD (0)
DAVIESS (1) WASHINGTON
DEARBORN (2) LAWRENCEBURG, MOORES HILL COLLEGE
DECATUR (1) GREENSBURG
DEKALB (3) BUTLER, GARRETT, WATERLOO
DELAWARE (1) MUNCIE
DUBOIS (0)
ELKHART (2) ELKHART, GOSHEN
FAYETTE (1) CONNERSVILLE
FLOYD (1) NEW ALBANY
FOUNTAIN (3) ATTICA, COVINGTON, KINGMAN
FRANKLIN (1) BROOKVILLE
FULTON (3) AKRON, KEWANNA, ROCHESTER
GIBSON (3) FORT BRANCH, OWENSVILLE, PRINCETON
GRANT (3) GAS CITY, MARION, VAN BUREN
GREENE (3) BLOOMFIELD, LINTON, WORTHINGTON
HAMILTON (5) ATLANTA, CARMEL, NOBLESVILLE, SHERIDAN, WESTFIELD
HANCOCK (2) FORTVILLE, GREENFIELD
HARRISON (1) CORYDON
HENDRICKS (4) BROWNSBURG, COATESVILLE, DANVILLE, PLAINFIELD
HENRY (2) KNIGHTSTOWN, NEW CASTLE
HOWARD (1) KOKOMO
HUNTINGTON (2) HUNTINGTON, WARREN
JACKSON (1) SEYMOUR
JASPER (2) REMINGTON, RENSSELAER
JAY (1) PORTLAND
JEFFERSON (0)
JENNINGS (1) NORTH VERNON
JOHNSON (1) FRANKLIN
KNOX (1) VINCENNES
KOSCIUSKO (4) MILFORD, PIERCETON, SYRACUSE, WARSAW
LAGRANGE (1) LAGRANGE
LAKE (9) CROWN POINT, EAST CHICAGO (2) PASTRICK & INDIANA HARBOR BRANCHES, GARY (3)
     MAIN, BAILEY & HOBART BRANCHES, HAMMOND, LOWELL, WHITING
LAPORTE (2) LAPORTE, WESTVILLE
LAWRENCE (2) BEDFORD, MITCHELL
MADISON (4) ALEXANDRIA, ANDERSON, ELWOOD, PENDLETON
MARION (5) INDIANAPOLIS: E. WASHINGTON, HAWTHORNE, W. INDIANAPOLIS, MADISON AVE.,
     SPADES PARK
MARSHALL (2) CULVER, PLYMOUTH
MARTIN (1) SHOALS
MIAMI (2) CONVERSE, PERU
MONROE (1) BLOOMINGTON
MONTGOMERY (4) CRAWFORDSVILLE, DARLINGTON, LINDEN, WAVELAND
MORGAN (2) MARTINSVILLE, MOORESVILLE
NEWTON (2) BROOK, KENTLAND
NOBLE (3) ALBION, KENDALLVILLE, LIGONIER
OHIO (1) RISING SUN
ORANGE (2) ORLEANS, PAOLI
OWEN (1) SPENCER
PARKE (1) ROCKVILLE
PERRY (1) TELL CITY
PIKE (0)
PORTER (2) HEBRON, VALPARAISO
POSEY (2) MOUNT VERNON, POSEYVILLE

234

Pulaski (3) Francesville, Monterey, Winamac
Putnam (3) DePauw University, Greencastle, Roachdale
Randolph (2) Winchester, Union City
Ripley (1) Osgood
Rush (0)
St. Joseph (2) Mishawaka, New Carlisle
Scott (1) Scottsburg
Shelby (1) Shelbyville
Spencer (2) Grandview, Rockport
Starke (1) North Judson
Steuben (1) Angola
Sullivan (3) Carlisle, Merom, Sullivan
Switzerland (1) Vevay
Tippecanoe (0)
Tipton (1) Tipton
Union (1) Liberty
Vanderburgh (3) Evansville Branches: Cherry, Chandler East, Franklin Park West
Vermillion (1) Clinton
Vigo (0)
Wabash (3) North Manchester, Roann, Wabash
Warren (2) West Lebanon, Williamsport
Warrick (2) Boonville, Newburgh
Washington (1) Salem
Wayne (1) Earlham College, Richmond
Wells (1) Bluffton
White (3) Brookston, Monon, Monticello
Whitley (0)

Indiana's Carnegie Libraries
National Register of Historic Places

Anderson, Bloomington, Colfax, Converse, Covington, Goshen, Greensburg, Hobart, Indianapolis Hawthorne Branch, Kirklin, Mishawaka, Moores Hill, Muncie, New Albany, North Manchester, Rennselaer, Thorntown

Indiana Carnegie Libraries
Indiana State Register:

Carmel, North Vernon, Walton

Select Bibliography: Carnegie Library Literature

Anderson, Florence. *Carnegie Corporation Library Program, 1911-1961.* New York: The Carnegie Corporation of New York, 1963.

Beckman, Margaret, et al. *The Best Gift: A Record of the Carnegie Libraries in Ontario, Canada.* Toronto: Dundurn Press, 1984.

Bial, Raymond and Linda Bial. *The Carnegie Library in Illinois.* Urbana: University of Illinois Press, 1991.

Blumenson, John J. G. *Identifying American Architecture: A Pictorial Guide to Styles & Terms, 1600-1945.* Nashville, Tennessee: American Association for State & Local History, 1977.

Bobinski, George Sylvan. *Carnegie Libraries: Their Histories and Impact on American Public Library Development.* Chicago: American Library Association, 1969.

Carnegie, Andrew. *Autobiography of Andrew Carnegie.* Boston: Houghton Press, 1920.

Carnegie, Andrew. *The Gospel of Wealth.* Indianapolis, Ind.: Indiana University Center on Philanthropy, 1990.

Carnegie Corporation. Library Correspondence, 1890-1922, microfilm and microfiche. New York: Columbia University, Rare Book Archives.

Carnegie Library Correspondence, 1901-1922. Indianapolis, Ind.: Indiana State Library, Library Development Office files.

Constantine, J. Robert. *The Role of Libraries in the Cultural History of Indiana.* Bloomington, Ind.: Indiana Library Studies, 1970.

Dunn, Jacob P. *"The Libraries of Indiana",* World's Fair Monograph. Indianapolis, Ind.: Wm. Burford Printing, 1893.

Frye, Lonn. *Carnegie Libraries: Restoration and Expansion.* Springfield: Illinois Historic Preservation Agency, 1993.

Harris, M. H. *"The Availability of Books and the Nature of Book Ownership on the Southern Indiana Frontier, 1800-1850."* Bloomington, Ind.: Doctoral dissertation, Indiana University, 1971.

Henry, W. E. *Municipal and Institutional Libraries of Indiana.* Indianapolis, Ind.: The Louisiana Purchase Exposition Commission of Indiana, 1904.

Jones, Theodore. *Carnegie Libraries Across America: A Public Legacy.* Preservation Press: New York: John Wiley Press, 1997.

Karl, Barry Dean. *Andrew Carnegie and His Gospel of Philanthropy: A Study in the Ethics of Responsibility.* Indianapolis, Ind.: Indiana University Center on Philanthropy, 1990.

Koch, Theodore Wesley. *A Book of Carnegie Libraries.* White Plains, New York: H. W. Wilson, 1917.

Library Occurrent (1901-1980). Indianapolis, Ind.: Indiana State Library, Public Library Commission and Library Development Office.

Martin, Robert Sidney, ed. *Carnegie Denied: Communities Rejecting Carnegie Library Construction Grants, 1898-1925.* Westport, Connecticut: Greenwood Press, 1993.

Miller, Durand R. *Carnegie Grants for Library Buildings, 1890-1917.* New York: Carnegie Corporation of New York, 1943.

OEHLERTS, DONALD ERVIN. *"The Development of American Public Library Architecture from 1850-1940."* BLOOMINGTON, IND.: DOCTORAL DISSERTATION, INDIANA UNIVERSITY, 1975.

PHILLIPS, CLIFTON J. *Indiana In Transition: The Emergence of An Industrial Commonwealth, 1880-1920.* INDIANAPOLIS, IND.: INDIANA HISTORICAL BUREAU & INDIANA HISTORICAL SOCIETY, 1968.

PUBLIC LIBRARY COMMISSION OF INDIANA. *Seventh Biennial Report of the Public Library Commission of Indiana, 1910-1912.* INDIANAPOLIS, IND.: WM. BURFORD PRINTING, 1913.

TAYLOR, M. V. *"Public Library Commission of Indiana, 1899-1925."* LEXINGTON, KENTUCKY: MASTER'S THESIS, UNIVERSITY OF KENTUCKY PRESS, MICROCARD PUBLICATIONS, SERIES B, NUMBER 3, 1953.

VAN SLYCK, ABIGAIL AYRES. *Free To All: Carnegie Libraries and American Culture, 1890-1920.* CHICAGO: UNIVERSITY OF CHICAGO PRESS, 1995.

WALTHER, L. A. *"Legal and Governmental Aspects of Public Library Development in Indiana, 1816-1953."* BLOOMINGTON, IND.: DOCTORAL DISSERTATION, INDIANA UNIVERSITY, 1957.

WELLS, JOHN ROY. *"Architecture of the Carnegie Libraries in Indiana."* MUNCIE, IND.: MASTER OF ARCHITECTURE THESIS, BALL STATE UNIVERSITY, 1981.

WERKLEY, C. E. *Mister Carnegie's Lib'ary.* NEW YORK: AMERICAN HERITAGE PRESS, 1970.

"The good that Mr. Carnegie has done for the library cause will live after him, and the coming generations will be blessed by his munificence."

WILLIAM E. HENRY, INDIANA STATE LIBRARIAN, 1904

"Thanks Laird Andy"

DRAWING BY BRETT VOLPP, ADAPTED FROM 1913 ORIGINAL